<u>Architecture on Common Ground</u>
<u>The Question of Land: Positions and Models</u>

Architecture on Common Ground
The Question of Land:
Positions and Models
Lars Müller Publishers /
University of Luxembourg

Florian Hertweck (ed.)

Florian Hertweck
The Question of Land Reloaded

«Study how a society uses its land, and you can come to pretty reliable conclusions as to what its future will be.»[1]

Ernst Friedrich Schumacher

A hectare of land recently changed hands twice in quick succession in a municipality near the capital of Luxembourg. First, a farmer sold the plot, which had been zoned for development by the municipality, to a local developer for 12 million euros. He in turn sold it to a foreign developer, who is now planning to develop it, for 18 million euros. Now the municipality finds itself confronted with a project that maxes out the amount of housing permitted. It is foreseeable that the developer will soon try to sell cheaply made apartments at high prices; otherwise, he wouldn't make money after paying the eye-watering price for the land. The fact that land can be bought and sold will not only have negative impacts on the quality of the urban design, the open spaces and the architecture at this location; it will also concentrate a particular segment of the population here, the only one that can still afford such residences – despite the requirement that 10 percent of the city's housing should be affordable. This can be observed in all exclusive locations today. The municipality would have liked to purchase the land itself, but as its total budget is 25 million euros, acquiring the land would have left it unable to do anything else. This common example of the process of housing production in Luxembourg shows once again that buying and selling land in highly sought-after areas has problematic effects on the production of buildings. And it makes clear that the housing question is, above all, a question of land.

The fact that land can be traded like any other good seems to be considered a law of nature in most Western democracies, as is its unequal distribution. In Luxembourg, where the public sector possesses only 10 percent of developable land, 1 percent of the population owns one-quarter of the entire country. The average real estate assets of each of these landowners are worth 21 million euros.[2] In England, 25,000 aristocrats, oligarchs, City bankers, and corporations, who constitute roughly 1 percent of the population, own no less than half the

1
Ernst Friedrich Schumacher, *Small Is Beautiful. A Study of Economics as If People Mattered,* London 1973, p. 73.
2
L'Observatoire de l'Habitat, *Le degré de concentration de la détention du potentiel foncier destiné à l'habitat en 2016,* ed. by Luxembourg Ministry of Housing and the Luxembourg Center for Socio-Economic Research, 2019, p. 1.

Florian Hertweck / The Question of Land Reloaded

entire country, whereas the public sector has only
8 percent of all land at its disposal, and all homeowners
taken together only 5 percent.[3]

Although the situation in Luxembourg and England
can be traced back to a particular economic culture
and history of land distribution, the symptoms of land
privatization and real estate speculation are simply
occurring in more extreme forms in their premier cities
than in other major cities that are similarly exposed
to financialization: the central areas are subject to
accelerated gentrification, turning them into residential
areas quite out of reach for new arrivals up to the upper
middle class. As shiny central districts, they become
clumps of insular, exclusive residences, gigantic
office complexes, and shopping centers. Because of
the concentration of jobs, they attract more and more
commuters, who settle further and further out in the
hinterland, depending on their incomes; in the case of
Luxembourg, the hinterland extends beyond the country's
borders. As social inequality between the center and
the periphery becomes more pronounced, commuting gets
more costly and time-consuming, and air pollution and
CO_2 emissions increase in turn – as does the nervousness
of all those who cannot get to work on foot or by bicycle.
Even those who profit from this development are now
critical of overburdened infrastructures and increasingly
monofunctional, growing cities, as they are surprised
to find themselves caught in traffic more often and bored
by the cultural homogeneity of their cities with the same
retail chain stores everywhere. Many businesses located
in the city have trouble attracting qualified employees
because they are no longer willing to put up with the
loss of quality of life due to the stresses described, even
for high salaries. So while a social and ecological time
bomb is ticking in our urban territories, legislatures are
not addressing the essential question of land, although
experts have been discussing the subject intensively
again in recent years. In the absence of legal reform,
even the most progressive municipalities are pushed to
the limits of what they can do. In contrast, land policy
oriented toward the public good can command a majority
in Switzerland, for example, as various referenda have

3
Rob Evans, «Half of England
Is Owned by Less than 1% of
the Population,» in:
The Guardian, April 17, 2019.
See also Guy Shrubsole,
*Who Owns England? How We
Lost Our Green and Pleasant
Land and How to Take It Back,*
London 2019.

Florian Hertweck / The Question of Land Reloaded

shown.[4] This would presumably also be the case in Germany and other European countries if the damage to the economy caused by land and housing speculation were quantified. The fact that far too little is happening at the political level has to do with the ideological history of the land question, in which antagonistic concepts of land clash.

Land As a Good

What seems to be a law of nature, namely that land is private property and a tradable good, has a long backstory reaching from imperial Rome to the enclosure of the commons in eighteenth-century England, to the sanctification of land ownership by Catholic bishops in the nineteenth century.[5] In early liberalism, which was oriented toward the image of the average landowner, owning land was considered to guarantee the economic security of the citizen striving for liberty – a view that extends to Germany's Civil Code, according to legal historian Dietmar Willoweit. «At the close of the Middle Ages, the newly self-confident and self-important individual had rid himself of old social ties, at least in the major cities, and had linked ownership with the notion of liberty.» From then on, ownership was seen in liberal thinking as a «free authority, as the right to dispose of a thing, to use it and abuse it as one desired.»[6]

The major wave of land privatization set in with the French Revolution. Contrary to Rousseau's and Robespierre's ideas, *liberté* trumped *égalité* in this re-distribution of land. In the Second Empire, the Saint-Simonists pressed ahead with large-scale land speculation. The modernization of Paris was to be financed by the value added to the land which had been expropriated, built up, and then resold. A new bank had to be established for this highly speculative endeavor – the beginning of a banking industry specializing in real estate lending. Since the landowners successfully litigated against this venture, it became necessary to increase compensation significantly and to authorize restitution. Public debt soared because profits plummeted,[7] yet the land did not even remain in public ownership.

At the same time, it was the real estate companies in Berlin – and not the municipality – that cut their lucrative

4
For example, the initiative «Boden behalten, Basel gestalten» (Keep the land, shape Basel), which prohibited the city of Basel from selling public land, received 67 percent of the vote, and no less than 76 percent voted for the initiative in Zurich to increase the share of cooperative housing in the city from 25 to 33 percent. Cf. «Die Politik behandelt den Boden wie Joghurt. Interview mit Jacqueline Badran,» in: Brigitta Gerber, Ulrich Kriese (eds.), *Boden behalten – Stadt gestalten,* Zurich 2019, p. 27.
5
See Rudolf Eberstadt, *Handbuch des Wohnungswesens und der Wohnungsfrage* [1917], Jena 1920, pp. 22–23.
6
Dietmar Willoweit, «Geschichtlicher Wandel des Eigentumsbegriffs. Grund und Boden in der gegenwärtigen Politik,» in: *Die neue Ordnung,* No. 5/1976, pp. 358–361. Willoweit invokes Italian jurist Bartolus von Saxoferrato (1313–1357) as the often-mentioned originator of this concept.
7
When George-Eugène Haussmann stepped down as prefect of the Département Seine, the per capita debt of Parisians was on average nine times higher than that of Londoners and 11 times higher than that of Berliners. See Michel Cornu, «Les finances de Haussmann. Le Bonneteau du Baron,» in: *Urbanisme,* No. 241/1990, pp. 39–47; Pierre Pinon, «Entreprises et financements,» in: Jean des Cars, Pierre Pinon (eds.), *Paris Haussmann,* Paris 1991, pp. 102–106.

Florian Hertweck / The Question of Land Reloaded

Fig. pp. 12/13:
Public properties in a
Luxembourg municipality,
2016
white: buildable, publicly
owned land / light gray:
buildable, privately owned
land

intermediate deals during the major expansion of the city planned by James Hobrecht. To simplify the transactions, the boundaries between the fields were retained as the boundaries between plots wherever possible. The real estate companies bought and provided access to the plots, which were much too large, and then resold them to developers, who built extremely dense tenement blocks on them to recoup the transaction costs; this was facilitated by the lack of effective building codes. The dreadful housing conditions, which were similar in all major European cities, not only brought proponents of land reform on the scene, but also motivated architects to direct their discipline toward jointly owned land.

After the Second World War, speculative builders pulled in large profits during the «fleeting dream of everlasting prosperity,» because transforming farmland into land zoned for building was not taxed and demand for housing was high during the wave of suburbanization.[8] An example on the outskirts of Munich: «in 1951, a plot used for grazing sheep was sold for 0.50 DM per square meter. In 1962, the city zoned the pasture for building, which raised the price to 30 DM per square meter. Then, it provided infrastructure, and the plot was developed. In 1971, a square meter cost 450 DM. Thus, the value of the land had risen by a factor of 900 within 20 years. Without taking the municipal fees for infrastructure development into account, this means that the value of a 20-hectare plot increased from 100,000 DM to 90 million DM.»[9] Even Bavarian politician Franz Josef Strauß, who was known to hate communism, criticized this at the CSU party convention in 1970: «Land prices in the Federal Republic of Germany are rising to such an extent that it is irresponsible to permit these profits to flow into the pockets of just a few without taxing them. For example, the city of Munich purchased land for roughly 650 million DM between 1957 and 1967. If it had bought all of it in 1957, that is, in the first year of this 10-year period, it would have paid just 148 million DM. Therefore, a few people have earned half a billion, and haven't even had to pay taxes on it, because of public services – the costs of infrastructure development.»[10]

Yet despite a major public debate about land in the Federal Republic of Germany in the seventies, and

8
Burkhart Lutz, *Der kurze Traum immerwährender Prosperität*, Frankfurt am Main / New York 1984.
9
Gesetzesvorlage zur Änderung des Bundesbaugesetzes: Deutscher Bundestag – 7. Wahlperiode, Drucksache 7/2496, p. 30.
10
Franz Josef Strauß, quoted in: *Materialien zum SPD-Parteitag vom 28.11. bis 2.12.1972 in Hannover*, Bonn 1972, p. 44.

Florian Hertweck / The Question of Land Reloaded

although the political parties had all established commissions for social land reform, nothing much changed. The party platform of Strauß's CSU even called for the introduction of land value capture of 80 percent to be paid on increased land values due to planning decisions, applicable in Munich. Yet in harmony with the tabloids, it stylized any and all land reform measures as communist work of the devil. Such measures included various forms of taxing increased land values to finance infrastructure. Hans-Jochen Vogel, then mayor of Munich and later Federal Minister of Regional Planning, Building and Urban Development, had proposed a system for areas subject to major development pressure in which the municipality had the right to make decisions about land and private individuals decided about the buildings on that land. As so often with the land question, it was falsely claimed that homeowners were to be expropriated, with the result that large parts of the population were frightened, even though Vogel never sought to have their real estate municipalized or subjected to higher taxes.

The Neoliberal Sellout

The neoliberal turn in the US and the UK in the eighties ushered in privatizations, including of public land and housing stocks. This policy was supported by influential economists such as Friedrich August von Hayek and Milton Friedman,[11] even if the latter held the view that a tax on land was still the least bad tax, comparatively speaking. The politico-economic soil on which the current situation has grown was tilled during that time. For even in an ordoliberal country like the Federal Republic of Germany – despite the fact that as a matter of principle ordo-liberalism[12] gave too little consideration to land – people fell for the laissez-faire idea that the state was to keep out of urban development and housing as far as possible since the business community was better at doing business and the free market would regulate itself; the question of land and housing would solve itself if only it were deregulated. The abolition of not-for-profit status for housing by Helmut Kohl's Christian Democratic/ Liberal government – he had proclaimed an intellectual and moral turning point following years of the Social

11
On the influence of neoliberalism on housing policy, see inter alia Anne Kockelkorn, «Wohnungsfrage Deutschland: Zurück in die Gegenwart. Von der Finanzialisierung der Nuller-jahre über den Niedergang der Neuen Heimat zum Ordoliberalismus der 1950er-Jahre,» in: Jesko Fezer et al. (eds.), *Wohnungsfrage,* Berlin 2017, pp. 106–142.
12
Ordoliberalism is the economic principle according to which the state provides a legal framework in order to guarantee free and fair competition, thus precluding the development of monopolies. Ordoliberalism was the basis in economic theory for the social market economy in the Federal Republic of Germany.

Florian Hertweck / The Question of Land Reloaded

Democratic/Liberal coalition – set the course for the privatization of public housing companies and their reservoir of land, which was carried out under the following Social Democrat/Green federal government. The public sector sold roughly half a million of its housing units between 1999 and 2006. The wave of privatization of public housing stock and the associated land went hand in hand with better-off residents returning to the city from the leafy suburbs and the streamlining of municipal government, including the building authorities. With the emergence of the shareholder-value principle, privatization encountered a new form of investors trading on the stock market who were neither aware of the context of the real estate they purchased, nor articulated any aspirations other than generating returns to be paid to shareholders.

In the early nineties, the decision to move Germany's capital from Bonn to Berlin, tax breaks on real estate investments, and a restitution policy for former East Germany that was oriented toward private property owners – land expropriated by the Nazi or East German governments had to be returned to its former owners or their descendants; alternatively, they received monetary compensation – triggered the «most dynamic increase in value that a piece of German land [Berlin] had ever experienced» without the federal or municipal government absorbing the «wealth that had landed in their laps.»[13] In the new federal states (former East Germany), business deals were now made by private parties again, and more than 80 percent of the plots affected by restitution changed hands. Yet the ownership problems following the political transition could have been solved with ground leases, as Social Democratic land law expert and architect Peter Conradi pointed out: «it would have been possible [in the new federal states] to return the property to the previous owners and to require them to grant the subsequent users ground leases limited to 50 years. That would have prevented many conflicts and much human suffering.»[14] After all, the Treuhand Agency, which the federal government instituted to privatize the state-owned businesses and properties of the German Democratic Republic, sold most of the real estate entrusted to it to

13
Heribert Prantl, «Heraus-forderungen der öffentlichen Liegenschaftspolitik in der wachsenden Stadt,» in: Gerber, Kriese 2019 (see note 4), p. 20.
14
Peter Conradi, «Ein soziales Bodenrecht – eine ungelöste/lösbare Aufgabe?,» in: Beate and Hartmut Dieterich (eds.), Boden – Wem nützt er? Wen stützt er?, Braunschweig/Wiesbaden 1997, p. 33.

Florian Hertweck / The Question of Land Reloaded

West German investors. «There are no East Germans who could lay claim to West German land,» said land reform advocate Hartmut Dieterich, «but countless West Germans who do so in East German cities.»[15]

Following the Berlin banking crisis, whose impact on the city's public budget rendered it hamstrung in 2001, selling off publicly owned real estate at the highest possible price was intended to fill the gaps in the public coffers. In this sense, Berlin was the avant-garde, since the same pattern was repeated worldwide after the global financial crisis seven years later: publicly owned land and infrastructure such as waterworks, railroad lines, and airports were sold on a massive scale to offset public debt. The revenues had little effect on public finances, but many cities now find themselves lacking any relevant reservoir of land. After German unification, the city of Berlin, for example, owned more than half the land zoned for development there, but elsewhere, most of the developable land in urban locations is privately owned, and almost all the land owned by the public sector is on the urban fringe.[16] At the same time, the real estate market was flooded with unfathomable amounts of money following the global financial crisis, particularly in cities whose land and real estate were not yet valued as highly as in Paris or London, because other markets no longer yielded returns even remotely as attractive. In Germany, where the home ownership rate is only 45 percent (in Berlin, it is a very low 18 percent), twice as much money – roughly 265 billion euros – was invested in real estate in 2019 as in the year of the global financial crisis.[17]

The international capital companies and pension funds were joined by an ever-growing number of family offices increasingly investing the wealth held by family-owned small and medium-sized enterprises in real estate. In his book *Capital in the Twenty-First Century,* economist Thomas Piketty showed how incomes from capital investments, a disproportionate share of which are in real estate, are seeing much stronger growth than the economy as a whole, with windfall profits making the wealthy ever richer.[18]

Hans-Jochen Vogel enjoyed provoking people by commenting that land prices in Munich have risen by a

15
Beate and Hartmut Dieterich, «Einführung,» in: ibid., p. 73.
16
See Berliner Senats-verwaltung für Stadtentwick-lung und Umwelt, *Stadt-entwicklungsplan Wohnen* 2025, 2014, p. 15.
17
«Immobilienumsätze in Deutschland haben sich ver-doppelt,» in: *Frankfurter Allgemeine Zeitung,* March 11, 2019.
18
Thomas Piketty, *Capital in the Twenty-First Century,* Cambridge, Massachusetts 2014.

whopping 20,000 percent since the 1950s, whereas gross incomes have increased by just 300 percent during the same period. In 2017 alone, the price of residential plots increased by about 30 percent there. Rent for a Munich apartment measuring 60 square meters has increased by 50 percent in the past five years, but in Berlin by more than 70 percent. As journalist Laura Weißmüller emphasizes, pensioners, single parents, and low earners especially, but now also the entire middle class suffer from the effects of capital investments in real estate and land speculation. Reinier de Graaf, a partner with OMA architects, says, «If I look at my friends in Amsterdam, people all roughly my age and with the same education and background, the financial divide runs exactly along the lines of who decided to buy a home in the nineties and who continued to rent.»[19] Fewer and fewer young people in Germany are able to buy a home, low interest rates notwithstanding. Since the amount of capital required is significantly higher than it was 20 years ago, and also because young people are losing interest in owning a home, the number of first-time home buyers has dropped to 60 percent of the figure from 20 years ago.[20] Discontent is gradually making itself heard; renters' movements, calls for expropriation, and projects to buy back real estate are coming to the fore. People are reclaiming the right to a city, which should be non-negotiable in a democracy, but is no longer valid today.

Land as a Commons
How old is the notion that land is not and should not be a tradable commodity? It reaches back to the nomadic peoples, who were certainly familiar with trading goods. Although it was true that until the sixth century B.C. oligarchies were the rule in the cities of ancient Greece, including oligarchic land regimes – aristocrats owned the best land – there was a turning point under a reign of tyranny by a small handful of aristocrats. These tyrants placed the other aristocrats in the service of the polity, which was therefore in a position to rid itself of the tyrants. The result was the formation of the Greek *poleis,* with the concept of the free citizen vested with political rights – excepting women, children, foreigners, and slaves – and

19
See the interview in this volume with Reinier de Graaf and Carolien Schippers.
20
Michael Voigtländer, Pekka Sagner, *Analyse der Wohneigentumsbildung; Gutachten für die Schwäbisch Hall AG,* Cologne 2019.

the self-government of the civic community. Every citizen involved in a new settlement was given land in a central location, even if the plots had different sizes depending on the citizen's social standing. Aristotle demanded that every citizen be allotted a plot near the central settlement as well as one at the outer edge of the territory.[21] Selling land was prohibited, which is why no real estate market existed at first. Settlers who arrived later could only lease land and had to do other kinds of work, so many people became skilled artisans and traders of other goods. Finally, the quasi-equality of the concept of citizens was mirrored in the urban planning of Hippodamus of Miletus; he developed a grid with a typology of two different plot sizes. Ildefons Cerdà took up this spatial expression of a quasi-egalitarian image of society again in the nineteenth century for Barcelona.

The medieval German city is often drawn upon as a – somewhat glorified – model of urban development without land speculation, or for today's ground leases. In *Die Stadt und ihr Boden* (Towns and the Land), architect Hans Bernoulli describes the founding of towns in the eleventh and twelfth centuries as an example of organic urban development which was liberated from land speculation; the settlers were allocated plots by the royal landlords: «the merchants received larger plots on the market square and the main road, the artisans and the farming burghers smaller ones, while an area outside the city was jointly managed as a commons to provide food. Now the settlers built […] their houses on the plots allocated to them. They paid the landlord an annual sum for the right to build on the allocated piece of land and to have and keep that building […]. Their right to land was hereditary; if the landlord agreed, the right including the building itself could be sold to a third party. In this way, the building and the land were legally differentiated most clearly.»[22] The story of «complete differentiation between the land and the building in twelfth- and thirteenth-century German real estate law» is also told by economist Rudolf Eberstadt in his *Handbuch des Wohnungswesens und der Wohnungsfrage* (Handbook of the Housing Sector and the Housing Question): «According to German law, the values created by capital and labor were not allowed

21
See Frank Kolb, *Die Stadt im Altertum,* Düsseldorf 2005.
22
Hans Bernoulli, *Die Stadt und ihr Boden,* Erlenbach-Zurich 1949 [first edition: 1946], p. 24.

Florian Hertweck / The Question of Land Reloaded

RUDOLF EBERSTADT

HANDBUCH DES

WOHNUNGSWESENS

DRITTE AUFLAGE

JENA

VERLAG VON GUSTAV FISCHER

Rudolf Eberstadt, *Hand-buch des Wohnungswesens und der Wohnungsfrage* (Handbook of the Housing Sector and the Housing Question). Third revised and expanded edition, Jena 1917 (first edition 1909)

Adolf Damaschke, *Marxismus und Bodenreform* (Marxism and Land Reform), Jena 1926 (first edition 1922)

Marxismus und Bodenreform

Von

Adolf Damaſchke

26.—30. Tauſend

Jena
Verlag von Guſtav Fiſcher
1926

to be combined with the right of the landowner.» House-builders «did not have to pay a purchase price for the land, but only a fee.» Nonetheless, there was a market for real estate in this period too: «In the flourishing cities we find a number of people who buy and own houses as a business, partly as an attractive capital investment, also for resale to turn a profit.» If a house was demolished and its owner refused «to build, or was not able to do so for lack of means, the plot was sold by order of the authorities.» And, according to Eberstadt, the «law relating to expropriation was regularly applied in the Middle Ages [with compensation].»[23]

French Enlightenment philosopher Jean-Jacques Rousseau in particular commented on the land question. In his *Discourse on Inequality,* he argued against the supposed law of nature that land was a monopoly of a ruling class: «The first man, who, after enclosing a piece of ground, took it into his head to say, ‹This is mine,› and found people simple enough to believe him, was the true founder of civil society. How many crimes, how many wars, how many murders, how many misfortunes and horrors would that man have saved the human species, who pulling up the stakes or filling up the ditches should have cried to his fellows: Be sure not to listen to this impostor; you are lost if you forget that the fruits of the earth belong equally to us all, and the earth itself to nobody!»[24] Land activist Thomas Spence took the same line 20 years later in his lecture *The Rights of Man, as Exhibited in a Lecture, Read at the Philosophical Society, in Newcastle.* In it, he criticized the enclosure of the commons, which set the course for the unequal distribution of land that still prevails today: «Thus were the first land-holders usurpers and tyrants; and all who have since possessed their lands, have done so by right of inheritance, purchase, &c. from them […]»[25] According to Spence, all land was to be transferred to the municipalities, which would lease it to third parties in order to finance all public functions through the rent of land.

Land Reform: Between Taxation and Socialization

Numerous thinkers later grappled with the land question: from Adam Smith to David Ricardo, from the physiocrats

23
Eberstadt 1920 (see note 5), pp. 44–45.
24
Jean-Jacques Rousseau, *Discourse on Inequality* [first edition 1755], Part II, Section I. http://faculty.wiu.edu/M-Cole/Rousseau.pdf
25
Thomas Spence, *The Rights of Man, as Exhibited in a Lecture, Read at the Philosophical Society, in Newcastle, to Which Is Now First Added an Interesting Conversation Between a Gentleman and the Author on the Subject of His Scheme,* London 1793, p. 9.

to the early socialists. But none of them were greeted as positively as US land reformer Henry George with his bestseller *Progress and Poverty,* first published in 1879, in which he shifted the land question from rural to urban areas. George's theorem was that the value of land was only realized through communal achievements. Private land ownership was «economically inefficient and unfair.»[26] Although he considered land to be a commons, he was against it being expropriated, and called for the «single tax» – introducing a tax on rent of land and simultaneously abolishing all other taxes. George's concept questioned whether society was to tax productive things such as labor, or simply land. This was a question that German land reformer Adolf Damaschke also raised in his most important work *Die Bodenreform* (Land Reform), first published in 1902, in which he devoted a chapter to Henry George. «Land is available just once where people need it, and that is the reason why the same economic cause that makes the products of labor cheaper must make land more expensive. Therefore, the products of labor and natural resources are completely opposite in terms of their economic nature. Our prevailing mammonistic system is wrong because it treats these two areas of the economy the same, namely land just like any product of human labor. Communism is wrong because it basically makes the same mistake, but goes to the other extreme: it too seeks to treat the products of labor the way one should treat land.»[27] Damaschke, who like most land reformers did not oppose the market economy per se, situated land reform in contrast to mammonism – the rule of money in capitalism – and communism. His approach was one of reform, not of revolution. Like George, he argued for taxation in order to absorb rent of land, now in the form of a tax on its basic value and another one on appreciation in value. Municipalities were not to sell their land, but only to grant ground leases and, if possible, expand their reservoirs of land, if necessary through expropriation. Damaschke also argued in favor of massively promoting cooperatives.

Even if German economic theorist Silvio Gesell and Damaschke shared a social-liberal view concerning land, Gesell argued for it to be nationalized in the interests

26
Dirk Löhr in his contribution in this volume, p. 56.
27
Adolf Damaschke, *Die Bodenreform,* Jena 1912 [first edition 1902], p. 53.

Florian Hertweck / The Question of Land Reloaded

of its social dimension. All land was to be transferred to public ownership and then leased out, whereas the buildings on the land were to remain private property that could be bought and sold. Gesell influenced numerous anarchists such as Gustav Landauer, who even appointed him finance minister of the short-lived Bavarian Soviet Republic. From Mikhail Bakunin and Peter Kropotkin on, the anarchists, who naturally opposed land ownership, linked the right to use land with cultivation of the land. «What we call value,» Landauer wrote in 1911 in his *For Socialism,* «thus arises only through work to improve the ground and to extract and further process the products of the earth.»[28] Only if the earth was no one's private property would humans be free. Landauer argued for continuous redistribution of land ownership so that an imbalance would never occur.

In the early twentieth century, notions of land as a commons and of communal housing reached the historic peak of their popularity in Europe. The land and housing reform movement influenced municipal and national policies in many countries. The municipality of Zurich first purchased large swaths of land in 1896 to build housing there. The Weimar Constitution took on key demands of the land reform movement, in particular that increases in the value of land were to be made utilizable to the community (Article 155). «A new guiding principle of housing in the community emerged everywhere: cooperatives were established by middle-class people, artisans, blue- and white-collar workers, even university professors»; as they «mobilized self-help, they were usually the only developers of new buildings, thereby taking a burden off the municipalities.» The cooperatives in turn received «support from municipalities in many ways: by providing municipal land through ground leases, by exemptions from fees, infrastructure costs, building regulations, etc.» in advance.[29]

In Vienna, the social-democratic city government implemented the most aggressive land policy in order to realize unprecedented amounts of housing. Since the municipality feared that the infrastructure costs *outside* the city would be high, it introduced strong tenants' rights and a high land appreciation tax, which made land

28
Gustav Landauer,
For Socialism [1911],
https://theanarchistlibrary.
org/library/gustav-landauer-
call-to-socialism#toc11,
section 7.
29
Klaus Novy, Michael Prinz,
*Illustrierte Geschichte der
Gemeinwirtschaft.
Wirtschaftliche Selbsthilfe
in der Arbeiterbewegung von
den Anfängen bis 1945,*
Berlin / Bonn 1985, p. 102.

Florian Hertweck / The Question of Land Reloaded

prices plummet and drove landowners *within* the city to sell their real estate at any price. This policy enabled the municipality to increase its share of land in Vienna from 17 percent in 1919 to 33 percent in 1930.[30] The now freely available plots were built up by cooperatives and other not-for-profit organizations, covering at most half of the surface area of the land – generally on the perimeters of the city blocks, leaving planted courtyards for communal use – compared with 85 percent in the previous high-density tenements. At the conclusion of Vienna's housing construction program, one-seventh of the urban population was living in not-for-profit and cooperative housing. «Neither the highest profitability nor a low average rate of return, not even recovery of the building costs were decisive for the economics, but rather the principle that there was no expectation of a return.» According to economist Klaus Novy, «housing as a good became a social service provided by the municipalities; it lost its character of being capital and a source of non-labor income, and it became a durable consumer good.»[31] Vienna, which to this day has continued to orient its urban development policy toward the public good, and which, in contrast to other cities, has not privatized its public land, ranks very high in quality-of-life surveys every year.

Ideal and Reality

Thinkers imagining land as a commons had tremendous influence on architects: Frank Lloyd Wright directly referenced Henry George in Broadacre City, which provided plots of the same size for all its residents, as did Spanish urban planner Arturo Soria y Mata in his Ciudad Lineal. Although not an architect, Ebenezer Howard created one of the most influential city models. His garden city referred, among others, to Thomas Spence: all land was to be owned by the municipality. Bruno Taut, architect of many housing developments built on public land in Berlin (which were privatized some years ago), referred to Pyotr Kropotkin in his book *Die Auflösung der Städte* (The Dissolution of Cities). After the Second World War, many architects such as Bernoulli, who based his vision on Silvio Gesell's theories, still considered it necessary to «liberate» land in order to conduct coherent and functional urban

30
Helmut Weihsmann, *Das Rote Wien. Sozialdemo-kratische Architektur und Kommunalpolitik 1919–1934,* Vienna 2002, pp. 32, 58.
31
Klaus Novy, «Der Wiener Gemeindewohnungsbau: ‹Sozialisierung von unten›,» in: *ARCH+,* No. 45/1979, p. 14.

design. In this regard, one should imagine the excitement Cornelis van Eesteren, former director of the CIAM (Congrès Internationaux d'Architecture Moderne), sensed in the sixties when he developed the plan for an entirely new city on the polders of Lelystad, near Amsterdam, a perfect *tabula rasa* not at all subdivided into plots. The Charter of Athens states: «This sharp contradiction [between modern urban design and limitless fragmentation of individually owned land] poses one of the most serious problems of our time: the pressing need to regulate the disposition of land on an equitable and legal basis, so as to meet the vital needs of the community as well as those of the individual.»[32] Yet it was beyond dispute to the authors of the Charter that «[p]rivate interests should be subordinated to the interests of the community.»[33] And in their *Programm für Stadterneuerung* (Program for Urban Renewal), which was also signed in the middle of the Second World War by architects and urban planners including Egon Eiermann, Fritz Schumacher, and Rudolf Schwarz, Walter Gropius and Martin Wagner made the following demand: Because «land speculation often [brings about] the deterioration of housing developments, the municipality itself should own the land. The individual plots should be leased, whereas the houses themselves can be owned individually.»[34]

The reality in the existing postwar cities in Germany was different, however. Land ownership was not oriented toward social responsibility, although this is even enshrined in the Basic Law of the Federal Republic of Germany. Hans-Jochen Vogel was confronted with the problem of widespread land speculation as mayor of Munich from 1960 to 1972. The massive land price increases, he said, made rents continue to climb, and social housing as well as «far too few necessary infrastructure projects such as hospitals, schools, or kindergartens could be built, if any at all.»[35] It was not by chance that Vogel, a jurist, launched his package of measures at the 49th Deutsche Juristentag, a major conference of attorneys, in 1972. Besides various fiscal reforms, it provided for a new legal institution in areas with high development pressure, namely splitting the public right to determine the use and the users of land on the one hand (*Verfügungseigentum*)

32
https://www.getty.edu/conservation/publications_resources/research_resources/charters/charter04.html, p. 93.
33
Congrès Internationaux d'Architecture Moderne (CIAM), *La Charte d'Athenes* or *The Athens Charter* [1933], translated by J. Tyrwhitt, Paris, The Library of the Graduate School of Design, Harvard University, 1946. https://www.getty.edu/conservation/publications_resources/research_resources/charters/charter04.html, sections 93, 94.
34
Walter Gropius, Martin Wagner, «Ein Programm für Stadterneuerung,» in: Ulrich Conrads (ed.), *Programme und Manifeste zur Architektur des 20. Jahrhunderts,* Basel 2013 [first edition 1975], pp. 139–140.
35
«Vorbemerkungen,» in: Landeshauptstadt München (ed.), *Initiative für eine Neuordnung des Bodenrechts,* no date, presumably 1971 or 1972, p. 1. Papers of Hans-Jochen Vogel, Friedrich-Ebert-Stiftung, Bonn.

from the private right to use buildings on the other (*Nutzungseigentum*), as called for by Gesell, Bernoulli, and others. Although this controversial idea in his land reform proposal is similar in principle to ground leases, Vogel deliberately avoided that term because he was not only concerned with the practice of its application for land already in public ownership, but above all with transferring centrally located plots subject to massive speculation to municipal ownership so that the municipality would again become capable of taking action. Vogel and his fellow campaigners from the Social Democratic Party invoked the unpopular Article 14 (3) («Expropriation shall only be permissible for the public good.») and Article 15 («Land […] may, for the purpose of nationalization, be transferred to public ownership […]») of the Basic Law. Politicians of other convictions, but also progressive land rights reformers such as Hartmut Dieterich, criticized the municipalization of land as simply shifting the monopoly from the private to the public sector, advocating instead for distributing land ownership across the population – and if possible among owner-occupiers – as broadly as possible. Other ideas were derived from this recommendation: the idea of *Mietkauf* (renting property with the option to purchase it later, whereby the rent already paid would be counted toward the purchase price), which was to be pursued further, as well as the subsidy for homeowners, which was introduced later, or the subsidy for homeowners with children, which still exists today; these measures intensified urban sprawl.

In the early nineties, one Belgian and 29 US economists, including four Nobel laureates, claimed in an open letter to Mikhail Gorbachev, the then president of the Soviet Union, that a state or municipal land monopoly could be a positive model. They welcomed the Soviet Union opening up to a market economy and praised the plans for freely convertible currency, free trade, and the separation of companies from the state. But the economists said that Gorbachev should not adopt one feature of a liberal economy: the collective privatization of rent of land. Since in Western countries taxation absorbed far less rent of land than was theoretically possible, incomes, sales, and capital values were taxed, which in

Florian Hertweck / The Question of Land Reloaded

Hans Bernoulli

Die Stadt und ihr Boden

Towns and the Land

Summary and Legends in English · 120 Abbildungen und Pläne · 2. Auflage

Verlag für Architektur · Les Editions d'Architecture · Erlenbach-Zürich

LANDESHAUPTSTADT MÜNCHEN

Initiative
für eine Neuordnung
des Bodenrechts

Municipal Department of
the state capital of Munich,
*Initiative for Reorganizing
Land Law,* working paper and
public hearing, 1970–1972

principle hobbled the economy. In contrast, the Soviet Union was to retain public land ownership and lease plots to users for a certain period of time. The rents of land collectivized in this way were to be spent on social policy, financing infrastructure, and removing burdens on productive areas such as labor. The economists' open letter was to underline that handling land in a manner oriented toward the common good was not only reasonable in social and ecological terms, but also made economic sense. In addition, like all efforts toward land reform, it made clear that contrasting land as a tradable good and as a commons does not, as often claimed, mean contrasting capitalism and communism but rather that the opportunity for a dialog between a market economy and the common good is established in the notion of land as a commons.

What Is the Question of Land Reloaded About?

Today, the question of land is about how land can be treated as a commons in a democratic society. How can we find a healthy middle ground between the two extreme ideological poles, namely the socialization of land on the one hand and privatization on the other? As economic historian Richard Henry Tawney stated as early as the 1920s: «the idea […] that private property in land capital is necessarily mischievous is a piece of scholastic pedantry as absurd as that of those […] who would invest all property with some kind of mysterious sanctity.»[36,37] Since the pendulum has swung to the extreme of privatization in recent decades, further privatization of land should be halted categorically (some municipalities are already doing so). At the same time, public and communal land policy and housing production should be tackled more actively and imaginatively (we present some good examples). The question of land is basically still about what Peter Conradi called for decades ago, namely «making land speculation more difficult, reducing windfall profits from land sales, making it more difficult to hoard developable plots, and encouraging the use of developable plots as stipulated by zoning.»[38]

Placed in this context, the dialog about the question of land, between land as a general good on the one hand and

36
R. H. Tawney, *The Acquisitive Society,* New York 1920, p. 86.
37
http://www.gesetze-im-internet.de/englisch_gg/englisch_gg.html#p0083.
38
Conradi 1997 (see note 13), p. 31.

houses being privately protected and tradable property on the other, does not contradict the social market economy.[39] Heribert Prantl, a lawyer and journalist with the daily *Süddeutsche Zeitung,* claims that a tax on land is «not a precursor to communism, but the actualization of the Basic Law,» if the social responsibility that ownership entails is taken into account.[40] Introducing a tax on land that applies only to the land itself and not to the value of any buildings on the land would be an important first step. But would that be enough in a situation in which many municipalities are basically unable to draw on a land reservoir if they are to prioritize development within built-up areas? Will fiscal measures suffice if one can assume that the value of land will continue to increase because of climate policy measures and the energy transition from fossil fuels to renewables, while migration to the cities continues to intensify? If some cities make their own land available only through ground leases, and preferably to cooperatives, will that have sufficient impact? If the answer to these questions is no, then how will the public sector be able to expand its land reservoir perceptibly? By systematically applying the right of preemption – as practiced in the city of Ulm, for example – which would require national or European financial support, especially for smaller or economically underdeveloped municipalities' land banks, or even through *städtebauliche Entwicklungsmassnahmen* (SEMs) and expropriation in some areas? Or do we need to think about land in an entirely different way, for example in the sense of citizens being shareholders in land? This model would anchor common responsibility in each and every one of us. Finally, the question of land is about much more than housing; it poses questions about the society we would like to live in, about the type and purpose of growth, about the type and the value of labor.

About This Book

Although the question about how land is apportioned, allocated, and used is literally fundamental to architecture, housing, and urban design, and thus to the development of cities and territories, only a few architects examine it closely. There are several reasons for this. First, the topic

39
The social market economy is based on the principle of ordoliberalism, according to which the state must set a legal framework within which economic activity can unfold. This is generally thought to include active policies concerning the economy, economic stabilization, and taxes as well as a network of social benefits for people who are elderly, sick, low-income, and /or unemployed.
40
Prantl 2019 (see note 13), p. 20.

forces architects to concern themselves with a complex subject matter that repeatedly challenged this book editor's intellectual grasp as well. When it comes to the land question, Rudolf Eberstadt's dictum still holds: studying it requires broad knowledge – from public administration to economics.[41] Architects have little training in these fields. As a result, with a few exceptions the land question has not been and is not being addressed by architects, but by economists, philosophers, politicians, activists, and politically engaged writers. Neither Henry George, Adolf Damaschke, Hans-Jochen Vogel nor Hartmut Dieterich had a background in architecture or urban planning. Regrettably, the latter two passed away this year. Second, it is difficult to deal with the question of land in an unideological way. Yet since architects strive to transfer their ideas into built reality and need clients for this purpose, be they public or private, they tend to produce an illusion of being political rather than actually taking positions. That is why most positions and concepts of the city developed by architects disregard the question of land. Very few – such as Le Corbusier's *The City of To-morrow and Its Planning* – hint at it subtly, and only in exceptional cases, such as the work of Hans Bernoulli or Frank Lloyd Wright, are such concepts explicitly made a topic of discussion. «There seems to be something wrong with land,» wrote Bernoulli in the introduction to *Die Stadt und ihr Boden,* «and for opaque reasons, everybody avoids going into this dis-concerting issue.»[42]

This book seeks to address this «disconcerting issue» head-on. Following the introduction, it presents historical models and events important to the question of land. Social economist Werner Onken, editor of the collected works of Silvio Gesell, summarizes the land reform movement. Fiscal economist Dirk Löhr, who issued a new edition of Henry George's magnum opus *Progress and Poverty,* explains George's hypotheses. Architect Manuela Kölke, whose research focuses on anarchy, explains why land was relevant to the anarchists in Vienna after the First World War. Architectural historian Sylvia Claus, co-editor of a new book on Hans Bernoulli, which was published in 2018, illuminates his approach of

41
Rudolf Eberstadt, «Aus dem Vorwort zur ersten Auflage,» in: Eberstadt 1920 (see note 5), no page number.
42
Bernoulli 1949 (see note 22), p. 6.

Florian Hertweck / The Question of Land Reloaded

municipalized land. Architect Giovanni La Varra relates an approach to land municipalization in Italy in the sixties that corresponds with Hans-Jochen Vogel's approach the following decade, which is described in the subsequent chapter by Florian Hertweck. Berlin urban planner and former member of the Bundestag (German federal parliament) Franziska Eichstädt-Bohlig traces the history of the sellout of not-for-profit housing in 2000s Germany, whose dramatic impacts are intensifying. Urban researcher Markus Hesse shines a light on various state approaches relating to the financialization of land markets and urban development using the example of small countries. In contrast, economic geographer Christian Schulz, whose research examines the circular economies of a post-growth economy, shows clearly which alternative options for action exist in post-growth contexts that are intentionally designed to be comprehensible. Journalist Laura Weißmüller, who was involved in getting the German media to take up the question of land, locates the issue within the current debate. This first section of the book concludes with a conversation with Berlin architects Christian Schöningh, known for the «Spreefeld» cooperative he co-founded, Arno Brandlhuber, who with filmmaker Christopher Roth devoted the film *The Property Drama* to the question of land, and Nikolaus Kuhnert, architecture critic and editor of the journal *ARCH+*, who has been writing and publishing about the question of land and housing since the seventies.

The second section discusses various models of the city in conversations with actors from public administration, foundations, academia, and planning practice. In Munich we discussed the principle of Socially Just Land Use (SoBoN) with Urban Planning Commissioner Elisabeth Merk and her predecessor Christiane Thalgott. In Amsterdam, where 85 percent of urban land is still owned by the public sector, we spoke with Carolien Schippers, Head of the Department of Urban Development, as well as Reinier de Graaf, a partner with OMA architects. In Basel, we talked with two representatives of foundations, Martin Weis of the Christoph Merian Stiftung and Klaus Hubmann of Stiftung Habitat, about their experiences with ground leases. Stefan Rettich presents how Singapore, where the right to housing is organized by the state, manages land. In contrast, we learned in the interview with Françoise Ged of the Observatoire de Chine and land law expert Miguel Elosua that socializing land does not necessarily bring about social and ecological urban development, as shown by the case of China. Neither the first nor the second section of the book aims to be comprehensive. Many other models of the city would have warranted discussion: Freiburg, Tübingen, Ulm, Ivry-sur-Seine, Zurich, and above all Vienna, which has, however, already been documented and discussed in depth many times.

In the third section, we touch on various models of architecture and urban design – from utopias such as Le Corbusier's *The City of To-morrow and Its Planning* to elevated projects that leave the land itself available for public uses, to models applying ground leases. Section Four is about Luxembourg, where the question of land is extremely virulent. A conversation with Sam Tanson, Luxembourg's Minister of Housing, and Member of the Council of State Mike Mathias goes into the question as to what kind of policies are able to respond to the problem of land and housing in a country with a very liberal constitutional and economic tradition. Finally, we present the contribution to Luxembourg's pavilion at the 16th Venice Biennale of Architecture, «The Architecture of the Common Ground.»

The present book is intended not to be a polemic but a contribution to the debate; although it does take a stance, that stance enables readers to develop various positions and options for action. Activists, pressure groups, renters' organizations, discussion groups, publications such as *Boden behalten, Stadt gestalten* (Keep the Land, Shape the City), edited by Brigitta Gerber and Ulrich Kriese, and concerned journalists – they all are bringing the question of land into the public sphere. It is no coincidence that it is beginning to mobilize more architects in the course of current attempts to re-politicize the discourse on architecture. This book especially addresses architects as well as urban and regional planners, who not only bring their stance on the question of land to bear on the concepts they realize in their architecture, urban design, and spatial plans, but who can also contribute to developing the narrative of a new sense of community and the commons, including land, to counter the neoliberal narrative. Of course, this is not intended to exclude other readers. This volume is thus an attempt to make fruitful for spatial production positions relating to the question of land as well as architectural and urban design models of socio-ecological land use, going beyond the debates in journals such as *ARCH+* and *Stadtbauwelt.* It does not aspire to be comprehensive, but seeks to make a contribution toward more architects and others involved in spatial planning once more taking a stand on this important issue. But above all, this volume was written for students, as was *Positions on Emancipation,* the most recent volume published by the Master's Program in Architecture at the University of Luxembourg. Let us hope that they grapple critically and productively with the major social and ecological questions of our time in their future work.

Positions

Positions

Werner Onken

Who Owns the Earth?
On the History of Thought Concerning Land, Resources, and the Atmosphere as Common Goods

Present-day land grabbing is not a new phenomenon, but rather the dramatic intensification of a problem with a very long history. From ancient times to the present day, an often bloody trail of conflicts around inequitably distributed land, water, and other resources has run through the history of humankind. People have sought to resolve this dilemma time and again.

An idea central to Judaism, Christianity, and Islam is the notion that the Earth belongs to God and that we humans are temporary «guests on this Earth» who are to be its good stewards. The beginning of the 24th psalm reads: «The earth is the Lord's, and everything in it, the world, and all who live in it.» This stance is also to be found in African lore; instead of ownership rights, it «merely» recognizes individual usage rights to common land. And «Mother Earth» is considered holy in the lore of the indigenous peoples of the Americas as well; it must not be made into a commodity that can be bought and sold.

Respect for land and nature as God's sacred creation has been lost in Western civilization since the transition from the Middle Ages to the early modern period. One of the reasons is quite understandable: the notion of over-arching divine and common ownership of land was abused by the nobility to legitimize their rule during the centuries of feudalism. They considered themselves to be God's worldly custodians of the Earth and claimed ownership of land accordingly. From their position at the top of the feudal pyramid, they granted fiefs (land) to their serfs and demanded labor services in return.

These feudal power relations had to be dismantled in the transition to the bourgeois rule of law and democracy. But what would replace them when it came to land?

Humanist and Enlightenment philosophers could not find guidance concerning egalitarian ways of dealing with land in the thinking of their predecessors in Antiquity. Aristotle wavered as to whether land was to be common or private property. He and other ancient philosophers tended to want to divide the land, which was concentrated in the hands of large landowners, into smaller, privately owned parcels.[1]

The original, religious idea that land and the Earth as a whole were merely loaned to all humans living today and in

1
Aristotle, *Politics*, translated by Benjamin Jowett, Oxford 1885, pp. 33–35, https://archive.org/details/politicsaristot05arisgoog/page/n204.

Werner Onken / Who Owns the Earth?

the future by a higher divine authority had been discredited by the abuse of the idea of feudal tenure. That is why the humanists and Enlightenment thinkers did not yet develop the idea that democratic republics would need commonly owned land or legally guaranteed private usage rights. Instead, philosophers John Locke in England and Immanuel Kant in Germany paved the way for putting the land under feudal ownership into private hands.

In *Perpetual Peace,* published in 1795, Kant presented his ideas about cosmopolitan law and deplored the inhuman behavior of Europeans in their colonies overseas. On the other hand, he justified the «conditions accompanying established states where the rights of property are assured.»[2] In the early nineteenth century, the Napoleonic Code sealed the fate of how land and resources would be treated as tradable commodities in the future. Thus, they were given the same status as the products of human labor. This certainly did not result from malicious intent but was made in good faith that it would be possible to break up the power previously connected to feudal land ownership by individualizing it and distributing it widely.

After Locke and Kant, Adam Smith and other classical representatives of liberalism envisaged an egalitarian bourgeois society as an alternative to the hierarchy of the feudal estates – a market society with many small and medium-sized enterprises that exchanged the products of their labor, including privatized land, on markets free of monopolies. And they considered the money used as a means of exchange to be a harmless, neutral medium with no influence whatsoever on real events.

In reality, however, money was much more than merely a means serving the purpose of exchange, and it certainly had structural power to orient production more toward profitability than toward human needs. From then on, the main goal of all economic activity became the use of money to make more money. Karl Marx summed it up in the formula (money – commodity – money): $M-C-M'$ or $M-M'$.

So what emerged in place of the feudal hierarchy of estates was not an egalitarian bourgeois society, but a new capitalist hierarchy of the grande and the petite bourgeoisie as well as proletarian underclasses. Combined with the intrinsic dynamics of money, the privatization of land

2
Immanuel Kant, *Perpetual Peace,* translated by Mary Campbell Smith, London 1903/1917 [first edition 1795], p. 148; John Locke, Second Treatise of Government, https://www.earlymoderntexts.com/assets/pdfs/locke1689a.pdf [first edition 1690], pp. 10–11, 12–14.

Werner Onken / Who Owns the Earth?

became a central problem of society. From the early nineteenth century on, land gradually came to be a tradable commodity. Contrary to the assumptions of the classical representatives of liberalism, the people in bourgeois-capitalist society did not have justly distributed opportunities to purchase a piece of land of their own through their own work. «Liberated» farmers could often only acquire or keep land if they mortgaged it. Since many of them could not carry that much debt, the land often reverted back to the feudal lords or fell into the hands of privileged bankers or industrialists who demanded rent or lease payments from the underprivileged.

Moreover, land became progressively scarce as a consequence of the rapidly increasing population density during early capitalist industrialization. Similar to monetary capital and real industrial capital, land that owners did not live on became not only a tradable commodity but also a capital good that was to generate returns for its private owners. Where cities grew because of a concentration of industrial facilities and became segregated into exclusive residential areas and impoverished quarters for the proletariat with unsanitary tenements, numerous opportunities emerged for speculation on the basis of the location of land. The growth of the big cities went hand in hand with the major waves of land speculation and also with longer distances between the places where people lived, worked, and shopped, which in turn generated more and more traffic.

From the early nineteenth century on, land reform movements emerged that sought to remedy these undesirable developments – first in England, Ireland, and the US, later on the European continent as well. These land reform movements did not aim to turn the clock back to feudalism. Instead, they sought alternatives to both feudalism and modern capitalism. They were concerned with drawing, in a historic sense, on the original religious idea that the Earth with all its treasures was entrusted and loaned to all of humanity by the deities. They also grappled with the question as to how this idea could be put into practice in constitutional democracies in their own time.

Three main currents evolved within the land reform movement. The first could be called the «realist» wing.

One of its leading representatives was the North American social reformer Henry George. He believed that private land ownership was so deeply anchored in modernist thinking that it was politically futile to seek to replace it with another form of property. So on the one hand, George accepted the existence of private land ownership as unalterable; on the other, he wanted to overcome its negative side effects by means of a «single tax.» The constitutional democracy was to tax land values and increases in land values to benefit the general public. At the same time, this was to be the state's only source of tax revenue. In other words, Henry George wanted to socialize not land ownership but only the rent of land.

In Germany, Henry George's ideas were popularized especially by Adolf Damaschke and the Bund Deutscher Bodenreformer (BdB, League of German Land Reformers) he founded in 1898. However, Damaschke watered them down inasmuch as he only wanted to tax increases in land value, partly benefiting the general public. Yet the BdB did succeed in having land reform goals included in Article 155 of Germany's Weimar Constitution in 1919. A regulation concerning ground leases was also enacted at the time; it gave municipalities and church communities the opportunity to contract out private usage rights to their land for a predetermined period of time – for example, 99 years – in exchange for continuous usage fees.[3]

The second, the «fundamentalist» wing of the land-reform movement, wanted to transfer ownership of privatized land, providing compensation, to the general public – either to the state or to the municipalities or regional administrative bodies. Social reformers Michael Flürscheim and Silvio Gesell developed the idea that public bodies were to allocate private usage rights to individual plots of land to the highest bidders in the form of ground leases, and use the revenues raised in this way for social purposes.

Even in the early twentieth century, Gesell considered socializing resources within the land, such as oil, besides the land itself, and having them managed as common property of humanity by an international institution such as the League of Nations. A fee would have to be paid for the private use of resources, analogous to the fee for the

3
Michael Silagi, *Henry George and Europe: The Far-Reaching Impact and Effect of the Ideas of the American Social Philosopher,* New York 2000 [first edition: 1973]; Hans Diefenbacher, Klaus Hugler, *Adolf Damaschke und Henry George – Ansätze zu einer Theorie und Politik der Bodenreform,* Marburg 2005; Dirk Löhr, *Prinzip Renten-ökonomie – Wenn Eigentum zu Diebstahl wird,* Marburg 2013; Rolf Novy-Huy, Stiftung trias (eds.), *Das Erbbaurecht – ein anderer Umgang mit Grund und Boden,* Hattingen 2015.

Werner Onken / Who Owns the Earth?

Even in the early twentieth century, Gesell considered socializing resources within the land, such as oil, besides the land itself, and having them managed as common property of humanity by an international institution such as the League of Nations.

private use of land. All of the revenue from this resource usage fee would be paid back to the global population, with each person receiving the same amount.

With the eyes of a global citizen, Gesell viewed equal rights for all people on Earth as the «number one human right»: «No matter what the colour of a man's skin, black, brown, white or yellow, the undivided earth belongs to him. … From this description of Free-Land it follows that such expressions as ‹English coal,› ‹German potash,› ‹American oil› and so forth can be understood only in a geographical sense. For everyone, no matter to what race he may belong, has the same right to English coal, German potash, and American oil.»[4]

The two main currents of the land reform movement aimed to put their goals into practice through political means, as a reform «from above.» As the prospects for success were uncertain, liberal-socialist land reformers such as Franz Oppenheimer, Theodor Hertzka, and the libertarian cultural philosopher Gustav Landauer tried out reforms «from below» by attempting to establish settlements on common land either in European countries or overseas. Oppenheimer also influenced the beginnings of Zionist settlements in Palestine and – as did Martin Buber – the later kibbutz movement. Settlement cooperatives like these were also connected to the garden city movement and cooperative housing.[5]

The three different currents of the land reform movement did not contradict one another. They could actually be complementary. People could establish housing cooperatives by simply getting together and finding suitable, affordable land rather than having to wait for a favorable political majority. Yet the reformers' hopes became reality in only a few cases.[6] Besides, state-owned land could be contracted out for private usage through ground leases. Instead of selling off public property and using the revenues to plug holes in public budgets, the state could make use of its right of preemption, purchasing more land over time, depending on political will and financial capabilities, and have this public property be used by private individuals and entities. And when land that was initially still in private hands was bought and sold, the state could tax the increases in

4
Silvio Gesell, «The Natural Economic Order,» translated by Philip Pye, Berlin 1929 [first edition 1916], pp. 89–126.
5
Gerhard Senft (ed.), Land und Freiheit – Zum Diskurs über das Eigentum an Grund und Boden in der Moderne, Vienna 2013.
6
Anne Feuchter-Schawelka, «Siedlungs- und Land-kommunebewegung,» in: Jürgen Reulecke, Diethart Kerbs (eds.), Handbuch der Reformbewegungen 1880–1933, Wuppertal 1998, pp. 227–244; Kristiana Hartmann, «gartenstadt-bewegung,» in: ibid., pp. 289–300.

Werner Onken / Who Owns the Earth?

land value and use those revenues to finance additional public land purchases.

As we have seen, the land reform movements of the nineteenth and early twentieth centuries were diverse. Even some renowned economists were sympathetic toward them. John Stuart Mill, as the last great socially minded classical economist, and leading neoclassical economists such as Hermann Heinrich Gossen and Léon Walras, took it for granted that land – in contrast to the products of human labor – could not be a marketable good, even though they otherwise followed the guiding principle of «free markets.»

By and large, economics has lost sight of the question of land, and with it also of the various approaches to land reform, ever since the neoclassical production function limited the definition of material prosperity to a function of the inputs of human labor, capital, and technical progress, with land being subsumed under capital.

Although from the early stages on, the proponents of land reform considered it an international goal affecting all of humanity, this perspective was also narrowed on nationalist grounds. In Germany, it devolved into the Nazi ideology co-opting land reform. Its «blood and soil» ideology was a nothing less than a diabolical perversion of the idea of a close connection between human beings and the land. The purpose of the Nazi ideology's land reform rhetoric was in reality a legitimation for «Aryanizing» agriculture by means of the Reich Hereditary Farm Law (*Reichserbhofgesetz*). Otherwise, land remained capitalist private property, both in the countryside and in the cities. This was complemented by the Nazi ideology of «a people without space,» which was just as dehumanizing and which was used to justify violent land grabbing in Slavic countries in central and eastern Europe.

Land reform experienced a second perversion in the Communist countries, where larger landholdings were expropriated without compensation and agriculture was collectivized by force.

The notion that the Earth could belong to God or to everyone, and that we are not due property rights to it but only usage rights in return for payment, became discredited again by the two major dictatorships of the twentieth century. After 1945, this idea became taboo in the West because of the Cold War. Article 15 of the Basic Law of the Federal Republic of Germany would have made it possible to transfer land, natural resources, and means of production to common ownership in return for compensation. However, in reality capitalist private land ownership was so dominant in the postwar decades that the Social Democratic Party, during its period of a new beginning in the early seventies, failed to push through even timid proposals for land reform, such as the introduction of land value capture. Then the topic vanished from the political scene again, not even re-emerging in the beginnings of the ecological movement, where it would have served as a reminder that the Earth is a commons belonging to all human beings and that, as such, it must be managed in a different way than private property.

After the political transition of the autumn of 1989, the Western ideology of private land ownership unfortunately also prevented compensation for the historical injustice of the East German land reform of 1945–1949. Instead, policy followed the counterproductive principle of «restitution rather than compensation.» Besides countless cases where investments were blocked, the unique historical opportunity was lost to grant private usage rights to public land on a large scale in return for payment, which would have sent a clear signal for land reform and triggered truly sustainable urban and regional development.

Inappropriate structures with respect to land owner-ship are similarly firmly entrenched in many Third World countries, where large-scale landholdings either keep countless small farmers dependent on quasi-feudal land-owners, who became established in colonial times, or make them entirely landless, thereby driving them to the slums of the megacities. Promised land reforms have often failed to materialize or were mishandled, resulting in disappointing outcomes; as a consequence, the idea of common land ownership lost ground in countries of the South as well.

Thus the global system that disadvantages small-scale food producers has benefited the large multinational agricultural and pharmaceutical corporations that believe they can guarantee the global food supply through patented genetic engineering instead of through land reforms. Driven by the dynamics of the accumulation of money, the modern growth-based economic system is advancing into and dominating more and more spheres of life, small and large, by colonializing natural resources, genes and seeds, health, knowledge, and the Earth's atmosphere. By transforming all of them into tradable goods, capital goods, and objects of speculation, as occurred when land was first appropriated, this economic system gradually subjugates all of life, as commodities, for the purpose of increasing financial assets. And in times when financial investments are becoming riskier, purchasing resources and land as capital investments is becoming another form of land grabbing, especially in Africa and Latin America.

Continuing urban sprawl and excessive land consumption, as well as the increasing global concentration of capital and humans in metropolitan areas with its corresponding transportation problems underline the fact that the West and the East, the North and the South must recognize that taming the capitalist growth dynamics of money and finding forms in which the natural foundations of all human beings' livelihoods can be managed as common goods are major tasks for interdisciplinary research. That is why the question of land as well as the question of money, both of which have long been neglected, should be integrated into the current discourses on sustainability so that they develop a deeper sociopolitical dimension rather than remaining on the technical surface, as «Green Capitalism» does.

The basic idea of land reform, namely a) treating land as a common good belonging to all humans, b) charging fees for its private use, and c) paying these fees back on a per-capita basis to the (global) population, could contribute to the development of just procedures effective in the long term, which can be applied not only to land but also to resources and the climate. Making it a reality that all people share equally in all the foundations of our existence is admittedly a major interdisciplinary task. Beyond the basic ideas, there are more open questions than answers, and a great need for research into the details. Nonetheless, it is necessary to shift from a domination-based way of managing the common foundations of our lives to a cooperative understanding of how to use them in socially and environmentally friendly ways. Elinor Ostrom's research on the commons can contribute to achieving this goal as well.[7]

7
See, for example, David Bollier, Silke Helfrich (eds.), *Wealth of the Commons. A World Beyond Market and State,* Amherst 2012; David Bollier, Silke Helfrich (eds.), *Patterns of Commoning,* Amherst 2015; David Bollier, Silke Helfrich. *Free, Fair and Alive. The Insurgent Power of the Commons,* Gabriola Island, BC 2019.

Dirk Löhr
Henry George: The Public Value of Land

The Life of Henry George

Henry George was born on September 2, 1839 in Philadelphia as the second of ten children; he grew up in modest circumstances. His life was eventful: As a 16-year-old, he first went to Australia and India as a cabin boy; afterward, he completed a printing apprenticeship, and then experimented for a short time as a gold digger – with little success. Finally, he settled in San Francisco where he started a family. There he worked as a typesetter and journalist. His skills, honed in autodidactic studies, soon paved the way to an editorship and even the position of editor-in-chief of the *San Francisco Times.* In 1867, he took over the management of the *Herald,* and in 1872 the *Evening Post* in San Francisco. Finally, George became editor of the workers' newspaper *The Standard.*[1]

Henry George watched the development of the American West Coast states with great interest. In his view, these states fast-forwarded through all the stages of development for which Europe and the East Coast states had needed many decades. More and more people followed the pioneers. Although land was initially free, ultimately more and more of it was occupied by a ruthless minority of speculators and railway companies. The majority of the population had no access to land, and large parts of the population slipped into misery. Yet, the most important impetus for the development of George's theories was a visit to New York during the 1860s. Here, he was able to experience the coexistence of prosperity and progress on the one hand, and bitter poverty on the other. This inspired him to entitle his major work, which appeared in 1879, *Progress and Poverty.*[2] According to George, social grievances were caused by the monopolization of land and natural treasures by a selfish minority. Actually, he believed that all people should have the same natural right to access the resources of earth. After initial difficulties, *Progress and Poverty* became a bestseller and was translated into 15 languages. It became the most widely read work of its time after the Bible. In the end, millions of copies were sold.[3]

However, Pope Leo XIII attacked Henry George for his rejection of land ownership. In the encyclical *Rerum novarum,* he contradicted Henry George's statements and

1
Werner Onken, «Henry George – ein Sozialreformer des Gedankens und der Tat,» in: *Fragen der Freiheit,* Issue 245, December 1997, pp. 3–18.
2
Revised edition with a new introduction: Marburg (Metropolis) 2017. Among others, this was followed by the books *The Irish Land Question* (1881), *Social Problems* (1884), *Protection or Free Trade* (1886), and numerous essays in magazines. Posthumous publications include *The Science of Political Economy* and a ten-volume edition of his complete works (1898–1901, German edition 1906–1911).
3
Alan Nothnagle, «Spiel mir das Lied der Gerechtigkeit,» in: Klaus Hugler, Hans Diefenbacher (eds.): *Ansätze zu einer Theorie und Politik der Bodenreform,* Marburg 2005, pp. 101–126, here p. 115.

justified the private ownership of land. George responded with «The Condition of Labor» (1893), initially published as an open letter to the Pope, which is often considered to be his masterpiece.[4] Among other things, George argues that private ownership of land cannot be justified; it is fundamentally different from private ownership of things that man has created. Also in 1893, *A Perplexed Philosopher* was published, in which George not only criticized Herbert Spencer for recanting his earlier critique of private land ownership, but also introduced a philosophical foundation of the land question.[5]

Politically, George was close to the workers' movement and related intellectual circles (such as the Fabian Society), but he was bitterly opposed by Marx and Engels and their followers. Henry George died in 1897 during the election campaign for mayor of New York; he had been nominated as the candidate of workers' organizations. The followers of Henry George range across the political spectrum of democratic parties and political movements – from the socialist to the liberal (even libertarian), all the way to the conservative political camp (Winston Churchill, among others, was influenced by reading Henry George[6]).

Land and taxation

In *Progress and Poverty,* Henry George set out a comprehensive economic and social theory. The constitutive elements of this theory can be found in those passages where land is treated. Among others, he picked up on the French physiocrats and further elaborated their theories. His gaze was directed mainly toward land and labor as factors of production. George saw the factor «capital» as derived from the factor «labor,» rather than as an original factor of production, much like the French physiocrats. Later, however, the emerging neoclassical theory succeeded in blurring the difference between capital and land.[7] To this day, economic science is strongly influenced by neo-classical theory, and therefore largely «groundless.»

In his land rent and land value theory, Henry George leaned on the work of David Ricardo, who (together with Johann Heinrich von Thünen) laid the foundations of land rent theory. Among other things, it posited that rent was the return on supra-marginal land, the level of which

4
Adolf Damaschke, «Das Leben und Wirken von Henry George,» in: Hugler, Diefenbacher 2005 (see note 3), pp. 81–99; here p. 92.
5
Onken 1997 (see note 1).
6
N.N., «Why Henry George Had a Point,» in: *The Economist,* April 2, 2015. Online: http://www.economist.com/blogs/freeexchange/2015/04/land-value-tax.
7
John B. Clark, «The Genesis of Capital,» in: *Yale Review,* November 1893, pp. 302–315.

Dirk Löhr / Henry George: The Public Value of Land

The emerging neo-classical theory succeeded in blurring the difference between capital and land.
To this day, economic science is strongly influenced by neo-classical theory, and therefore largely «groundless.»

Dirk Löhr: Simplified
representation of Henry
George's theorem

National income as a function of the population (own illustration)					
Composition		Distribution		Character	
Private goods and services	⟷	Wages (labor factor)	⟷	Costs	
		Interest (capital factor)	⟷		
Public goods and services (provision costs)	⟷	Rent of land (land factor)	⟷	Residual (social surplus)	

is driven by population growth. However, Henry George emphasized that the value of land is an achievement of the community – no private landowner creates land's value. This also distinguishes land from capital (and consumer goods), which is valorized by its producers. Among others, Alfred Marshall [8] (a teacher of J. M. Keynes) endorsed George on this point: In addition to the forces of nature and other external effects («spillovers»), rents of land, i.e., the benefits yielded by the land, are created mainly by public works.

George's basic idea was developed in the last decades of the twentieth century by modern economists. Of particular note is the theorem named after Henry George (also called the «golden rule» of local public finance), which, among others, was also formulated by Arnott and Stiglitz. [9]

According to the Henry George theorem (see simplified representation on the left), rents of land are generated by the provision of public services. On the other hand, the Henry George theorem might also be read in reverse, meaning that under certain conditions, the fixed costs for the provision of public services (infrastructure, security, education, health) may be fully funded by the rents of land. However, the marginal costs of public services should be covered by fees (which are not highlighted in the adjacent figure).

These findings led to the concept of a «single tax,» which had already been proposed by the physiocrats. [10] Henry George, however, had a broad understanding of «land» that included all natural resources. Therefore, many modern Georgists would like to absorb all sources of rents that emerge within the context of using physical space (ranging from taxi licenses to raw material resources, to the use of broadcasting frequencies). [11] Therefore, the «single tax» could more aptly be called the «Henry George principle.» [12]

However, privatizing rents of land favors a minority, as it means that rents of land do not flow into public finances. The public budget must instead be financed by taxing the mobile factors of production, labor and capital, as well as consumption.

Henry George regarded the private appropriation of the fruits of public works as «theft»; this brought him into a certain proximity to the French socialist Pierre-Joseph

8
Alfred Marshall, *Principles of Economics*, 8th edition, London 1947, pp. 794–804. See also Mason Gaffney, «Land as a Distinctive Factor of Production,» in: Nicolaus Tideman (ed.), *Land and Taxation*, London 1994, pp. 39–102, here p. 50.
9
Richard J. Arnott, Joseph E. Stiglitz, «Aggregate Land Rents, Expenditure on Public Goods, and Optimal City Size,» in: *Quarterly Journal of Economics*, 93/1979, pp. 471–500.
10
Unlike George, however, they wanted to tax those who used the land, not the landowners.
11
Jürgen Backhaus, «Ein Steuersystem nach Henry George als Denkmodell und Alternative oder zur Ergänzung der Ökosteuer,» in: *Zeitschrift für Sozial-ökonomie*, Vol. 36., 1999, pp. 26–32.
12
Joseph E. Stiglitz, «Reforming Taxation to Promote Growth and Equity,» White Paper, Roosevelt Institute, 1999. Online: http://rooseveltinstitute.org/wp-content/uploads/2014/05/Stiglitz_Reforming_Taxation_White_Paper_Roosevelt_Institute.pdf.

Dirk Löhr / Henry George: The Public Value of Land

Proudhon («property is theft»).[13] In contrast to the German-Argentine land and money reformer Silvio Gesell, George rigorously rejected compensation for the expropriation of landowners.

Henry George considered private ownership of land to be both economically inefficient and unfair – a thought later reasserted by Mason Gaffney (one of the leading contemporary Georgists) in his «philosophy of reconciliation.»[14] According to Gaffney, the contrast between «efficiency» and «justice» postulated by neoclassical economists is misleading. By ignoring the problems with the private ownership of land and the privatization of benefits yielded by the rents of land, neoclassical economics presents the general public with false alternatives.

First, private ownership of land is not economically efficient. External effects are an important cause of market failure. Actually, the private value of land is always the result of external effects. And indeed, the private land market is currently failing, as evidenced by speculation in under- and unused land, and by the crises generated by the bursting of real estate bubbles (which are actually land price bubbles[15]). The last striking example was the 2008 crisis in the US, which was initially a crisis in the real estate market that spread into financial crises all over the world.

Secondly, private ownership of land is unfair. From an intertemporal point of view, eternal rights of use on the planet are granted at the expense of accessibility for future generations.[16] Moreover, the distributional imbalances resulting from the privatization of land and its income constitutes a social problem. For Henry George, wages and interest are residuals left over after the demands of land-owners have been met. Nowadays, most of his current supporters have a different view, according to which rent of land represents a residuum.[17] For instance, income and wealth distribution in Germany did not improve during the low-interest phase of recent years – the opposite is especially true with regard to wealth distribution. Obviously, the major beneficiary of reduced capital income was not labor income but the rent of land. Indications for this include the sharp rise in rents in metropolitan areas. Because profitable investment opportunities became more

13
Pierre-Joseph Proudhon, *Was ist das Eigentum?* New edition of the first memorandum from 1896, Graz 1971, p. 1.
14
Francis K. Peddle, «Das Wesen des Gemeinwohls – Mason Gaffneys Philosophie der Versöhnung,» in: Dirk Löhr, Fred Harrison (eds.), *Das Ende der Rentenökonomie,* Marburg 2017, pp. 145–161.
15
Eighty percent of the price increases of real estate since the Second World War are accounted for by increases in land prices. Katharina Knoll, Moritz Schularick, Thomas Steger, «No Price like Home: Global House Prices, 1870–2012,» in: *American Economic Review,* 107/2018, pp. 331–353.
16
John S. Mill, *Grundsätze der politischen Ökonomie nebst einigen Anwendungen auf die Gesellschaftswissenschaft* [1848], Vol. 2, Hamburg 1952, chapter II, § 6.
17
See Mason Gaffney, «The hidden taxable capacity of land: enough and to spare,» in: *International Journal of Social Economics,* 36/2009, pp. 328–411, here p. 378.

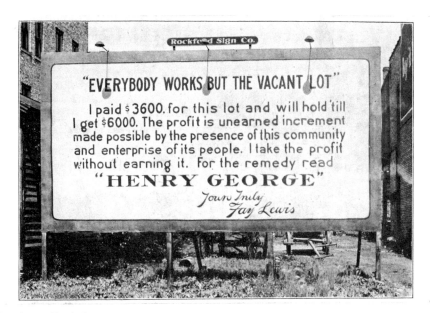

Henry George, «Everybody
Works But the Vacant Lot»
(postcard, undated)

Private ownership of land is not economically efficient.... as evidenced by speculation in under- and unused land, and by the crises generated by the bursting of real estate bubbles (which are actually land price bubbles).

and more scarce, asset prices – especially for land – were
«inflated.»[18]

Although Henry George basically rejected the private
ownership of land, he nevertheless realized the mindset of
his fellow citizens, in particular that of smallholders.
For this reason he pleaded for preserving private property
in form but «hollowing» it out by collecting taxes on
land that were high enough to transfer the entire value of
the land into the hands of the community. Other land
reformers, such as Michael Flürscheim[19] and Silvio Gesell[20]
preferred the nationalization of land, which was then
to be allocated via a lease auction to the highest bidder.

Henry George, Here and Today

The land value tax propagated by Henry George is not
a panacea. In this regard, George was too optimistic.
Independent (economic) political goals must be pursued
with different instruments.[21] In addition, a land value
increment tax is not primarily a steering tax; where it is
used, it serves merely to decrease the counterproductive
steering effects of other taxes. The land value increment
tax is neutral with regard to the production factors of
labor and capital as well as consumption. However, the land
value increment tax is also called «super-neutral» because
of its positive «collateral benefits.»[22] Some examples
for benefits to urban development include the following.

The land value increment tax gives an incentive to
follow planning guidelines. Those owners who underuse
their property pay the same tax they would for an optimal
use according to the land use planning. With a more
compact design (multifamily dwellings), the land value
increment tax is distributed among more housing units,
thereby burdening apartments within compact settlement
designs less than those which consume more land. At
the same time, the tax encourages re-compacting building
designs within the scope of the planning guidelines,
and urges landowners to build on unused or underused
land. The planning premise of «internal development before
external development» is thus supported. In addition,
the tax impedes land speculation.

The land value increment tax also indirectly supports
affordable housing and construction. In a freely financed

18
Dirk Löhr, «Boden – die
verkannte Umverteilungs-
maschine,» in: Zeitschrift für
Sozialökonomie, Vol. 55/
November 2018, pp. 3–19.
19
Michael Flürscheim, Rent,
interest and wages – or,
the real bearings of the land
question (private rent the
mother of interest, the cause
of commercial depressions &
social misery), London 1891.
20
Silvio Gesell, Die Natürliche
Wirtschaftsordnung durch
Freiland und Freigeld, 9th ed.,
Lauf bei Nürnberg 1949.
21
Jan Tinbergen, On the
Theory of Economic Policy,
Amsterdam 1952.
22
Terry Dwyer, «Taxation:
The lost history,» in: American
Journal of Economics and
Sociology, Annual Supplement
73/2014, pp. 751–756.

housing market, it increases supply by putting pressure on unused and underused land. However, social housing is also supported if the cost rents are reduced as a result of falling land prices.[23] The same applies to housing cooperatives. At least in the longer term, it is much more difficult to pass on to tenants a land value increment tax than property taxes, which include the building in their tax base.

The controversial debate on the land market and property tax reform in Germany shows that the work of Henry George is anything but a historical curiosity; indeed, it is of utmost relevance in the present.

23
Of course, this requires the support of planning or targeted property-tax exemptions in order to prevent a multiple burden on the rent of land.

Manuela Kölke
Life without Property.
The «Groundlessness» of Anarchist Settler Movements

1
Statement by the nihilistic protagonist Tyler Durden in David Fincher's dramatic film *Fight Club*, 139 min., USA 1999. Based on Chuck Palahniuk's novel *Fight Club* of 1996.

2
See Giorgio Agamben, *The Kingdom and the Glory: For a Theological Genealogy of Economy and Government*, Palo Alto 2011; Ernesto Laclau, Chantal Mouffe, *Hegemony and Socialist Strategy. Towards a Radical Democratic Politics*, Brooklyn, NY 1985.

3
See Jakob Böhme, *De incarnatione verbi* (The Incarnation of Jesus Christ) [1620], Whitefish, MT 1993.

4
See Francisco Varela, Humberto Maturana, Ricardo Uribe, «Autopoiesis: The Organization of Living Systems, Its Characterization and a Model,» in: *Currents in Modern Biology*, No. 4/1974, pp. 187–196, as well as Vilém Flusser, *Bodenlos. Eine philosophische Autobiographie* (Groundless. A Philosophical Autobiography), Bensheim / Düsseldorf 1992.

5
See Emmanuel Levinas, «Humanism and An-archy» [1964], in Emmanuel Levinas, *Humanism of the Other*, Chicago 2003.

6
See *Meister Eckhart, Meister Eckharts Mystische Schriften. Aus dem Mittelhochdeutschen in unsere Sprache übertragen von Gustav Landauer* (Meister Eckhart's Mystical Writings, translated from Medieval German by Gustav Landauer), Berlin 1903.

7
«Van Eeden praises Multatuli's lack of principles, as principles set for a lifetime can hinder the free growth of a personality» (translation by Manuela Kölke), in: Frederick van Eeden, *Logische Grundlage der Verständigung*, Stuttgart 2005, p. 67.

Many people find it difficult to imagine life without property. Property creates normative orders of production and promises security. It is regarded as constitutive of human freedom and thus as an indispensable component of social organization. And yet, even the philosophers of classical antiquity and many other cultures attributed the origin of social conflicts, like slavery and exploitation, to the greed (*pleonexia*) for material goods and in social hierarchies. Property was, thus, often perceived as a burden or an obstacle – «The things you own end up owning you.»[1]

Such a critique of the modernist concept of property is most strongly expressed in *anarchism,* which regards property not as a solution but as a cause of social conflict.

The ancient Greek term *arché* means beginning, origin, ground, matter, principle and rule. The negation of this concept, *an-arché (ἀναρχία)*, from which «anarchism» is derived, stands for lack of beginning, baselessness,[2] unground,[3] groundlessness,[4] lack of origin,[5] lack of matter,[6] lack of principles,[7] and lack of rule. The rejection of a fixed status, and the critique of the need for an overarching state, even when representationally «elected,» is common to all anarchist positions. With this critique often comes the concurrent rejection of restrictive bourgeois institutions and moral concepts such as the church, marriage, family and property, since they are secured by the same super-ordinate structures. But this «rejection» can only take place on a voluntary basis, because anarchy is naturally free of all constraints. The negation of principles itself must not become a principle by any means. Society is therefore understood as a voluntary union of individuals who live and work together on an equal footing, self-determined, decentralized, in federal and self-governing collectives and cooperatives of various kinds. Material resources such as land are understood as common property that is available to everyone. In that sense it belongs to all and yet to no one.

Anarchist Critique of Property and Mutual Aid

The French economist and sociologist Pierre-Joseph Proudhon (1809–1865), who was the first to describe himself as an anarchist, articulated early arguments for the anarchist critique of property in his 1840 work *Qu'est-ce que la propriété? Ou recherches sur le principe du droit et du gouvernement.* (The first complete English edition of 1890 was published under the title *What is Property? Or, an Inquiry into the Principle of Right and of Government*). From this work originates the well-known dictum: «Property is theft.» Property is the prerequisite for an income without doing work yourself and generates profits which are not based on work. Thus, economic growth or gains are based on the exploitation of man by man, since collectively generated value is retained only by individuals. Ownership of the means of industrial production, land, and also housing, leads to unjustified enrichment and is thus at the core of criticism of the prevailing political and social conditions under capitalism. In contrast to Marx's «authoritarian socialism,» according to anarchists, private property and the bourgeois state that protects it are to be fought directly and immediately replaced by self-organized forms of common property. Marx accused Proudhon of being only interested in a reformist regulation of property and thus not in a fundamental change of social conditions, but clearly Proudhon was interested in a large-scale reorganization of society.

For Proudhon, ownership is not based on natural law, as many are excluded from ownership. Proudhon criticizes both the *occupation theory* and John Locke's *labor theory of property* used for the legitimation of property ownership. Both initially presuppose a fictitious equality of access, that is, the availability of sufficient resources for all to appropriate.[8] It is in accordance with the behavior of capitalist processes, however, that property leads to scarcity and inequality. Inheritance of property, for example, slows down its redistribution and thus supports existing power structures. Greater justice can only be achieved if property is distributed evenly and the distribution is adapted to the respective circumstances. For Proudhon, labor invested in land or means of production does not automatically entitle the workers to turn it into their property, because the results of the labor, such as the harvest to which they are entitled, are not the same as land or means of production themselves. Property therefore does not protect against social conflicts but is rather their object and cause. There is no legitimate justification for the transition from original common property to bourgeois

8
John Locke, *Two Treatises of Government II. An Essay Concerning the True Origin, Extent, and End of Civil Government,* London 1689, §27, p. 28.

Manuela Kölke / Life without Property

For Proudhon, there is no legitimate justification for the transition from original common property to bourgeois private property. Land ownership should therefore remain with the municipalities and be given to smaller tenants for a limited period of time.

private property. Land ownership, according to anarchists, should therefore remain with the municipalities and be given to smaller tenants for a limited period of time, or should be managed by «voluntary workers' associations» (autogestion[9]) in a decentralized manner. Products are exchanged according to the principle of voluntary reciprocity – that is, according to the simple law of value – through granting interest-free credit, the formation of cooperatives, and mutual agreements. Such anarchistic groupings enable the flexible adjustment of production rates to match the needs of society.

Mikhail Bakunin (1814–1876) and Pyotr Kropotkin (1842–1921) devoted themselves in particular to the question of the organization of social coexistence without property. Kropotkin, who came from a Russian noble family and was a member of the Imperial Russian Army, conducted research on the local self-government of the province of Transbaikalia in Siberia from 1862–1867. On further geographical expeditions he familiarized himself with Proudhon's works, and in 1872 he confessed to being an anarchist. Through his experiences with the animal world and human coexistence in the region, he began to question the relevance of competition in Charles Darwin's theory of evolution. In 1872 he traveled to Western Europe to join revolutionary circles. Starting from the observation that social organization in the form of the state is not able to provide the best care for all, he developed his critique of capitalism in his 1892 publication *The Conquest of Bread*.[10] In 1902 he published his best-known work, *Mutual Aid: A Factor of Evolution*.[11] Therein he uses Proudhon's principle of reciprocity in an attempt to establish a scientific basis for anarchism. Numerous examples – such as the pelican fishing cooperative or clan societies, reciprocity customs in village communities or medieval guilds, right up to modern associations – are meant to show that the most successful development strategy in evolution is based on socializing in small groups, mutual aid and support, and not on the «survival of the fittest.»

The short lifespan of the Paris Commune in 1871 – which existed for only a few months due to a lack of supply from the surrounding countryside, its own territorial isolation, and insufficient agricultural and garden areas –

9
Companies and projects that are self-governed primarily on a grassroots basis or through democratically represented councils.
10
Pyotr Kropotkin, *The Conquest of Bread*, London 1892. Translated into German by Bernhard Kampffmeyer, Berlin 1921.
11
Pyotr Kropotkin, *Mutual Aid: A Factor of Evolution*, New York 1902.

Manuela Kölke / Life without Property

prompted Kropotkin to draw up proposals for securing an economically independent supply for communal settlements. In his book *Fields, Factories and Workshops,* published in 1898, Kropotkin therefore advocated for cooperative associations, combining and supplementing mental and physical work, joint education and care, for example, in kindergartens, by abolishing private ownership of means of production and land, and above all by integrating industry and agriculture. «The well-being of all is the goal; expropriation is the means.»[12] In addition to the focus on the joint cultivation and farming of the land, the strong interdependence with science, industry and handicrafts promotes optimal self-management. Interior colonization – that is, the distribution of production sites and settlements within the country – and diversity of employment should prevent dependency on one sole employer.

However, Bakunin and Kropotkin pursued different approaches to the distribution of manufactured goods within the free workers' associations. Bakunin's anarcho-collectivism aimed to maintain the remuneration system (in different forms) on the basis of working hours so that this income could be used to purchase items on a municipal market. In this hybrid form of individualism and collectivism, individuals possess their own tools, but land and means of production remain in communal ownership. Kropotkin's anarcho-communism, on the other hand, is based on the socialization of the spheres of production and distribution – that is, on the abolition of wage labor, means of payment, and the market – and on the free consumption of goods by all: «each according to their needs.»

«The Earth is Nobody's Property» – Decentralized Settlement Models or the Fertile Soils of the Turn of the Century
Kropotkin's ideas, in particular, fell on fertile ground in Europe and worldwide in the face of the rapid industrialization of large cities, the increasing scarcity of housing and the poor supply situation by the state, especially during and after the First World War. At the same time as the international debates on land reform, ever more anarchist-inspired settlement movements were emerging, such as the Dukhobors settlements in Saskatchewan,

12
Kropotkin 1892, (see note 10).

Manuela Kölke / Life without Property

«Brettldorf»
(informal settlement) in
Vienna, view toward
Bruckhaufen, c. 1935

Manuela Kölke / Life without Property

Canada (supported by Kropotkin himself), workers' settlements and squats in Spain, fish crate settlements in Hamburg, *bidonvilles* in France, and «Brettldörfer» (informal settlements) in Austria – settlements which have been largely forgotten in the face of today's vast *favelas* of the Global South. Even if direct anarchist influences on the inhabitants of such settlements are difficult to prove, the construction of social housing projects and cooperative settlements in Germany, in particular, bears witness to the significant influence of anarchist manifestos as such.

At the end of the nineteenth century, Gustav Landauer (1870–1919) – following Proudhon, Kropotkin, Tolstoy and Nietzsche, and in contrast to Max Stirner's individualistic anarchism – developed the idea of a social anarchism that advocated a new generality, unity and community and was based on free association without coercion and competition in communities of solidarity. He advanced what was also known as an eco-liberal alternative, advocating the revaluation of social relationships and a return to nature. In the context of the *Friedrichshagener Dichterkreis*[13] near Berlin, in 1895 Landauer presented a plan for the creation of socialist islands within capitalist society through consumer and production cooperatives, whose exemplary character was to inspire further dissemination. In *Call to Socialism,* he demanded the abolition of property and the socialization of land, following Proudhon's example: «Out of private ownership of the land and its corollary, non-ownership, there arise slavery, subservience, tribute, rent, interest, the proletariat. … The earth is no one's private property. Let the earth have no masters; then we men are free. … Out of this rebirth [the abolition of private property] a mighty redistribution of property will follow, and […] there will be the permanent intention to redistribute the land in future times at definite or indefinite intervals again and again.»[14]

Together with Franz Oppenheimer's work *The Settlement Cooperative* (*Die Siedlungsgenossenschaft*) of 1896, Landauer's ideas served as the basis for the *Neue Gemeinschaft* (new community) founded in Schlachtensee in 1900, which implemented the concept of the communal kitchen. They anticipated much of Ebenezer Howard's idea of the *Garden City* and had an enormous influence on

13
The *Friedrichshagener Dichterkreis* (Friedrichshagen Poetry Circle) was a loose association of naturalist writers, artists and intellectuals, who from 1888/89 initially met in the house of Gerhard Hauptmann in Erkner, where they sought the peace and quiet of the Mark Brandenburg countryside near the cosmopolitan city of Berlin. Later they met in the homes of Wilhelm Bölsche and Bruno Wille in Friedrichshagen near Lake Müggelsee. Motivated by the desire to reform their lives while living a bohemian lifestyle many of them settled in Friedrichshagen around 1890. The ideas circulating in this circle stimulated the foundation of the fruit-growing cooperative Eden (Obstbau-Genossenschaft Eden) and the New Community (Neue Gemeinschaft).
14
Gustav Landauer, *Call to Socialism (Aufruf zum Sozialismus)*, Berlin 1911. Available at: https://theanarchistlibrary.org/library/gustav-landauer-call-to-socialism.

Manuela Kölke / Life without Property

the German Garden City Society (Deutsche Gartenstadt-Gesellschaft, DGG), founded in 1902, and later on the kibbutz movement.[15] In *To-Morrow: A Peaceful Path to Real Reform,* published in 1898, Howard (1859–1928) also called for the relocation, or more precisely the decentralization of residents and industry to agrarian-industrial settlements outside the congested cities. He did not explicitly name Kropotkin as a source, although he was familiar with his ideas. Strong proof of the lively exchange between the anarchists and the (Berlin) settler movement were their friendships with Kropotkin. Both Landauer and Bernhard Kampffmeyer, one of the founders of the DGG, translated Kropotkin's works and, later, Howard's writings into German. Despite the anarchist influences, however, many of the garden city settlements, tended to remain more oriented toward social reform.

The Extraordinary Dynamics of the Self-governing Settler Movement in Vienna

The example of the Viennese settlements shows how, through self-administration and large-scale investment in mutual aid – namely, facilitating self-help, the challenges posed by housing shortages and land speculation could be dealt with far more radically than the idea of the garden city initially intended them to be. As early as 1900, poor garbage collectors and working-class families settled spontaneously and illegally in Brettldörfer, clusters of temporary wooden huts near the city boundaries and in the Vienna Woods, in order to escape high rents and social hardship and to improve their food supply through horti-culture and animal husbandry, which was restricted by the state. Characteristic of these settlements were wild land seizures, often by means of deforestation. The growing settlements rarely complied with the building regulations of the period. Already during the First World War these settlements were able to sell their surpluses, and thus contribute to supply Vienna's entire population with food.[16]

According to Klaus Novy, the development of the Viennese settlement movement can be understood in four phases.[17] The «wild settlements» initially developed from 1900 to 1920 as a grassroots emergency project. Despite the appropriation of land and the existential necessity

15
«Ebenezer Howard ‹almost certainly› heard [Kropotkin] speak in London […],» see Teresa Harris, «Models of Co-operative Association in the German Garden City Movement,» in: *The German Garden City Movement: Architecture, Politics and Urban Transformation, 1902–1931*, Dissertation, Columbia University, New York 2012, pp. 48–51.
16
Friedrich Hauer, Andre Krammer, «Das Wilde Wien. Rückblick auf ein Jahr-hundert informeller Stadt-entwicklung,» in: *dérive – Zeitschrift für Stadtforschung*, No. 71/2018, p. 12; «Bidonvilles & Bretteldörfer. Ein Jahrhundert informeller Stadtentwicklung in Europa,» *Dérive – Radio für Stadt-forschung.* May 1, 2018. Available here: https://cba.fro.at/373781.
17
Klaus Novy, «Selbsthilfe als Reformbewegung» (Self-Help as Reform Movement), in: *ARCH+*, No. 55/1981, pp. 36–38.

Manuela Kölke / Life without Property

of self-management, there was no uniform ideology regarding the form of self-organization to be implemented. Not all residents had the primary goal of social-spatial and emancipatory self-empowerment. Many were concerned with pure survival in often unsanitary and impoverished conditions. Although the settlements were politically oriented to the left, they were still heterogeneous collectives overall. On the one hand, Kropotkin's theory of mutual help is confirmed by the example of these settlements – occasional conflicts were resolved independently and without superordinate rules. On the other hand, the formation of associations over time also led to the development of common principles that enabled stronger community organization, such as the publication of journals and public protests, which put massive pressure on the city administration around 1920.

The second phase, between 1921 and 1923, was characterized by the development of a large-scale system of organized self-help. By 1914, the lack of a «petty-bourgeois–individualistic–ownership» allotment garden association encouraged the socialist orientation of projects such as «Eden,» «Zukunft,» and «Menschenfrühling,» the Tolstoy colony and other settlements that combined elements of the garden city with Landauer's ecoliberal alternative. These direct references were not a surprising development, since Hans Kampffmeyer, cousin of Bernhard Kampffmeyer and Secretary General of the DGG, was appointed Chairman of the Settlement Office of the City of Vienna in 1919, before Adolf Loos took office in 1921. Otto Neurath (1882–1945), Social Democrat economic planner and friend of Landauer until his assassination in 1919 in Munich, founded the Institute for Communal Economy (Institut für Gemeinwirtschaft) in 1921, became chairman of the Association for Settlements and Small Gardens (Verband für Siedlungs- und Kleingartenwesen), and was decisive in the creation of the Non-profit Institute for Settlement and Building Materials (Gemeinnützige Siedlungs- und Baustoffanstalt, «GESIBA») in Red Vienna.

Through these associations, Neurath organized direct aid for the settlers and the subsequent integration of infrastructures to ensure the communal food supply. The radical rent protection policy reduced land prices to 20 percent of their prewar value, which enabled the municipalities to acquire land at favorable prices and to grant land to cooperatives as ground leases at favorable interest rates. There was a lively barter trade between the settlements. Construction activity was structured as a mixed system: the work was remunerated according to hours or market value. With this, together with the mobilization of the settlers to construct the buildings themselves and new methods of financing based solely on the settlers' work rather than equity capital, the general framework was established for the development of the settlers' activities.

Neurath's settlement exhibition in the Vienna town hall square in 1922/23 and the founding of the Museum for Settlement and Town Planning (Museum für Siedlung und Städtebau) in 1923 mobilized more and more supporters. It focused mainly on education – that is, helping people to help themselves in planning their own settlements. In the settlement school, architects shared their knowledge, looked after and accompanied the settlers. Josef Frank devoted himself to methods of economical building. Adolf Loos saw himself as a teacher of spatial design. He designed the «House with One Wall,» quite similar to Martin Wagner's «Growing House,» as a minimum structure with possibilities for expansion and large gardens for the «Heuberg» teaching settlement. The «Friedensstadt» settlement, developed by Margarete Schütte-Lihotzky with Loos' assistance, typified settler's huts and a «core house type.» She rationalized the domestic economy with her «Frankfurt Kitchen» and founded a commodity trust (*Warentreuhand*) as an advisory office for housing furnishings. In contrast to the garden city movement's standardization of building types, here an anarchistic tendency was also at play: Schütte-Lihotsky's core house types did not comply with the applicable building regulations but were very successful, despite Loos' vehement criticism.

In this way, the phenomenon of settlement housing, which was otherwise regarded as rather bourgeois-conservative, was in keeping with its proletarian-socialist orientation. «[Neurath's] thinking revolves around the problem of how social dynamics can be organized in such a way that the interests articulated in the movement are

Manuela Kölke / Life without Property

not institutionalized as particular interests, but can be brought to mediation with others through overarching organizations and thus generalized into common emancipatory interests.»[18] Novy distinguishes between two contrasting types of settler. According to the ideas of the individualistic property settlers (IPS) individual housing interest can best be secured by private property. For Neurath, however, individual housing interest must be transformed into a general housing interest. This can only be achieved by cooperative settlers (COS), who, as nonprofit property owners, are capable of keeping co-operatives from being transferred into the private sector. «Allotment gardeners and settlers want to maintain solidarity among themselves and with the community as a whole; they therefore fight all efforts to isolate individuals and to give them free right of disposal over their land and house.»[19] Only in this way could Neurath transfer the guild organization (as already analyzed by Kropotkin) to the settlers' association, in order to successfully establish it as the overarching organization of all umbrella organizations, thus «bypassing the state»: «The aim of this guild would be the complete elimination of the private building industry and the private ownership of apartment buildings.»[20] With the help of this form of guild socialism, which had hitherto involved one million people, the Settlers' Association wanted to radically decentralize housing construction and housing administration through cooperatives.

Along with the City of Vienna's renewed efforts to protect and restore private property, which began in 1924 with a new taxation policy, the previous land occupations were legally recognized, and the respective areas rededicated as the basis for the formation of official settlement cooperatives and community housing estates. In this third phase, the communal appropriation of the settler idea led to the stagnation of the settler movement as such. Settler colonies were evacuated and unemployed families were resettled in so-called «super blocks» controlled by the city administration, or in «people's housing palaces» (*Volkswohnpaläste*) that were built as part of the community building program, or on abandoned estates in the countryside, where they were once again left to their devices as far as general food supply was concerned.

18
Ibid., p. 35.
19
Otto Neurath, *Österreichs Kleingärtner- und Siedler-Organisation*, Vienna 1923, p. 24.
20
Novy 1981 (see note 16), p. 35.

Manuela Kölke / Life without Property

The city administration, therefore, treated the «wild» cooperative settlements in a very contradictory way as a «tolerated alternative» to the model of the communal apartment building, to the «super block» of Red Vienna. Existing anarchist and similarly alternative projects were increasingly opposed.

As a result of the global economic crisis and a strengthened central government in Austria, housing settlements for the unemployed in the urban periphery were restructured as «emergency projects from above,» transformed from grassroots, self-governing cooperatives into externally governed municipal communities during the final phase from 1930 onwards. The entry thresholds to the settlements were disproportionately raised by increased work requirements. Community facilities were neglected. Only after the Second World War did the housing shortage slowly decrease, so that the last colonies still existed into the early 1960s.

Using this «example of history withheld from us,» Novy shows that settlements can organize themselves in solidarity, guided by grassroots democracy, into cooperatives, even if their settlements have only a single housing type. The decisive factor for this is the ability to communalize individual interests. However, the larger the institutions become, the more difficult this task becomes, as more and more interests must be served by generalization. Klaus Novy considered the Viennese «settler movement as the social engine of the new housing policy,»[21] because, despite its eventual appropriation by the municipalities, it triggered a successful debate on housing and forms of life.

The groundlessness of the anarchist settler movement is thus only without ground – that is, «without roots,» «absurd,» «senseless» and «without a reasonable basis,» as Vilém Flusser imagines human existence to be[22] – to the extent that, despite its ambivalence and controversy, it generates the energy that is necessary to overcome itself on another level with the help of community cohesion and solidarity. No form of housing has fixed validity. It must, therefore, be developed anew in each case through the confrontation with concrete suffering.[23]

21
Ibid., p. 39.
22
Flusser 1992 (see note 4), p. 9.
23
Novy 1981 (see note 16), p. 39.

Sylvia Claus
Who Owns the City?
Hans Bernoulli's Political Urban Planning

«In urban planning questions, what matters is not the next
instant, but the next century.»[1]

Hans Bernoulli

The Schweizerische Städtebau-Ausstellung (Swiss Urban
Planning Exhibition) took place at Kunsthaus Zürich
from August 4 to September 2, 1928. Organized by the
Bund Schweizerischer Architekten (Federation of Swiss
Architects) it had been developed by Camille Martin,
Director of the Geneva Urban Planning Authority, and
Hans Bernoulli, one of Switzerland's most internationally
influential architects, theoreticians, and urban planners.
Bernoulli and Martin knew each other from their days
as students in Munich and Karlsruhe. They were united
by their interest in artistic urban planning in the style of
Camillo Sitte. Bernoulli contributed drawings for the
French translation of Sitte's *City Planning According to
Artistic Principles* (1889), published by Camille Martin
in 1902,[2] and advocated the formal principles of aesthetic-
pictorial urban planning both in his journalistic and his
architectural works.[3]

    However, if anyone was expecting a show of «beautiful»
Swiss urban planning in 1928 in urban planning typologies,
paradigmatic zoning plans, and exemplary cityscapes,
they were disappointed. Martin and Bernoulli, collaborating
with the relevant authorities and various colleagues,
presented instead a systematic comparative analysis of
the urban planning situation in ten Swiss cities, which they
also published in 1929 under the title *Städtebau in der
Schweiz – Grundlagen.*

    Presentation boards, arrayed to emphasize comparabil-
ity, bore strikingly eye-catching graphics of the topography
(relief, spread of development, how the traffic network
related to the relief and development), the traffic network,
the use plans, and the distribution of green spaces. These
boards would later serve as the core of the Swiss section
of the International Town Planning and Housing Exhibition
at the major German Building Exhibition in Berlin in 1931,
organized by that city's Director of Urban Development,
Martin Wagner. Aerial photographs of several Swiss cities
provided a quick overview of the entire city being depicted
and included a sketch highlighting a key message in each

1
Hans Bernoulli to the
architect and urban planner
Hans Bernhard Reichow in a
letter of September 20, 1948
2
Camillo Sitte, *L'art de bâtir les
villes. Notes et réflexions
d'une architecte,* translated
and completed by Camille
Martin, Geneva / Paris 1902.
3
See on this Sylvia Claus,
«Stadtbild und Bodenfrage.
Zum Verhältnis von
Architektur und Gesellschaft
bei Hans Bernoulli,» in:
Sylvia Claus, Lukas Zurfluh
(eds.), *Städtebau als politische
Kultur. Der Architekt und
Theoretiker Hans Bernoulli,*
Zurich 2018, pp. 8–27.

Sylvia Claus / Who Owns the City?

Public and private properties
in Bern and Zurich in 1928.
Panel from the Schweizerische
Städtebau-Ausstellung (Swiss
Urban Planning Exhibition)
curated that year by Camille
Martin and Hans Bernoulli

Gelb: Öffentlicher Besitz; weiss; Privater Besitz

BERN

Bund, einschl. SBB	96,6 ha =	1,9 %
Stadt Bern, einschl. Gewässer	219,8 ha =	4,3 %
Einwohnergemeinde	768,6 ha =	14,9 %
Burgergemeinde, einschl. Wald	1691,5 ha =	32,8 %
Kirchgemeinden	6,0 ha =	0,1 %
Private, einschl. Privatbahnen, Spitäler etc.	2375,3 ha =	46,2 %

Der ausgedehnte öffentliche Bodenbesitz, zirka
53,8 % des gesamten Stadtgebietes, liegt in den
Händen von Bund, Staat, Einwohnergemeinde und
Burgergemeinde. Der Hauptanteil fällt auf die Burgergemeinde, in deren Besitz sich die schönen Wal-
dungen um die Stadt befinden. Durch Ausscheidungs-
vertrag vom Jahre 1852 zwischen Burgergemeinde
und Einwohnergemeinde ist die Einwohnergemeinde
zu einem ansehnlichen Grundbesitz gekommen. Die-
ser ist besonders im letzten Dezennium systematisch
durch Ankauf vergrössert worden und ist das Er-
gebnis einer zielbewussten Bodenpolitik. Der private Bodenbesitz ist mehr in Kleinparzellen aufge-
teilt. Weder in privaten Händen noch in der Hand
von Terraingesellschaften befinden sich grössere,
zusammenhängende Komplexe.

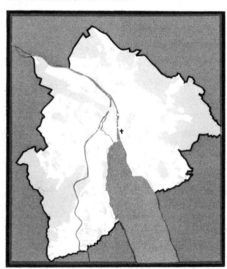

Maßstab 1 : 100 000

ZÜRICH

Das Gebiet der Stadt Zürich mit einer Gesamtfläche von 4912,11 ha
verteilt sich nach Grundeigentum auf:

	ha	ha	%
Eigentum des Bundes:			
Bundesbahngebiet	130,00		
unveräusserliche Liegenschaften	9,68	139,68	3,2
Eigentum des Kantons Zürich			
Liegenschaften	118,72		
Wald	159,34		
Allmend und Kasernenareal	24,74	302,80	6,8
Wasserfläche (See und Flüsse)		496,70	(11,2)
Eigentum der Stadt Zürich (1928)			
unveräusserliche Liegenschaften	138,69		
öffentliche Fonds u. Stiftungen	316,44		
städt. Wohnkolonien	12,26		
städt. Werke	63,92		
realisierbare Liegenschaften	869,38	1400,69	31,7
öffentliche Strassenfläche		343,17	7,8
Öffentliches Grundeigentum total		2682,32	
Privates Grundeigentum		2229,79	50,5

* Die prozentuale Verteilung bezieht sich auf die Gesamtbodenfläche
nach Abzug der Wasserfläche = 4415,4 ha.

Vom Grundeigentum der Stadt Zürich sind
751,15 ha Wald und ca. 68,80 ha Allmend; vom
privaten Grundbesitz sind ca. 181 ha Wald und
ca. 4 ha. private Strassenfläche. Das städtische
Grundeigentum wird systematisch durch Zukauf
vermehrt. Die Abgabe von realisierbaren städtischen
Liegenschaften erfolgt grösstenteils an Genossenschaften mit gemeinnützigem Charakter. Der Pri-
vatbesitz ist im wesentlichen in Kleinparzellen aufge-
kauft. Die Bebauung der Splitterparzellen erfolgt
in den letzten Jahren zum überwiegenden Teil durch
private und gemeinnützige Genossenschaften. Aus-
serhalb der Stadtgrenzen hat die Stadt Zürich ca.
1542 ha Grundeigentum, zum grössten Teil aus Wald
bestehend.

case. Each aerial image was complemented by one photograph and sectional drawing of a characteristic residential street in each of the cities studied. What the exhibition showed best of all was how public and private property were distributed in the cities concerned.

Even though it was not Bernoulli but the Geneva architect and urban planner Maurice Braillard, a close associate of Martin's, who was responsible for the section on public and private property, the importance conferred on this aspect of urban planning was due to the collective efforts of Bernoulli and Martin. In the introduction to the exhibition, they formulated their view clearly: «If one gets to the bottom of things, it soon becomes apparent that the main problem posed by urban expansion is the use of the land; this applies not only to use of the land that remains free in the immediate vicinity of the city, but even more so to use of the land in the wider surroundings, which is to serve urban planning further into the future. If a site belongs to the public, the choice of when, where, and how to build is completely free. The first task of urban planning today is thus to return to the authorities a power which it previously had, the power over urban land.»[4]

Allocation, Nationalization, Communalization?

The expropriation of land is a key problem that has been a controversial topic of discussion in urban planning theory since its emergence at the end of the nineteenth century. Initially, the issue concerned the ability to plan areas slated for construction that were fragmented into many pieces of real estate with different owners.[5] Only the possibility to reallocate and expropriate land allowed larger-scale city planning designs to be realized. Opponents of this process, among them Camillo Sitte, advocated instead for cautious planning that took consideration of property rights as well as existing traffic routes. This would allow a development structure to emerge more or less on its own. In this way, Sitte justifiably rejected the rigid schematism of strictly axial development. However, he also downplayed the issue of land expropriation, claiming, «The law of expropriating urban private property is a problem for site planning.»[6]

The fact that the issue of property ownership was far more than a «problem for site planning» was vigorously

4
Städtebau in der Schweiz – Grundlagen, ed. by Bund Schweizerischer Architekten, Camille Martin, Hans Bernoulli (eds.), Zurich 1929, p. 1.
5
Reinhard Baumeister, *Stadt-Erweiterungen in technischer, baupolizeilicher und wirthschaftlicher Beziehung,* Berlin 1876, pp. 355–384.
6
Camillo Sitte, «Enteignungsgesetz und Lageplan,» in: *Der Städtebau,* No. 1–3/1904, pp. 5–7, 17–19, 35–37.

introduced into the urban planning discussion by Rudolf Eberstadt, an economist associated with the Seminar für Städtebau (Seminar for Urban Planning) at the Technische Hochschule Charlottenburg, the first of its kind. «From the provision and apportionment of land for building, to the ownership of the completed homes, the organization of urban planning and commerce in land values are surrendered to speculation. Subdividing land is a matter of speculation. The design, the shape of the building and the production of housing are determined by speculation.»[7] With this assertion Eberstadt touched on a sore spot: What drives up property prices, and with them rental prices – back then as today – are anticipated returns.

One solution for this problem would be the communalization of land, as Hans Bernoulli had advocated ever more assertively since the urban-planning exhibition. With this demand Bernoulli synthesized a wide spectrum of professional experiences – as chief architect of the Deutsche Gartenstadtgesellschaft (German Garden City Association), a melting pot of land reform approaches in the first decade of the twentieth century; as lecturer and titular professor for urban planning at the Eidgenössische Technische Hochschule (Federal Institute of Technology) in Zurich; as a protagonist of the Freiwirtschaft (Free Economy) movement since 1923; as the initiator of cooperative settlements in Switzerland; as author and editor of a wide variety of newspapers and journals; as national councilor and politician; and finally, as an expert on European reconstruction after World War II.

The English garden-city movement was especially seminal for Bernoulli, as he emphasized in a lecture on the occasion of the 1928 exhibition: «Only Ebenezer Howard, with his Garden City Association, proceeded systematically in the communalization of urban building land, by acquiring each entire area upon which a ‹garden city› was to be built, and allocating it to the municipality as inalienable property. The individual buildings were built exclusively by private persons or cooperatives, but the land remained public property. The legal form for this separation of ownership was the English leasehold system.»[8]

The Deutsche Gartenstadtgesellschaft also had important theoreticians of social and land reform at its

7
Rudolf Eberstadt, *Die Spekulation im neuzeitlichen Städtebau. Eine Untersuchung der Grundlagen des städtischen Wohnungswesens, zugleich eine Abwehr der gegen die systematische Wohnungsreform gerichteten Angriffe*, Jena 1907.
8
Hans Bernoulli, «Rationelle Stadterweiterung,» in: *Das Werk*, No. 10/1928, pp. 323–329.

Sylvia Claus / Who Owns the City?

disposal: Adolf Damaschke, founder and long-time chairman of the Bund Deutscher Bodenreformer (Federation of German Land Reformers), and Franz Oppenheimer. While Oppenheimer actually demanded the abolition of private ownership of land, which he called the root of all social evils, Damaschke was more moderate: he wanted to curb land speculation by taxing profits from appreciation and sales. Silvio Gesell's *Freiwirtschaft* theory was also based on these considerations. Gesell advocated communalizing land in exchange for compensation and then leasing it to the previous owners. The rent charged by the public authorities was to be adjusted regularly so that the land's appreciation in value would accrue to the general public.[9]

Bernoulli, who had participated in the first Internationaler Freiland-Freigeld-Kongress (International Congress on Free Land and Free Money) in Basel in 1923, where he encountered Gesell,[10] espoused his new friend's arguments. In 1926, well before the Städtebau-Ausstellung, he presented the ideas of *Freiwirtschaft* at the International Housing and Town Planning Conference in Vienna: «Even the Freiwirtschaftsbund (Free Economy Federation) prescribes full compensation of landowners in accordance with their self-assessment.» Primarily, however, «this land ownership reform is conceived as part of a reform of national money, which targets lowering the interest rate and ultimately eliminating interest completely.» Only in this way could the state cope with these expenditures «without becoming a slave to a monstrous debt burden with continuous interest payments.»[11]

For Bernoulli (as for Gesell), land policy and monetary policy were thus two sides of the same coin. This explains Bernoulli's proposals for monetary policy and critique of the central bank during the legislative terms he served on the Great Council of Basel as a representative of the Freiwirtschaftsbund (1935–1942) and on the National Council (1947–1951) for the Alliance of Independents.

Above all, however, Bernoulli had become acquainted with the practice of cooperative housing construction as chief architect of the Deutsche Gartenstadtgesellschaft in 1910/11. After returning to Germany in 1912, and especially from the 1920s on, Bernoulli built numerous residential estates and large developments in Switzerland

9
Adolf Damaschke, *Die Bodenreform. Grundsätzliches und Geschichtliches zur Erkenntnis und Überwindung der sozialen Not* [1902], 3rd edition, Berlin 1904; Silvio Gesell, *Die natürliche Wirtschaftsordnung durch Freiland und Freigeld,* Berlin 1916.
10
Riccardo Rossi, «Zwischen Kredit und Hypothek. Das strategische Expertentum Hans Bernoullis und die schweizerische Freiwirtschaftsbewegung,» in: Claus, Zurfluh 2018 (see note 3), pp. 118–127.
11
Hans Bernoulli, «Grundbesitz und Stadterweiterung,» Switzerland, in: *International housing and town planning congress. Vienna 1926. Papers = Congrès international de l'habitation et de l'aménagement des villes. Vienne 1926. Rapports = Internationaler Wohnungs- und Städtebaukongress. Vienna 1926. Vorberichte,* ed. by the International Federation for Housing and Town Planning, Vienna 1926, pp. 114–120, here p. 116.

«The municipality sells no land that belongs to it. The municipality purchases land that is privately owned whenever possible. The municipality allows private entities to use its land by granting them a right to build on this land it owns.»
Hans Bernoulli

on a cooperative basis, for which he himself often initiated the founding of the building and residential cooperatives. Therefore he was well aware of the economic conditions of building in urban expansion zones when he organized the Schweizerische Städtebau-Ausstellung of the Bund Schweizer Architekten BSA and demanded regulatory power over urban land.

The Future of the City

Bernoulli elaborated at length on how this power would be reclaimed in his 1942 tract «Die organische Erneuerung unserer Städte» (The Organic Renewal of Our Cities), and then underpinned these insights historically in the 1946 book *Die Stadt und ihr Boden* (Towns and the Land), which was translated into many languages.[12]

Although Bernoulli certainly addressed the issue of land speculation in these works, his primary focus was on farsighted urban planning for the benefit of the city and its residents. He adhered more closely to the tradition of the city planners of the turn of the century than the life and society reformers of the garden city movement. Bernoulli's goal was to renew the city step by step, district by district, in what he called, using the characteristic style of his day, an «organic,» cyclical process: «Is it possible that the entire structural capacity of a city, even if it is privately owned, renews itself on its own after [the] expiration of its normal service life, without compulsion, without intervention into private rights?»[13]

Bernoulli proposed the separation of land and buildings. A building may be private property, but the land should be leased by the municipality to the builder for the service life of the building. For this, of course, land must be transferred into municipal ownership. Yet Bernoulli's proposals are hardly radical, and perhaps for this very reason, so highly controversial: «The municipality sells no land that belongs to it. The municipality purchases land that is privately owned whenever possible. The municipality allows private entities to use its land by granting them a right to build on this land it owns.»

The municipalities were to cautiously buy back private real estate, without compulsion or time pressure, and then make it available to potential builders in the form of

12
Hans Bernoulli, *Die organische Erneuerung unserer Städte, ein Vorschlag,* Basel 1942 (2nd, expanded edition Stuttgart 1949 = *Aufbau-Sonderhefte* 9); idem., *Die Stadt und ihr Boden / Towns and the Land,* Erlenbach-Zurich 1946 (2nd edition 1949, 3rd, expanded edition 1991); idem., *La città e il suolo urbano,* ed. by Luigi Dodi, Milan 1951 (2nd edition 1952); idem., *La città e il suolo urbano,* ed. by Mireille Senn, Venice 2006.
13
Bernoulli 1946 (see note 12), p. 20.

Hans Bernoulli, «Two methods
toward sanative improvement
and renewal.» Diagram from
his book *Die Stadt und ihr
Boden* (Towns and the Land),
1946

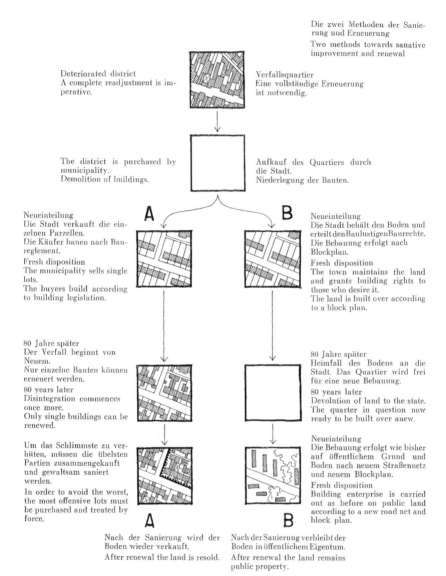

Die zwei Methoden der Sanierung und Erneuerung
Two methods towards sanative
improvement and renewal

Deteriorated district
A complete readjustment is imperative.

Verfallsquartier
Eine vollständige Erneuerung
ist notwendig.

The district is purchased by
municipality.
Demolition of buildings.

Aufkauf des Quartiers durch
die Stadt.
Niederlegung der Bauten.

A

Neueinteilung
Die Stadt verkauft die ein-
zelnen Parzellen.
Die Käufer bauen nach Bau-
reglement.

Fresh disposition
The municipality sells single
lots.
The buyers build according
to building legislation.

B

Neueinteilung
Die Stadt behält den Boden und
erteilt den BaulustigenBaurechte.
Die Bebauung erfolgt nach
Blockplan.

Fresh disposition
The town maintains the land
and grants building rights to
those who desire it.
The land is built over according
to a block plan.

80 Jahre später
Der Verfall beginnt von
Neuem.
Nur einzelne Bauten können
erneuert werden.

80 years later
Disintegration commences
once more.
Only single buildings can be
renewed.

Um das Schlimmste zu ver-
hüten, müssen die übelsten
Partien zusammengekauft
und gewaltsam saniert
werden.

In order to avoid the worst,
the most offensive lots must
be purchased and treated by
force.

80 Jahre später
Heimfall des Bodens an die
Stadt. Das Quartier wird frei
für eine neue Bebauung.

80 years later
Devolution of land to the state.
The quarter in question now
ready to be built over anew.

Neueinteilung
Die Bebauung erfolgt wie bisher
auf öffentlichem Grund und
Boden nach neuem Straßennetz
und neuem Blockplan.

Fresh disposition
Building enterprise is carried
out as before on public land
according to a new road net and
block plan.

A

Nach der Sanierung wird der
Boden wieder verkauft.
After renewal the land is resold.

B

Nach der Sanierung verbleibt der
Boden in öffentlichem Eigentum.
After renewal the land remains
public property.

117

ground leases, for a limited period of time and in return for payment of a leasehold fee: the ground rent. The duration of the leasehold was to correspond to the presumed service life of a building, whereby Bernoulli anticipated around 80 years. To finance the purchase of land, the city was to issue bonds and raise loans. The debt interest would be financed by the leases, while the debt repayment would be guaranteed by the appreciation of land values.

Bernoulli was thus by no means aiming for an expropriation of private property that would cause social upheaval. His *Freiwirtschaft* ideas were not revolutionary. On the contrary, they were grounded in his interest in the urban development of the city. Bernoulli was well aware that his plans would also prevent speculative profits, exorbitant rents, and the loss of public spaces. He was a political animal, and thought of himself as an architect with a responsibility to society. This stance cost him his professorship at the ETH Zurich during the «Spiritual National Defense» campaign in 1938, and made him a sought-after expert on urban planning and questions of building law during the era of reconstruction after World War II.[14] And it continues to make his work highly relevant today. For architecture is always part of an overarching context of the landscape, urban planning and society. Taking responsibility for this means taking political action – today more than ever.

14
Hubertus Adam, «Ordnung in das verworrene Wesen unserer Städte bringen. Stadterneuerung und Wiederaufbau als Konstante im Denken Hans Bernoullis,» in: Claus, Zurfluh 2018 (see note 3), pp. 128–143.

Sylvia Claus / Who Owns the City?

Giovanni La Varra
The Italian Job. The Value of Land in the Years of the Italian Economic Miracle

One Hundred Million Italians

Between 1955 and 1970, around 17 million Italians migrated from the south of the country to the north, from small towns to big cities, from the mountains to the plains, from the fields to the factories. The Italian peninsula had a population of about 55 million at the time. This massive migration put quite a strain on Italian society, its cities, and thus, on its urban planning. Italy's spatial and urban policy framework had just prevailed over the emergency of necessary rebuilding after the war, and Italy was thoroughly occupied with building modern structures like freeways, airports, universities, and hospitals. Urban planning is one of the instruments governments have at their disposal to navigate through such sweeping social upheaval.

Italy's urban planning legislation goes back to the year 1942, meaning that it was passed by the Fascist regime during World War II. It provides for various urban planning instruments on different levels. By law, land management is based on the general land-use plan (*Piano Regolatore Generale,* PRG) that was to be adopted by all 8,000 Italian municipalities. As so often in Italian legislation, there were no explicit provisions for cases in which municipalities did not adhere to these requirements – which happened often, especially in smaller and medium-sized towns. In part they were not fulfilled because the necessary technical means were lacking; in other cases, non-compliance was due to imprudent agreements with private property owners, for whom the lack of development plans presented an opportunity to continue handling urban development without any restrictions or obligations. Yet at the same time, Italian building culture was at a very high standard, with many Italian urban planners – nearly all of whom had received their professional training and cultural imprinting during the Fascist period – working both as teachers at the universities and in construction praxis. *Urbanistica,* which was edited by Giovanni Astengo in the 1960s and continues to appear today, was one of the world's most respected journals, not least because of the outstanding quality of its images.[1]

The cities of northern Italy, and all cities with a commitment to political responsibility, agreed that urban-planning instruments were needed to control internal

1
«Under the direction of Giovanni Astengo in the years from 1948 to 1976, it was the most esteemed journal for urbanism in the world,» claims Vezio de Lucia in: *Se questa è una città* [1989], Rome 2006, p. 19.

The citizens of Naples
protesting against speculation
and the demolition of their
apartments in «Le mani sulla
città,» a sociocritical film by
Francesco Rosi that received
the Golden Lion in Venice
in 1963

emigration and immigration as well as industrial development. However, the first urban-development plans – even those that were created by the most influential urban planners – were based on exorbitant growth forecasts.

One term is found over and again in the explanatory texts on the development plans in Italy at the time: necessity. Cities were growing under the impact of immigration and demand for a higher standard of living. The plans proceeded from the assumption that the most important Italian cities would possibly grow by around 50 percent in the 1960s, and in some places even by 100 percent.[2] In the subsequent period, cities did grow considerably through immigration, but by no means to the extent and in the forms foreseen in the plans. The prognoses turned out to be highly exaggerated, and it was hardly possible to reconcile the actual developments with the programs drafted by Italy's urban planners. Yet the idea of inexhaustible growth, combined with the political pressure to include an ever-larger group of owners of agricultural areas in the surroundings of the city, persuaded architects and urban planners to develop excessive visions. Exaggerated growth forecasts served, on the one hand, the political objective of keeping everyone satisfied; on the other hand, they ensured that public authorities were able to exercise their discretion to favor certain property owners.[3] Thus, municipal authorities, having little to no interest in purchasing land of their own, at least safeguarded their option to select the land for which they issued building permits. As a result, the exorbitance of urban planning came to be a form of preserving power.

A Christian, Democratic Country

In the turbulent postwar years, Italy chose to belong to the West. The decisive moment for this was the parliamentary election of 1948, from which a new party emerged: founded underground during the final years of the war, Democrazia Cristiana (Christian Democracy, DC) won the election, and from that time on went on to rule alone for the entire decade of the 1950s. The opposition was made up of the Italian Communist (Partito Comunista, PCI) and Socialist (Partito Socialista, PSI) parties, along with

2
«The urban land-use plans of most Italian cities today [1967] have housing forecasts at their disposal for at least double today's potential» in: Giuseppe Campos Venuti, *Amministrare l'urbanistica,* Turin 1967, p. 38.
The prognoses upon which the Italian urban development plans of the 1960s were based proceeded from a future national population of 100 million.
3
Marco Romano, *L'urbanistica in Italia nel periodo dello sviluppo,* Venice 1982, p. 167.

Giovanni La Varra / The Italian Job

a few smaller liberal and conservative parties. DC was a large, broadly based party that attracted representatives of all social strata. Its success was based on an extensive communication network through public speakers, and the Roman Catholic Church's interventions in its favor. The party achieved the impressive feat of socially and politically integrating millions of Italians who had rendered homage to the Fascists for years into a party that made a clean break with the past and led the population onto a new, democratic stage. Democrazia Cristiana offered a great opportunity for collective atonement.

At the end of the 1950s, however, DC found that exercising power on its own was abrogating politics, making it difficult to address new societal demands. In the early 1960s the party opened negotiations, first in Milan and then on the national level, to form a coalition government with the PSI, which had since left the Popular Democratic Front with the PCI – and thus also escaped the Soviet Union's influence to which the PCI was bound, especially on foreign policy. The first governments of the 1960s, although still without PSI participation, attempted to bring new social concerns into politics and to prepare the country for a center-left government. Against this background, an urban planning reform that was careful to distribute the scarce resources of housing and public institutions became a disputed topic in debates with the socialists.

Urban Planning Activity in a Catholic Country
At the start of the 1960s, the outskirts of Italian cities were among «the ugliest in the world.»[4] At that time a young Christian Democrat, Fiorentino Sullo, Minister for Public Works in 1962, launched a debate that yielded two important urban planning laws. The first of these – Legge 167 of 1962 – laid down the criteria according to which municipalities were allowed to expropriate land in order to build public housing. The law provided for the specification of detailed plans (*Piani Particolareggiati,* PP) that were subordinated to the general land-use plan (PRG). Areas for public housing construction were to be plotted in these detailed plans, along with the parameters for their purchase from private owners at capped prices. After the land was purchased, the new districts were built with public funding.

4
Campos Venuti 1967 (see note 2), p. 35.

Immediately, the law was extraordinarily successful, even though the quality of the new neighborhoods was often quite low in terms of their architecture, structural engineering, and urban planning aspects. Also problematic was the fact that many of them were built too far from the existing city limits, as unscrupulous agreements with private landowners meant that the areas located furthest from the city were often the first to be developed, so that public funds were needed to pay for the missing roads and canalization. Only after these remote areas were connected to the city did private investors develop projects within the areas that already enjoyed urban infrastructure at the taxpayers' expense. For this kind of development, «the community bears the costs and the landowners benefit.»[5]

In spite of all of these problematic developments, at that time Italy introduced a far-reaching social housing program. Just a little later, in late 1962, it was once again Sullo who formulated a further ambitious goal: he wanted a new law regulating private development projects in cities. The objective was to reduce the yields realized by private landowners when the general land-use plan designated previously agricultural lands as prospective or actual development areas, instantly multiplying their value. Twenty- to 30-fold value appreciations were not uncommon.

With this bonus in their pockets, the landowners became private investors, taking up residential construction themselves. Yet their projects took a minimalist view of urban planning measures: the ensembles and districts they built had hardly any streets or parking spaces, and no green spaces were created; only the bare minimum of space was left free for public institutions like schools, churches, community centers, and the like, and these were built, mostly not until years later, with public funds. Neither did the private sector invest in any modern traffic network, such as metro rail or trams. With the support of prominent Italian urban planners like Giovanni Astengo, Luigi Piccinato, and Giuseppe Samonà,[6] Minister Sullo endeavored to correct this imbalance, which, on the one hand, generated yields that were not reinvested in public measures, and on the other, allowed markedly monofunctional cities to emerge.

5
Ibid., p. 41. Expressed in other words: «No costs are borne by the landowners; it is the community that has to perform a huge transfer of wealth,» in: Giovanni Ferracuti, Maurizio Marcelloni, *La Casa. Mercato e programmazione,* Turin 1982, p. 62.
6
A comprehensive research project on the Italian urban planners of the era (Piccinato, Marconi, Samonà, Quaroni, De Carlo, Astengo, Campos Venuti) is found in: Paola di Biagi, Patrizia Gabellini (eds.), *Urbanisti italiani,* Bari 1992.

Giovanni La Varra / The Italian Job

The draft law proposed that the authorities expropriate the land to be used for new construction in the city, develop the urban area with public funds, and ultimately auction the rights of use to build on this land.

Sullo pursued an approach as simple as it was courageous. The draft law he submitted proposed that a) detailed plans also be submitted for new private sector construction in the city, and that these plans account for the public interest, b) the land to be used for these detailed plans be expropriated by the authorities, who would pay market prices for farmland and thus eliminate unproductive profits for the landowners, c) the areas, once they had become public property, also be integrated into urban planning with public funds, and d) the rights of use (*diritto di superficie*) for the land produced by these measures be awarded in public auctions open to all interested economic actors. In other words: Even in the case of privately owned land, the city administration prepares the plans, expropriates the areas, develops the urban area with a purposefully structured road network and supply system, and ultimately auctions the real estate to builders. It was a revolutionary, and from today's perspective, in some respects exaggeratedly liberal scheme, with performance, transparency, and competition between various actors at its core. The original ownership of land conferred no rights and no added value at all. Sullo's land use rights were thus an instrument allowing the ownership of land to be decoupled from ownership of buildings. Concretely, this meant that land first became public land through expropriation, so that the persons to whom the real estate was awarded by auction were able to erect and sell buildings, but could not purchase the real estate. According to Italian law, land use rights can be awarded permanently or for a limited time.

Sullo did not envision granting use of the properties for a limited period; he was well aware that the residents of Italy – which enjoyed the highest rate of property ownership in Europe, then as it still does today – love to live in their own home. His project did, however, disturb the real estate lobbyists, known in Italy as «*blocco edilizio*,»[7] as well as the coalition of landowners, a reactionary bourgeoisie striving for unbridled profits. What bothered them most was the instrument of the auction as a free-market economic principle that precluded surprising appreciations in value, much more than the imponderables of land use rights. It was Sullo's primary aim to «leave landowners

7
The term *blocco edilizio* in the Italian press and in academic literature designates the implicit contract between politics and large landowners, whose structure of clientelistic relations had negative effects on the development of urban policy. It must be emphasized that the real estate bloc also included companies owned by the Vatican and important religious communities, which are historically the largest landowners in Italy.

8
Romano 1982 (see note 3), p. 172.
9
Also involved were daily newspapers and magazines like *Il Sole 24 ore, Corriere della sera* and *Borghese*. The last of these dared, in a country marked by bigotry and moralizers, to allude to Sullo's homosexuality as a defamatory tool to discredit him politically.
10
Il Popolo, April 13, 1963. Ferracuti and Marcelloni note: «Sullo pointed out, to no avail, that the right of use was already present in our legislation, that home owner-ship remained completely unaffected by this and was an institution in capitalist industrial countries, which was accepted without compunction and without accusation of Marxist collectivism,» in: Ferracuti, Marcelloni 1982 (see note 5), p. 74.
11
Ivan Blecic (ed.), *Lo scandalo urbanistico 50 anni dopo. Sguardi e orizzonti sulla proposta di riforma di Fiorentino Sullo,* Milan 2017, with contributions from: Dino Borri, Emanuele Boscolo, Sergio Brenna, Paolo Carrozza, Arnaldo Bibo Cecchini, Mario Cerasoli, Vezio De Lucia, Giulio Ernesti, Franco Farinelli, Paolo Pileri, Luciano Vettoretto.
12
«At home even my closest relatives asked me, more out of consternation and confusion than curiosity, whether I intended to take their homes away from them…. And I admit that I no longer knew how I should strike back against this incredibly general misperception.» Fiorentino Sullo, *Lo scandalo urbanistico,* Florence 1964, pp. 17–18.

entirely unaffected by the decisions of the general land-use plan.»[8] In spring 1963, one month before the national elections, the real estate lobbyists launched a media campaign against Sullo,[9] accusing him of ramming his legislative proposals through parliament. Italy's most important daily newspapers were mobilized against his initiative. Faced with this targeted press campaign, the DC, Sullo's own party, left him foundering. Two weeks before the election, *Il Popolo,* the official daily of the DC, sent up a casually formulated, but nevertheless clear signal: «To the extent that certain provisions [of the law proposed by Sullo] can be assessed, it is clear that the Democrazia Cristiana is in no way involved in the scheme. As stated quite clearly in its election platform, the party is pursuing the goal of making home ownership available to all Italians, and to do so without restriction and in the traditional state of this law.»[10] The choice of words was blunt and amounted to a definitive rejection. After the election, a new government was formed and new ministers selected. Fiorentino Sullo was not appointed to the new government, and did not become minister again until 1968, when he served in the cabinet for three months (Education), and once more for four months in 1972 (Science Research and Technology). He left parliament for good in 1987, passing away in the year 2000. He is occasionally remembered in tracts on urban development even today, whereby he is commended for his political courage and his methodical determination (a rarity in the Italy of his day), which he applied in order to develop an economic model that appeared to be liberal and meritocratic, but in fact privileged certain interest groups and was oligopolistic.[11]

The cool, decisive tone with which the DC ditched Sullo was a signal to the real estate lobby that nothing would change. Sullo reacted in 1964 by publishing a book vindicating his behavior,[12] but this step served only to isolate him further.

The election of 1963 yielded a DC/PSI coalition government, the first center-left government – an epochal event for Italian politics and society. Yet there was no more talk of reforming urban planning for many years.

Not until 1968 was legislation proposed that preserved the advantageous conditions for the real estate lobby,

Giovanni La Varra / The Italian Job

which did not affect the principle of value appreciation for properties included in the general development plan, but did specify minimum standards whose application private persons would have had to consent to the state applying in the case of urban development. A minimum number of square meters of green spaces, parking, and facilities to serve the public welfare were required for each future resident. These «minimum numbers» may have been a purely quantitative guarantee, yet the fact that certain standards were to be upheld in urban development, albeit with certain restrictions, was in itself a significant success for urban planning in Italy – especially considering that just a few years previously, private property owners had enjoyed practically unlimited power and boundless privileges.

In the early 1970s the responsibility for urban development was delegated to the regions, and thus to the level between the state government and municipal authorities. The regional administrations initiated a cumbersome process in which they established administrative structures and developed plans in order to control urban development. In essence, however, because of sustained submissiveness to supposedly sacrosanct private property, not even this shift in responsibility produced any radical changes in administrative conditions.

The quality of structural, formal, and urban architecture remained poor. Despite the introduction of the minimum standards discussed above, new urban construction in Italy turned out to be chronically insufficient in terms of the provision of public institutions and infrastructure: green spaces, social infrastructures, streets, sidewalks and parking spaces, regional and urban rail networks.

As long as Italian cities were growing constantly, meaning up to the mid-1980s, urban planning authorities were not able to successfully counter a *modus operandi* in which public actors nearly always reconciled with private stakeholders without imposing many conditions. The situation did vary from one region to the next, of course, but there is no doubt that the term «submissiveness» best describes the behavior that was characteristic for the development of Italian cities from the postwar era up to 1989.

A Sea of Houses at the Foot of a Volcano

At least until the mid-seventies, there was continuously high demand for houses, even though the numbers actually indicate the opposite. In 1971, 63 million *stanze* (livable rooms) were available for 54 million Italians.[13] So apparently there were enough buildings, but they were not located in the places to which the population had moved. In the 1980s, Italy experienced a consolidation and propagation of prosperity that transformed it from a «dense» to a «dispersed» country. The trend toward single-family homes took hold of enormous areas, with sparsely settled towns emerging on previously agricultural land. Public investments in social housing were suddenly cut, although by this time it was obvious that alternative projects endeavoring to apply the ideas of rationalistic urban planning in order to create *quartieri autonomi* (self-sufficient neighborhoods) had fundamentally failed. With increasing prosperity, some Italians were even building second and third homes, while in the heterogeneous manufacturing sector, which was strongly marked by family structures, incredible numbers of small, cheap production buildings were erected side by side in small, isolated enclaves.

Italy entered the twenty-first century in a situation unique to all of Europe: The country is characterized by extremely high land usage; every second house in the south is illegal, that is, was erected without a building permit and in violation of urban planning regulations,[14] the construction of infrastructure is chronically underfinanced, and a general dilapidation of public spaces can be observed. What is more, the financial crisis of 2008 resulted in further structures and towns being left to their own devices: On wide expanses of land, second homes constructed for tourists remain unsold; multitudes of production facilities stand unused, especially in northern Italy; historic city centers in the south, whose population numbers are falling, are suspended in a state of deterioration that is difficult to halt and in the Apennines and the Alpine foothills, the comprehensive problem of abandoned hamlets persists. Nobody in Italy wants to live at altitudes over 500 meters anymore.

There is probably no more impressive image of the urbanistic irrationality predominant in Italy than the view

13
Romano 1982 (see note 3), p. 179. A *stanza* is an Italian parameter that measures the number of rooms available in housing per inhabitant. At that time a ratio of 1:1 was considered acceptable.
14
In 2015, 47.3 percent of the real estate in the south was built illegally; this percentage was 18.9 percent in the central regions, and 6.6 percent in the north (Dati Istat, Bericht BES Benessere Equo e Sostenibile, 2015).

of the areas around Vesuvius, the only active volcano on the European continent. Around 600,000 people live in the *zona rossa* (red zone), the area with the highest hazard level, which includes 18 communities around the crater. One out of every 100 Italians lives at the foot of the volcano.

Today the struggle no longer concerns yields, but land use. Next to the inhabited Italy there is an Italy that consists of buildings and productive spaces «on ice»: they are either abandoned or underutilized. The problem of land use is certainly concrete and topical, but it also lends itself to frivolous instrumentalization. The option of zero consumption of land may well be enforced radically by some municipal and regional authorities, but, as always, hard standpoints can turn out to be extremely over-simplified when they are applied to space and urbanity. There is no doubt that land has been consumed ruthlessly in Italy, and that the environment in some areas has suffered severely as a consequence. In our day, however, the inevitable task to be faced is to once again address the «porosity» of a city that has spread out raggedly and forfeited consistency in a few compact districts. The urban planning of the coming years must stipulate certain forms of intervention for the purpose of rededicating the country's pervasive commercial spaces. These are frequently monofunctional and built unsustainably; over time, this has made them unattractive even as real estate. Either larger cities must be provided with the infrastructure that was not created during their original development, whereby consideration must be taken of certain new forms of city-specific mobility that are gradually gaining ground, or the poor structural quality that has resulted even in newer Italian cities suffering from a lower quality of services must be improved. Today, the simplest technology is used to build too many buildings with too much energy consumption – this is today's structural reality in Italy. It would also be necessary to penalize violations of building law more strictly – for instance, the common practice of erecting buildings directly on the most sensitive areas of riverbanks. This has caused not only environmental damage but also the indirect risk of death for the inhabitants of these buildings, who frequently become victims of natural catastrophes. In addition, the entire Apennine region should be considered. It is losing population, and its physical integrity is becoming ever-more sensitive as a consequence, bringing landslides and flooding.

Urban development continues to be a stage on which particular interests – often represented politically – are prevailing over a long-term overall vision. Italy's territory was weakened, even wiped out, in the twentieth century. Italy's land has been exhausted and has new imbalances to master. If the present landscape of neoliberal politics – albeit diluted by local and reactionary influences – again places emphasis on the question of land ownership, this would address only one of the problematic issues. Today we can develop the idea of something «new» only if we work with the gigantic mass of existing building stock and find a different purpose for these structures.

Giovanni La Varra / The Italian Job

Florian Hertweck
Hans-Jochen Vogel's Program for a Public Right of Disposal over Land[1]

The lawyer and SPD (German Social Democratic Party) politician Hans-Jochen Vogel (1926–2020) had been mayor of Munich for 10 years when proposals for a far-reaching land reform program were put forward in 1970. Upon his initiative, a land rights commission was created in Munich's city administration, which presented the results of its session in a brochure entitled *Initiative für eine Neuordnung des Bodenrechts* (Initiative for a Reorganization of Land Rights). The introduction describes Munich as a city that «suffers most under the injustices and inadequacies of the land rights currently in force and under the abuses and excesses of speculation and profiteering with land.» The report lamented price increases of more than 100 percent within a year for real property in prime locations, which were driving rents ever higher; the construction of public housing was nearly impossible, and «urgently required infrastructure projects» like hospitals, schools, and kinder-gartens could only be «built in much smaller quantities than needed or not at all because of the high land prices.»[2] In fact, land prices all over the country increased by 54 percent between 1969 and 1972,[3] while the real values of land used agriculturally fell by more than one third. Therefore, in 1970 the Social Democrats set up a land rights commission on the federal level as well, with Vogel as a member, which would build on the municipal policy experiences of its members to discuss the topic and formulate proposals.

Two years later, at the special federal SPD convention in Dortmund shortly before the national election, Chancellor Willy Brandt announced his intention in the coming legis-lative period to strike out «in a new direction on the basis of our legal order and system of property ownership.» The intention was to prevent «a few speculators dispensing a commodity as essential as land at society's expense.»[4]

On the second day of that convention, Vogel gave a keynote speech in which he placed the consequences of land speculation in a larger socio-ecological context: «The absolutization of the economic principle [is] challeng[ing] our foundations. This system initiated the commercialization and exploitation of all assets, all riches and reserves of nature.… Land development is eating into our landscape like tough slurry.… Like a cancerous tumor, office buildings

1
This chapter is an abridged and slightly edited version of my article «Hans-Jochen Vogels Projekt eines neuen Eigentumsrechts des städtischen Bodens – Ein Protokoll in 20 Punkten,» in: *ARCH+*, No. 231/2018, pp. 46–53.
2
«Vorbemerkungen,» in: Landeshauptstadt München (ed.), *Initiative für eine Neuordnung des Bodenrechts*, undated, presumably 1971 or 1972, p. 1. From the papers of Hans-Jochen Vogel at the Friedrich Ebert Foundation in Bonn.
3
From 1960 to 1969, the price rose from 38,000 DM to around 95,000 DM per hectare, followed in 1970 by an increase to 111,000 DM per hectare, to 121,700 DM per hectare in 1971, and in 1972 the price rose to 146,500 DM per hectare. *Bericht des Ministeriums für Ernährung, Landwirtschaft und Forsten*, signed by Dr. [Ernst-Ulrich] Pfingsten, from the papers of Hans-Jochen Vogel, 1973.
4
Bundesvorstand der SPD (ed.), *Außerordentlicher Parteitag der SPD, am 12. bis 13. Oktober 1972 in Dortmund, Westfalenhalle, Protokoll der Verhandlungen*, Bonn 1973, p. 66. In the federal election of November 19, 1972 the SPD received 45.8 percent of the secondary vote.

are proliferating in the outskirts of our cities and driving people away from their ancestral neighborhoods. Soon only the rich will be able to afford the luxury of a home near the city center.» While «entire areas are becoming empty,» others are brimming over with people, with the consequence that «armies of cars [are jamming] our streets and [generating] poisonous clouds of exhaust, which hang over entire districts in sulfur yellow.» These were no fantastic visions but rather observations presented by municipal politicians during the «Save Our Cities Now!» conference of the Association of German Cities in Munich in May 1971, prepared and chaired by Vogel, its president. The situation thus demanded fast action: «How can we [counter]act this? With conservative inaction, with laissez-faire policies? […] Nothing,» Vogel continued, will «sort itself out in the end.»[5]

In the same year, in an article for the 49th Deutscher Juristentag (conference of the German Bar Association), which is frequently cited today in the debate about land reform, he outlined a far-reaching program. This would first have to include «an amendment to federal town planning law,» in order to give municipalities «the general powers to issue orders for construction, modernization, and demolition» as well as «their competence to regulate the way real properties are used»; second, laws on expropriation and compensation would have to be reformed to make compensation easier, to separate the procedures for expropriation and compensation, and to introduce a right to preemptive purchase; third, the reform would have to provide land value capture so that planning-induced land value increases would benefit the municipality and not only the landowner, as a complement to the compensation a municipality has to pay landowners when planning measures cause the value of their land to decrease; fourth, «a land value tax» should be introduced «on extraordinary appreciations,» insofar as these «are not brought about through their own merits»; fifth, land valuation must be reformed «through a transition to monitored valuations by the landowners themselves.»

However, because Vogel believed that these five measures – all of which were compatible with the existing system – would not be sufficient, what was needed right

5
Ibid., p. 164.

away were «concrete ideas about a further phase in which [land ownership] will be redefined» – in the sense that it «is conceived to include only those rights and powers which do not contradict social responsibility.» This could be guaranteed only if «the existing ownership of land [is] divided into *Nutzungseigentum* (‹ownership of usage›) and *Verfügungseigentum* (‹ownership of disposal›), and the right to Verfügungseigentum [is transferred] to the public, which [bases] its cancellable or limited *Nutzungseigentum* of the individual tracts of land on contracts stipulating the kind of use, the level of compensation for use, and the duration of the rights of use.»[6]

At the abovementioned congress in Munich, the division of ownership into *Nutzungseigentum* and *Verfügungs-eigentum* was the subject of an exchange between Vogel, Munich city councilors and administrative staff, as well as others including Gerhard Leibholz, an influential judge on the Federal Constitutional Court. Leibholz believed it would be possible, according to Article 15 of the Basic Law, to divide property rights into *Verfügungseigentum* and *Nutzungseigentum.*[7] With this assertion he was able to cite precedence in a 1967 decision by the Federal Constitutional Court, which, like the Bavarian constitution, had rejected the purely market-oriented utilization of land: «The fact that land is unrenewable and indispensable forbids leaving its use completely up to the inestimable free play of market forces and the discretion of the individual; on the contrary, an equitable legal and social order requires the public interest in land to be taken into account far more than in the case of any other property.»[8] Although frequently cited, this decision, like similar provisions of the constitutions in Bavaria and Bremen, had not been reflected in policy, but this was to change in the subsequent period.

In his governmental address after the SPD election victory in January 1973, Chancellor Willy Brandt declared reform of the land law to be one of the emphases for the coming legislative term. The coalition of Social Democrats and Liberals planned to introduce a land value increment tax, whose purpose was to «inhibit the nuisance of irresponsible speculation with land.» Brandt asserted that, just as private property is protected, his government would ensure that «the social obligations [associated with

6
Hans-Jochen Vogel, «Boden-recht und Stadtentwicklung,» offprint from the *Neue Juristische Wochenschrift,* No. 35/1972, pp. 1544ff., cited here from Arno Brandlhuber, Florian Hertweck, Thomas Mayfried (eds.), *The Dialogic City. Berlin wird Berlin,* Cologne 2015, pp. 651–655.
7
Initiative für eine Neuordnung des Bodenrechts, Munich 1970, p. 173. Article 15 of the Basic Law reads: «Land […] may, for the purpose of nationalization, be transferred to public ownership or other forms of public enterprise by a law that determines the nature and extent of compensation.»
8
BVerfG, January 12, 1967 – 1 BvR 169/63. Cited in English at http://www.europarl. europa.eu/doceo/document/ TA-8-2017-0197_EN.html, Article I.

property] were also in good hands.»[9] Although Brandt did not explicitly mention Vogel's proposal for *Nutzungseigentum,* with this statement he already implied that the reform of the Basic Law with relation to land ownership would have to take both components into consideration, which was already reflected in principle by the program of the coalition government and could be found in the differentiation between land and buildings.

At the Social Democratic Party convention in Hanover in April 1973, Bremen's Mayor Hans Koschnick (SPD), Chairman of the Commission for Land Law Reform, introduced a working paper by the commission, whose membership included not only Koschnick and Vogel but also the architect and director of construction in Stuttgart, Peter Conradi.[10] Right at the start the paper points to the deplorable state of existing land law, which treats «land like any other good in principle,» allows «price to be determined by the market principles of supply and demand,» and leaves «land value and rents of land essentially to each respective private property owner.» Within the bounds of federal town planning law, «the decision about the use of property is the up to the owner.»[11] Because the commission believed this arrangement to be erroneous from the very outset, it proposed a catalog of measures that essentially corresponded with all of the items in the reform Vogel had outlined to the bar association the previous year: a revision of the procedure for expropriation and the provisions for compensation, introduction of land value capture, a land value increment tax, and monitored self-valuations. A new arrangement would also be possible immediately for land that was already publicly owned: For federal land, legislation was to stipulate that «a sale to private entities is ruled out in principle.» Instead, «the allocation of *Nutzungseigentum* [was] to be chosen.» The parliaments of the federal states were asked to enact the same kind of regulations to govern the land they owned. And «to the municipalities [it should] be recommended,» Vogel called out to his colleagues in the plenum of the party convention, «from now on to cede only ground leases, and no more full ownership of any real property.»[12]

While the commission recommended that the party convention pass these measures, a new commission was

9
Willy Brandt, *Regierungserklärung des zweiten Kabinetts Brandt / Scheel, vom 18. Januar 1973,* Presse- und Informationsamt der Bundesregierung, Berlin 1973, pp. 25, 34.
10
Further members included Detlev Rohwedder, state secretary in the Ministry of Economics, who was later murdered by the RAF, and Karl Ravens, who would later become Federal Minister for Regional Planning, Construction and Urban Development.
11
Materialien zum Parteitag vom 28.11. bis 2.12.1972 Hannover. Vorschläge zur Reform der Bodenordnung, submitted by the Commission for Land Law Reform to the Party Executive of the SPD, 1972, p. 11. The party convention was ultimately postponed until April 1973.
12
Vorstand der SPD (ed.), *Parteitag der Sozialdemokratischen Partei Deutschlands,* April 10–14,1973, Stadthalle Hannover, Bonn 1974, p. 524.

Florian Hertweck / Hans-Jochen Vogel's Program

«We can no longer content ourselves with administrative measures. Neither can we continue to be content with mere building and planning laws. We need truly new ownership structures.» Hans Koschnik, 1973

to be charged with working out a final concept for public *Verfügungseigentum* and private *Nutzungseigentum* in the foreseeable future. In so doing, the commission concluded that more time would be needed in order to submit a balanced, politically viable concept to deal with this legally controversial and politically charged issue. «It would be unrealistic to believe,» Koschnick stated in his presentation to the convention, «that it would be possible to realize a complete package of these proposals in the present legislative term.» However, «the development of a solution concept [should be] tasked immediately, [in order] to fully preclude speculative investment» and so that «the competition of demand for building land [could] be oriented only on its potential use.» Further, he continued «We can no longer content ourselves with administrative measures. Neither can we continue to be content with mere building and planning laws. We need truly new ownership structures.»[13]

In May 1973 the Christian Democratic Union (CDU) presented a special publication on «Social Land Law,» which summarized the first results of its land law commission in preparation for the party convention in Hamburg. The Christian Democrats also aspired to create «social property,» but they understood it to mean «the expansion of access to land ownership for broad sectors of the population.»[14] The SPD's plan to introduce «a general separation of the conception of property into *Verfügungseigentum* [and] personal *Nutzungseigentum* is categorically rejected by the CDU,» because it would effect «a contraction of access to land ownership for broad sectors of the population.» The transfer of land ownership to municipalities would give them too much power. The commission also opposed the introduction of a land value increment tax, because it would be «socially unjust and technically unfeasible.»[15] In contrast, it suggested providing state funds to promote the accumulation of capital by less wealthy sectors of society, and raising the income tax on speculative profits from real estate sales. It saw a further solution to the problem in a more intensive mobilization of land supply for building. Creating new areas ready for construction, the commission claimed, would lower land prices.[16]

In addition to the SPD and the CDU the other two parties, FDP and CSU, set up similar commissions of their

13
Ibid., pp. 432, 537.
14
«Vorschläge für ein soziales Bodenrecht. Entwurf der Kommission ‹Bodenrecht›,» in: *Union in Deutschland,* special edition No. 22/1973, p. 7.
15
Ibid., p. 9. On this there still appears to have been discord within the CDU. The resolution of the party executive in October of the same year mentions «offsetting valorizations and losses as a consequence of public development and investment» as one of its aims. Cf. CDU-Bundesgeschäftsstelle, *Vorlage des CDU-Bundesvorstands für den 22. Bundesparteitag in Hamburg, Soziales Bodenrecht,* resolved on October 5/6, 1973 in Bonn, p. 4.
16
Ibid., p. 13.

Florian Hertweck / Hans-Jochen Vogel's Program

Materialien

Vorschläge eigentumsrechtlicher Lösungen zur Reform der Bodenordnung

vorgelegt vom Vorstand der Sozialdemokratischen Partei Deutschlands

„Nach ausführlicher Erarbeitung und Diskussion der verfassungsrechtlichen, rechtlichen und wirtschaftlichen Aspekte und unter Berücksichtigung von zu erwartenden Belastungen der öffentlichen Hände sowie der Erörterung von Einführungskriterien und Praktikabilitätsüberlegungen kommt die Kommission Bodenrechtsreform zu der mit großer Mehrheit gefaßten Empfehlung, eine Neuordnung der Eigentumsstruktur an Grund und Boden langfristig für städtebauliche Problembereiche durch ein Modell ‚Verfügungs- und Nutzungseigentum nach Art. 14,3 GG' anzustreben."

Hans Koschnick

Florian Hertweck / Hans-Jochen Vogel's Program

SPD
Sozialdemokraten

argumente

2

Warum Bodenrechts- reform?

Zersiedelte Landschaft

Verbaute Seeufer

Stadtrandzonen als Spekulationsgürtel

Stadtplanung unter dem Druck der Meistbietenden

Überangebot an teuren Eigentumswohnungen in Luxusgebieten – menschenunwürdige Unterkünfte in Elendsgebieten

Leere Innenstädte

Weitläufige Wohngebiete ohne wichtige öffentliche Einrichtungen

Misere des öffentlichen Nahverkehrs

Verkehrsfallen durch Spekulation

Spekulative Baulücken

Bodenpreissteigerungen, die wie ein Schatten bestimmten öffentlichen Einrichtungen folgen

Publication on land reform
by the German Social
Democratic Party, 1974

Florian Hertweck / Hans-Jochen Vogel's Program

own. There were debates in the Bundestag and legislative proposals, but all attempts to make land law more socially equitable failed, be it through instituting *Verfügungseigentum* or a land value increment tax. Even the repeated demand not to sell public land for building fell on deaf ears. Besides recognizing that the land issue was broadly discussed in the early seventies, it is clear from the debates at that time that the different land reform concepts of the two main parties were also based on different conceptions of urban planning. While the Social Democrats wanted to communalize publicly owned land in order to consolidate cities and towns and intermix them both functionally and socially by attracting renters, the CDU and CSU aspired to the larger-scale mobilization of building land in order to spread land ownership as widely as possible.

Postscript:
Over the last two years, Hans-Jochen Vogel increasingly joined in the renewed debate, asserting that, over time, the impression has been created that we must live with Germany's price increases of 1,600 percent for land and 491 percent for rent from 1962 to 2015, compared with only a 302 percent increase in the consumer price index. Only a few years ago, the 91-year-old Vogel expressed his astonishment that Munich land prices had risen by «believe it or not, 34,263 percent,»[17] as though society were no longer interested in this subject.

17
Hans-Jochen Vogel, «Die verdrängte Herausforderung der steigenden Baulandpreise,» in: *Süddeutsche Zeitung,* November 11, 2017.

Franziska Eichstädt-Bohlig
From Not-for-Profit Housing to Financial Market Roulette

The question of housing is inextricably linked to the question of land, as landowners wield considerable influence over the type and the price of land use. This is true especially when the political community rolls out the red carpet for private landowners to exploit capital freely. How the part of the housing stock in Germany that previously had not-for-profit status was handled is an instructive example.

It all began in 1982 when the weekly newsmagazine *Der Spiegel* exposed that board members of the housing company Neue Heimat, which was owned by trade unions, had illegally helped themselves to company assets and were doing business deals that were impermissible according to the law regulating not-for-profit housing. This scandal around Neue Heimat paved the way for abolishing not-for-profit status for housing in 1988.

The Death Blow for Not-for-Profit Status for Housing

Tucked away in the Tax Reform Act 1990, the law regulating not-for-profit housing was abolished by the government of Chancellor Helmut Kohl and the parliamentary majority of the political parties CDU/CSU (conservative) and FDP (liberal), taking effect as of January 1, 1990.[1] The reason given was the elimination of the tax benefits granted to compensate for the restrictions applying to not-for-profit enterprises. It was also claimed that the not-for-profit status for housing had been introduced to promote reconstruction following World War II, and that since reconstruction had been successful that status was no longer necessary and could no longer be justified to the private real estate industry.

This decision, which eliminated the more than century-old tradition of not-for-profit housing cooperatives and housing companies in Germany, was hardly noticed by the general public. From 1990 on, the housing companies were free market actors, which many of them welcomed. Almost 3.5 million rental units and the tenants living in them became fair game for new real estate deals. Not-for-profit status meant that if a housing company was liqui-dated or lost its not-for-profit status, then its rental units, land, and further assets had to be transferred to other not-for-profit housing companies. When the law governing

1
Article 21 of the Tax Reform Act 1990 as promulgated on July 25, 1988, *Federal Gazette* I, p. 1093.

F. Eichstädt-Bohlig / From Not-for-Profit Housing to Financial Market Roulette

From 1999 through the end of 2006, Germany's federal, state, and municipal governments sold roughly 500,000 publicly owned rental units to global financial investors at the highest price achievable, though the average price per unit was just 42,000 euros!

not-for-profit status for housing was abolished, that condition was lifted. The only consolation for renters: rents in previously not-for-profit housing could be raised by at most 5 percent for a transition period of five years in areas with increased demand for housing.[2]

Public Residential Properties on the Global Bargain Markets

The end of the Cold War was followed by a major rush of neoliberal capital exploitation. Shareholder value, deregulation, privatization, and the lean state became the dominant guiding principles in many parts of the world. In Germany the process was initially about privatizing major public companies such as the postal service and the airline Lufthansa, and about selling the federal government's stakes in ports, airports, Volkswagen, and the energy company VEBA. The rail service was privatized in its legal structure. Since then, its real estate holdings that are «not required for rail service operations» have been bought and sold at top prices throughout the country.

In former East Germany, the previously municipal housing companies were transformed into municipal limited liability companies and thus forced to privatize some of their housing stock. The housing cooperatives there were given the land on which their housing stood.[3] The real estate previously «owned by the people,» (i.e., by the state) was given back to those who had owned it before it had been nationalized, or sold to private and institutional investors from the West.

From 1999 through the end of 2006, Germany's federal, state, and municipal governments sold roughly 500,000 publicly owned rental units to global financial investors at the highest price achievable, though the average price per unit was just 42,000 euros![4] The first sale of a housing company owned by the federal government – namely, the one belonging to the rail service, with 114,000 units – was initiated by Chancellor Helmut Kohl's CDU-led government and completed in 2000 by the coalition of the SPD and Green parties. The deal involved selling 64,000 units to Deutsche Annington Immobilien GmbH, which had previously belonged to the Japanese Nomura consortium and has been the largest private housing

2
Ibid., § 4 Authorization.
3
Treaty of August 31, 1990 between the Federal Republic of Germany and the German Democratic Republic on the establishment of German unity (Unification Treaty), Article 22 (4).
4
These and most of the following data in: Bundesamt für Bauwesen und Raumordnung, *Veränderung der Anbieterstruktur im deutschen Wohnungsmarkt und wohnungspolitische Implikationen,* BBR Forschungen issue 124, Bonn 2007 and the BBSR database *Wohnungstrans-aktionen* on https://www.bbsr.bund.de/BBSR/DE/Veroeffentlichungen/ministerien/BMVBS/Forschungen/2007/Heft124.html?nn=395966

F. Eichstädt-Bohlig / From Not-for-Profit Housing to Financial Market Roulette

company in Germany since 2015, under the name Vonovia SE. The remaining 50,000 units were transferred to housing companies owned by the federal states, most of which were later privatized themselves.

In 2004, the Federal Insurance Institute for Employees (now part of German Pension Insurance) sold its previously not-for-profit housing company Gagfah, with 82,000 units, to the US financial investor Fortress. In 2006, Fortress transformed the company into a joint stock company under Luxembourgian law, which was bought by Deutsche Annington in 2014. Fortress absorbed NILEG, the Development Corporation of Lower Saxony, and its 30,000 rental units in 2005, as well as WOBA, the Municipal Housing Company Dresden, with 48,000 units in 2006. These rental units were initially allocated to the new for-profit company Gagfah S.A. and now belong to Vonovia.

Berlin pioneered the sale of large housing companies owned by the federal states. As early as 1998, Berlin sold its majority interests in the housing company GEHAG (32,000 units), which was renowned for its 1920s housing developments that were pathbreaking in both architectural and in social terms, including the Hufeisensiedlung in Berlin-Neukölln, Onkel Toms Hütte in Berlin-Zehlendorf, Wohnstadt Carl Legien in Berlin-Prenzlauer Berg, and others. Deutsche Wohnen acquired 100 percent of GEHAG in 2007 after some detours. In 2004, the Senate of Berlin also sold the not-for-profit housing company GSW with 66,000 units to the US consortium Cerberus Capital Management and the Whitehall Fund. Cerberus had GSW listed on the stock market in 2008; in 2013 Deutsche Wohnen also absorbed GSW, which at the time had just under 60,000 units.

During this period roughly 332,000 rental units owned by municipal companies were sold. The most important private-sector transactions for the Ruhr area were the sale of Viterra AG with 150,000 company-owned rental units by E.ON (the successor to the state-owned energy corporation VEBA) to Deutsche Annington, and the sale of 40,000 company-owned rental units by ThyssenKrupp to Corpus/Morgan Stanley in 2004/05.

By selling BauBeCon (20,000 rental units), a successor of Neue Heimat Lower Saxony, to Cerberus in 2005,

Sellout of a World Heritage
Site.
Top: The Weisse Stadt
(White City), Aroser Allee,
Berlin. Architect: Bruno
Ahrends.
Bottom: Ringsiedlung
Siemensstadt,
Jungfernheideweg, Berlin.
Architect: Hans Scharoun

Top: Hufeisensiedlung,
Berlin. Architects and urban
planners: Bruno Taut,
Martin Wagner. Landscape
architect: Leberecht Migge
Bottom: Wohnstadt Carl
Legien, Berlin. Architects:
Bruno Taut, Franz Hillinger

the German Trade Union Federation also played financial market roulette. BauBeCon was resold multiple times before Deutsche Wohnen took over the company for 1.24 billion euros in 2012.

Setting the Pace for Aggressive Real Estate Deals

Once housing companies had been purchased for the first time, the roulette of reselling major housing companies and packages of units began right away. In the process, the first and second investors did not invest in the real estate, but took the maximum amount of money possible out of the privatized companies before passing them along to the next profiteer or listing them on the stock market. Money set aside for maintenance was rebudgeted, and maintenance and repairs were curtailed to a minimum – as were the services provided by facility managers. Renters have often been treated very poorly.

Rental units in good locations have been remodeled and sold as condominiums. Low-income renters find themselves in less attractive housing developments – often on the urban fringe. That is where investors prefer to concentrate people dependent on public rental subsidies. In this way, neighborhoods are being segregated by social status, one building at a time. In the Ruhr area, an entire region that deindustrialized since mines were closed, dealing a blow to the local economy, the «locusts» often leave behind dilapidated properties that they simply do not maintain, and the municipalities have to pick up the pieces.[5]

This commercial exploitation roulette paused briefly during the financial crisis of 2008, only to set in again a short time later. The «locusts» moved on as soon as they had had their fill. Other actors reorganized as stock companies and became large corporations intending to rent out housing long-term. Two huge companies have ended up as the winners: Vonovia SE, which currently has 485,000 units, and Deutsche Wohnen SE with 160,000 units, 110,000 of them in Berlin. These two companies have become the nemesis of renters and symbols of a particularly cynical form of capitalism. At the same time, their business model opened the door for real estate speculation driven by the financial market, which has taken large German cities hostage since the financial crisis.

5
Landtag Nordrhein-Westfalen, *Abschlussbericht der Enquetekommission I in der 16. Wahlperiode, Wohnungswirtschaftlicher Wandel und neue Finanzinvestoren in NRW,* Landtagsdrucksache 16/2299–2013.

F. Eichstädt-Bohlig / From Not-for-Profit Housing to Financial Market Roulette

Today, the federal government and most of the federal states hardly own housing any more. Most cities and municipalities have become cautious about privatizing housing since the financial crisis. Yet up to this day, the differences between a housing industry oriented toward the public good and global real estate capitalism have been obscured in the political discourse. After all, the federal government, states, and municipalities sold their housing companies as share deals, including their names signifying not-for-profit status.[6] The first G in Gagfah still stands for «gemeinnützig» (not-for-profit), as does the first G in Berlin's GSW and GEHAG. Previously oriented toward the not-for-profit housing industry and cooperatives, the trade associations and their umbrella organization GdW (today Bundesverband deutscher Wohnungs- und Immobilien-unternehmen e.V., the Federal Association of German Housing and Real Estate Companies) now represent the interests of large private funds as well as those of real estate corporations and socially oriented housing cooper-atives and municipal housing companies. So it is not difficult to suspect conflicting goals!

The affected renters are still led to believe that their apartments are not-for-profit, while they are actually being handed recklessly from one owner to the next and the renters must constantly live in fear of being driven out of their homes. Although «social charters» were agreed upon for some housing developments, which provided or still provide some protection from drastic rent increases and terminations of rental contracts for a limited period of time, compliance has been monitored only sporadically. Also, they do not protect new renters, and clever lawyers working for the owners can usually find a way around them.

Housing Policy in Shambles
The public sector's privatization strategy was part and parcel of a generally irresponsible handling of housing and land policy. Besides not-for-profit status for housing, Germany's social housing program was dismantled as well. For many years, hardly any new social housing has been built, and for the older units, the requirement that they be rented to low-income tenants no longer applies. The federal government, the states, some municipalities,

6
Share deal refers to the purchase of shares of a real estate company, whereby no real estate transfer tax is due and the new owner is not registered in the land register.

and companies owned by the public sector have been selling land to the highest bidder regardless of social, ecological, or urban planning criteria. The law permits rent increases significantly higher than net income increases. The responsibility for housing policy was transferred from the federal government to the states in 2006.

The relevance of privatizations for land policy has not been discussed at all to date. General data about the land sold along with the rental units is not available, because entire housing companies were sold and the number of units was used as the measure of value. Since most of them are housing developments from the 1950s and 1960s with potential for building additional housing and densification, the public sector has often given up more than just rental housing – namely, also this land and its development potential. That is why it is to be expected that the new owners will opt for demolition and new construction in the near future, initiating the next phase of lucrative real estate exploitation.

The sales of rental property have already had dire consequences for the municipalities. Privatizations had positive impacts on public budgets in the short term. But long-term, not-for-profit housing is the far more important societal good. In financial terms, a considerable amount of the 11.5 billion euros per year necessary to provide housing subsidies for the needy could be saved.

The greatest political problem, however, is that by selling the not-for-profit housing to investors driven by the financial market, the business model of speculative profit maximization now sets the pace for the real estate industry in major cities. Although 48 percent of landlords in large cities of more than 500,000 are private individuals with a few units,[7] their traditional business model – namely, that an apartment building is to bring in moderate, but long-term and low-risk returns – is on the decline.

This trend has been accelerating and intensifying since the financial crisis of 2008. The policy of low interest rates has been driving capital from around the world into the major German cities to achieve the highest possible returns quickly. This is true of private equity funds, of the new, large housing companies mentioned above, and of clever individual investors – all of whom push through their own

7
Institut der deutschen Wirtschaft, *Mieten, Modernisierungen und Mieterstruktur – Vermietergruppen in Großstädten im Vergleich*, IW-Report 11/19, Cologne 2019.

interests at the expense of renters and people purchasing individual apartments. Rental law has various gray areas and provides legal tools that make this possible. Of course, land prices then rise accordingly. The land price of the Gründerzeit buildings in Berlin-Charlottenburg was 400 euros per square meter in 2007; today it is 10 times as high, making the building of new housing at affordable prices unviable.

Drastic rent increases, the transformation of rental units into condominiums, demolitions, and the construction of luxury housing have become the central problems in large cities since 2010. And yet the demand for affordable housing is increasing twofold: first, because people are continuing to move to urban regions; and second, because gentrification is displacing many people from centrally located residential neighborhoods. And gentrification does not only mean that a high earner who just relocated to Berlin moves into the apartment where a nurse used to live. A very large number of units are sold to well-off people from China, Russia, and/or Dubai as second and third homes. Others are bought by wheeler-dealers renting them out at excessively high prices as vacation rentals or furnished apartments.

As important as the existing protective instruments in German planning law are – they can only prevent a certain number of renters from being driven out of their urban neighborhoods. These instruments are only symbolic drops in a very large ocean – even though they require considerable bureaucratic time and effort.

«Crazy High Rents» and «Expropriate Deutsche Wohnen and Co.»

Since 2015, the federal government has sought to tackle the housing problems in big cities with an «Alliance for Affordable Housing and Building.»[8] The states are once again to receive financial support for social housing. The *Mietpreisbremse* (literally, «brake on rents,» a limited form of rent control) was tightened somewhat, the percentage of modernization costs that owners can add to the rent was lowered modestly from 11 to 8 percent, and a subsidy has been made available to families with children building a home. But none of these measures can put

8
Federal Ministry of the Interior, Building and Community, *Gemeinsame Wohnraumoffensive von Bund, Ländern und Kommunen, Ergebnisse des Wohngipfels am 21. September 2018 im Bundeskanzleramt.*

F. Eichstädt-Bohlig / From Not-for-Profit Housing to Financial Market Roulette

out the housing-policy firestorm because the neoliberal policies driving real estate prices up are systematically disregarded.

As a result, protests by renters in major cities are becoming more and more intense. Countless tenants' initiatives are rebelling against excessive rents, outrageous rent increases after modernizations, and the demolition of their homes for new luxury construction. More than 200 groups have formed in Berlin alone, demanding their right to housing and organizing large and powerful demonstrations against «crazy high rents.»

In early 2019 a coalition of tenants' initiatives attacked the real estate industry in Berlin directly: by initiating a petition for a referendum to «expropriate Deutsche Wohnen and Co.,» the renters seek to force Berlin's government to take rigorous and consistent action.

The coalition invokes Article 15 of Germany's Basic Law: «Land, natural resources and means of production may, for the purpose of nationalization, be transferred to public ownership or other forms of public enterprise by a law that determines the nature and extent of compensation […]» It simultaneously invokes the Constitution of the State of Berlin, which guarantees the right to adequate housing in Article 28.

The aim is to have a referendum calling on Berlin's House of Representatives to adopt a law expropriating private housing companies that own more than 3,000 units in exchange for compensation.[9] Simply by announcing this referendum and breaking a market economy taboo, the initiators achieved a great deal. Using the word «expropriation» and invoking the Basic Law and the Constitution of Berlin shook up the political community, the real estate industry, and the media, breathing new life into fears of class struggles that many believed had long been overcome. Of course, the real estate trade associations criticized the call for expropri-ation sharply and warned of blocking investment. But some investors suddenly began to act very cautiously. The political and business communities sense that the demand for a fundamental change of course is on the agenda.

Surveys show that many Berliners do have a positive view of expropriating the owners of large amounts of

9
Julia Löhr, «Plötzlich ist der Sozialismus wieder ganz nah,» *Frankfurter Allgemeine Zeitung,* April 6, 2019. Many more reports on the topic appeared in the media in the first half of 2019.

F. Eichstädt-Bohlig / From Not-for-Profit Housing to Financial Market Roulette

private rental housing. Few people doubt that the initiators, who submitted 77,000 signatures when they formally applied for the referendum in June 2019, will successfully clear the next hurdle, which requires 175,000 signatures, and the formal referendum, which needs at least 613,000 votes in favor. Yet this referendum would not be legally binding. Even if successful, Berlin's House of Representatives would not have to implement it.

The matter addressed by the referendum is controversial, but it is certainly considered legally permissible, although (or also, because) Article 15 of the Basic Law – expropriation for the purpose of nationalization – has never been applied in practice. However, people are puzzling over the amount of compensation and whether it could be legally disputed. The Berlin Senate estimates that compensation would total 29 to 36 billion euros. The initiators assume 9 to 18 billion euros. The government debt of the city of Berlin is already extremely high, at 58 billion euros.

Besides Deutsche Wohnen SE, with 111,500 units, 11 other private housing companies could be affected by expropriation, including Vonovia SE with 44,000 units in Berlin, and Akelius with 13,700 units, both of which are considered particularly aggressive in their way of doing business. But the Protestant Hilfswerk-Siedlung GmbH, which has 10,000 units and operates in the tradition of not-for-profit companies, would also be affected.

The first response of the SPD–Left–Green coalition government in Berlin was to roll out a tough instrument of rental law. On June 18, 2019, the Senate decided to introduce a «cap on rents» effective immediately; it was to block rental increases for five years and lower particularly high rents. In terms of procedural law, this tough measure is legitimized by the transfer of responsibility for housing policy from the federal government to the state governments. In terms of substance, the reason given for it is the tense situation on the housing market because of owners' increased expectations of returns and the Berlin population's below-average net household income.

Following this decision, the share prices of Deutsche Wohnen and Vonovia plummeted. Some investors announced they would no longer invest in their housing

F. Eichstädt-Bohlig / From Not-for-Profit Housing to Financial Market Roulette

stock. Others threatened to sell off more units as condominiums. In other cities such as Munich and Frankfurt
am Main, renters' coalitions formed immediately to demand
«caps on rents» there as well. The initiators of the Berlin
referendum welcomed the Senate's decision, but
declared that they would continue to pursue their desire
for expropriation of major private housing companies.

As of August 2019, the positions of the three parties
in Berlin's ruling coalition differ widely: the Left,
which as a governing party bore part of the responsibility
for privatizing GSW and GEHAG 15 years ago, supports
expropriating Deutsche Wohnen and other housing
companies and is collecting signatures for the referendum.[10]
The Greens consider expropriation to be a last resort. They
see the referendum above all as a challenge to demand
the social responsibility that ownership entails in the
political arena and to reinvigorate orientation toward the
public good.[11] Berlin's SPD has not yet taken a position;
it had promised to consult about how to deal with the
referendum in the fall of 2019.

The Christian Democratic Union (CDU), the Free Democratic Party (FDP), and the Alternative für Deutschland (AfD)
reject both calls for expropriation and the «cap on rents»;
they consider them dangerous first steps toward socialism,
which has been overcome. Investors, they claim, would
be scared off, and no new housing would be built. The FDP
found the simplest formula: it seeks to put an end to the
renters' protests by simply cutting Article 15 from the Basic
Law. However, it overlooked Article 19 (2) of the Basic Law,
which states: «In no case may the essence of a basic right
be affected.»

Most of the political parties and actors involved in the
debate limit solutions to the housing question to «build,
build, build.» Fast and cheap new construction, more public
support for construction, and cheap newly zoned land for
building would quickly help the market balance out supply
and demand. Yet the prices for construction and land
are already so overheated in the big cities that affordable
new buildings are almost impossible to implement. In
addition, all experts know that newly built housing is always
the most expensive, especially if it is to be sustainable and
ecologically responsible. Only when the loans have been

10
«Berlin hat Eigenbedarf!
Deutsche Wohnen und Co.
enteignen!,» Leaflet of the
party Die Linke for the
election to the European
Parliament 2019.
11
Bündnis 90/Die Grünen,
Landesverband Berlin,
*Beschluss des Landesaus-
schusses vom 15. Mai 2019*.

paid off does the time come when real estate can continually yield appropriate returns, even if rents are modest.

New construction is surely necessary in high-growth cities and regions. But the 300,000 new housing units built in Germany in 2018 increased the housing stock of 42 million by just 0.7 percent. Even if construction were doubled, that would only complement, but could not replace, what is urgently needed according to Article 14 (2) of the Basic Law: «Property entails obligations. Its use shall also serve the public good.» This is the urgent challenge to the political community to limit property owners' rights to capital exploitation in order to prevent displacement of renters.

At the same time, it is essential to reestablish municipal land banks as well as not-for-profit status for housing in order to guarantee sufficient housing stock reserved for low-income renters – even if it will take one to two generations for these measures to have structural impacts. Germany has more than 150 years of experience with the fact that the market alone will solve neither the question of housing nor the question of land. This is all the more true when financial investors dominate market activity and threaten social harmony in our cities.

F. Eichstädt-Bohlig / From Not-for-Profit Housing to Financial Market Roulette

Markus Hesse
«Property States» and the Financialization of Urban Development [1]

«Shady Deals»

The process of globalization of the economy and society has fundamentally changed the realities of life in cities in recent decades. The same is true of the perspectives of urban development. The emergence of a global trade and production regime that was only able to fully develop in the past century because of comprehensive political regulation was followed by the globalization of services. Technological innovations in data processing made current trends such as digitalization and the online platform economy possible. The greater impact of the financial markets on the real economy has further exacerbated these trends. Traditional boundaries between economic sectors or territories have been removed and global and local frames of reference are becoming indistinguishable. As a good that simply is not mobile, land is increasingly included in the sphere of the global exchange economy, as an asset. The mobilization of financial assets is followed by the large-scale valuation of real estate; as a consequence, local lifeworlds are subject to heightened pressure to achieve high rates of return.

Two examples from Berlin are textbook cases of how local circumstances change under the influence of world-wide capitalization. One is the story of the Büchertisch (Book Table) in Berlin-Kreuzberg, a not-for-profit initiative to promote the culture of reading, which collects book donations and passes them on to schools and many other institutions. When the Taliesin Property Fund, head-quartered on the island of Jersey, bought the property where the Büchertisch had rented space since 2004, it drastically raised the rent. The iniative could no longer afford the rent and had to find new premises.[2] This well-known pattern of capitalization, gentrification and displacement of local users is increasingly apparent in many cities. Another example in Berlin is the activities of the British billionaire family Pears, which became the subject of public debate because of current research by the press. The family is alleged to own about 3,000 rental apartments in Berlin.[3] This large amount of housing yields high returns, but is subject to only minimal taxation because of share deals that involve global regulation constructs and gaps. As the structure of ownership remains concealed within

1
Revised and expanded version of the essay «In Grund und Boden. Wie die Finanzialisierung von Bodenmärkten und Flächennutzung Städte unter Druck setzt,» in: *ARCH+*, No. 213/2018, pp. 78–83.
2
Adrian Garcia-Landa, Christoph Trautvetter, «Düstere Deals,» in: *Der Tagesspiegel,* November 15, 2016.
3
Recherchezentrum Correctiv, «Das verdeckte Imperium,» in: *Der Tagesspiegel,* May 31, 2019.

Markus Hesse / «Property States» and the Financialization of Urban Development

The Berlin Büchertisch before
it was displaced

the web of transnational investments, so too does the presence of owners remain discreet on the ground; their representatives are hardly visible or do not appear in public.

Both cases exist because of a complex web of ownership structures, offshore financial transactions, and ways to reduce taxes that developed only recently. Both are based on a complex and intricate network of companies and investments; shareholders use it to generate high returns and to reduce the tax burden on their profits. Their causal relationships are global: they extend from the built portfolio in Berlin to financing structures in the UK and Germany, to tax-optimized management in Luxembourg and Cyprus, all the way to company headquarters on the British Channel island of Jersey or the British Virgin Islands. The «shady deals»[4] enabled by such constructs, whose primary aim is to reduce taxes, have increasingly made cities the pawns of global profit interests.

Political Economy of the City

These more recent changes have taken place against the background of urban structural transformation spanning a number of decades. Whereas financialization is a recent phenomenon, the days of urban economies' local autonomy are long gone. As early as the period of industrialization, the economic base of many cities was essentially exchange with other locations – their export base was considered the key to economic success. In contrast, the political field in which decisions were made was determined locally; it shifted the urban development trajectory toward growth and competition. Alliances of important actors from the business community, chambers of commerce, trade unions, and political parties played a role then as now. They consider the city to be a growth machine, a seedbed, for prosperous development of national economies as well.[5]

Land has always been a key resource for such growth policies. As Swiss political scientist Sébastien Lambelet recently found in a study using the cities of Bern and Zurich as examples, land is one of five strategic resources that urban regimes can draw on to guide urban development.[6] This was the case even before the emergence of financial capitalism, and it has been discernible in a growing number

4
Garcia-Landa, Trautvetter 2016 (see note 2).
5
Harvey Molotch, «The City as a Growth Machine. Toward a Political Economy of Place,» in: *American Journal of Sociology*, No. 2/1976, pp. 309–332; David Wachsmuth, «Competitive Multi-City Regionalism. Growth Politics beyond the Growth Machine,» in: *Regional Studies*, No. 4/2017, pp. 643–653.
6
Sébastien Lambelet, «Filling in the Resource Gap of Urban Regime Analysis to Make It Travel in Time and Space,» in: *Urban Affairs Review*, No. 5/2019, pp. 1402–1432.

of countries since the late seventies / early eighties. Since then, major urban projects have typically been built at strategically important locations, including those beyond the traditional paths of urban expansion (outward growth). The decline of old industries and the transformation of the port and logistics sector opened up new land reserves within cities that could be made accessible for lucrative development projects. These areas not only served as locations for new services (for example, Docklands in London, Battery Park in New York City, La Défense in Paris or Luxembourg-Kirchberg, as well as countless projects to revitalize urban waterfronts); because of the rent gap, they made it possible to siphon off enormously high returns from the often derelict land. Drivers of urban growth and private profits coalesced in these projects.

What's New?
The most recent developments in the course of the internationalization of the economy and the expansion of the financial industry, in particular, have fundamentally changed this system and accelerated the corresponding dynamics of exploitation. The sharp increase of services within the economy as a whole has resulted in strong demand for office space, especially in urban areas. Against the background of the financial industry becoming decoupled from the real economy, the real estate sector is being integrated into the financial sector. Larger and larger volumes of capital are invested in real estate, both by real estate companies themselves and by third parties in the context of diversified investment strategies. Land is increasingly becoming a tradable good, and speculation is determining what happens on increasingly volatile markets.

The strong influx of international investment capital into the cities is intensifying this trend. As early as the late seventies, Scottish urbanologist Neil Smith identified this development as the actual core of what was later euphemistically called «reurbanization» – alleged evidence of a return of the cities that had experienced decades-long decline.[7] As a consequence, the volume of investments in downtown locations identified as attractive has expanded

7
Neil Smith, «Toward a Theory of Gentrification. A Back to the City Movement by Capital, not People,» in: *APA Journal,* No. 4/1979, pp. 538–548.

Initially welcomed by urban planners and architects, interest in living in central locations is now expressed in broad waves of modernization sweeping across entire neighbor-hoods, triggering the chain reactions of changes in ownership, modernization, and displacement.

considerably, initially with a view to realizing large shopping malls, multiplex movie theaters and the like, later also to building high-priced residences. Growing delocalization of the real-estate sector is to be observed in parallel – that is, the spectrum of companies holding real estate is becoming broader, it is increasingly dominated by anonymous (for example, institutional) investors such as investment funds, and it is becoming decidedly international. In times of low-cost loans, private households are also thronging to invest in real estate. Real estate is successively being transformed from a good that is used to one that is traded. «In contrast to 30 years ago, most investors in financial hubs such as Frankfurt are no longer owner-occupiers, but are interested in real estate as investment property.»[8]

This development has been accelerated by the policies of central banks flooding national economies with cheap money in an attempt to overcome the financial crisis of 2008/09 – a structural crisis that began, as is well known, when uncollateralized real-estate loans were granted and then traded on second- and third-order markets. In this sense, land markets are no longer primarily a reflection of the local interplay of supply and demand for land but are also increasingly determined by the abstract imperatives of the financial markets and the capital investment strategies of anonymous actors lacking any connection at all to the location in question.

In the shadows of the gentrification of city centers and neighboring quarters, interest in living in central locations or owning residential property there has increased. Although urban planners and architects initially welcomed this, it is now expressed in broad waves of modernization sweeping across entire neighborhoods, triggering the chain reactions of changes in ownership, modernization and displacement outlined above. «Gentrification» no longer seems sufficient as a theoretical and conceptual apparatus to properly describe the dimensions of these changes.[9] In the meantime, «financialization» has prevailed as an analytical concept, specifically in urban research, to do justice to the ramifications these changes have for cities.[10]

The Role of the State

Inspired by classical globalization discourses, scholars

8
Susanne Heeg, «Was bedeutet die Integration von Finanz- und Immobilien-märkten für Finanzmetro-polen? Erfahrungen aus dem anglophonen Raum,» in: Susanne Heeg, Robert Pütz (eds.), *Wohnungs- und Büroimmobilienmärkte unter Stress. Deregulierung, Privatisierung und Ökonomisierung,* Frankfurt am Main 2009, pp. 123–141, here p. 130.
9
Philip Lawton, «Unbounding Gentrification Theory: Multidimensional Space, Networks and Relational Approaches,» in: *Regional Studies,* 2019, https://doi.org/10.1080/00343404.2019.1646902
10
Manuel B. Aalbers, *The Financialization of Housing: A Political Economy Approach,* London/New York 2016; Ludovic Halbert, Katia Attuyer, «Introduction: The Financialisation of Urban Production. Conditions, Mediations and Transformations,» in: *Urban Studies,* No. 7/2016, pp. 1347–1361.

often interpret the conflicts that this development entails along a dichotomy of global vs. local, according to which the cities are one-sidedly seen as victims of this development. However, the various scales are closely intertwined, and winners and losers from this policy can easily be found on both sides. In principle, global and local mechanisms are interdependent rather than mutually exclusive. Many cities have themselves set out on the risky path of growth-machine policies; some engaged in negligent speculation before and during the financial crisis and subsequently found themselves in great hardship.

A central element in this discourse is the state: first, as a motor and financier of economic development policies; second, as the guarantor of social balance. After all, the social responsibility that ownership entails also applies to land in many countries. The unleashing of the financial sector would have never been possible had it not been for regulations allowing it and the primacy of privatization. The same is true of multinational corporations' aggressive tax-saving strategies, which were only able to fully unfold thanks to deregulation and tax competition. The victims of these policies that transcend borders are the public budgets of states and other territorial authorities that have been deprived of large amounts of money. Small business owners and renters unable to pay the rents exploding because of real estate owners' high expected returns are displaced from central locations and find themselves at the other end of the chain of cause and effect. The problematic consequences for cities have been obvious ever since people on normal incomes who are key to their functioning – for example bus drivers, teachers, police officers or nursing staff – have been displaced from them.

When the mechanisms of land capitalization throw the community into disarray, the question arises as to whether underlying conditions exist under which an alternative way of handling the problem might be possible. Various alternatives are imaginable: one could aim for corrections within the logic of the prevailing system – viewed pragmat-ically, that is the popular variant, as manifest interests remain untouched. But approaches of this kind may have limited effects, as efforts to cap rents in major German cities have shown, for example. Not only does expropriation

Markus Hesse / «Property States» and the Financialization of Urban Development

of property have to fulfill many legal prerequisites but it can also be very expensive for municipalities due to the compensation that they have to pay. Collaborative practices of different kinds try to escape from the logic of capitalization and to ensure users are part of the profits — for example in the case of co-housing projects, which are increasingly popular. Yet niches are likely to remain niches.[11] It is possible to envisage changes on the basis of new legislative frameworks, especially regulation and an active role of the state. The welfare state considers providing housing for the population to be a core public task. According to the prevailing doctrine, this is no longer possible in times of globalization and in light of strapped public budgets. But is this hypothesis true? To answer this question, I will present two admittedly very dissimilar cases. They represent in starkly contrasting ways what Finnish professor of Urban Studies Anne Haila calls the «property state.»[12]

«Property States» – Catalysts of the Crisis or Strategic Response?

The first case is the city-state of Singapore, one of the Asian Tigers that have seen very dynamic development since the mid-twentieth century and are often considered prototypes of high-density Asian urbanism. After gaining independence from the British Crown in 1963 and separating from Malaysia two years later, the then-backward country was faced with the challenge of designing a robust development strategy. The population was projected to grow, necessitating the construction of large amounts of housing.[13]

The two goals were attained by creating and/or actively exploiting niches of sovereignty. They offer much greater scope for action to small states and city-states than to federal systems. Singapore is a city within a state – and a state within a city. Under these circumstances, financial and strategic means can be deployed in a much more concentrated fashion than would ever be possible in large countries. The smaller the territory and the more limited the internal market, the greater the necessity to integrate into overarching – if not global – networks and associations. This is the only way to compensate for

11
Nathalie Christmann, Markus Hesse, Christian Schulz, «Tracing the Place of Home,» in: LUCA & Gouvernement du Grand Duché de Luxembourg (eds.), *Tracing Transitions*, Luxembourg 2016, pp. 36–50.
12
Anne Haila, «Real Estate in Global Cities: Singapore and Hong Kong As Property States,» in: *Urban Studies*, No. 12/2000, pp. 2241–2256; Anne Haila, *Urban Land Rent. Singapore as a Property State*, London 2016.
13
See the contribution by Stefan Rettich in this volume, pp. 258–267.

the small size of the country's territory. It is by no means coincidental that services, and above all financial activities, are a domain of small countries, islands and political enclaves.[14]

A specific way of managing a scarce resource – land – corresponds to this external orientation of the economy. The pressure on land is much higher in small countries than in large ones, and at the same time land management is strategically oriented toward the state's goals for economic exploitation. When the state of Singapore was established in 1965, the opportunity arose to implement a housing policy under complete territorial and economic control and in harmony with the country's political economy, practically under laboratory conditions. The same is true of a policy for securing reserves of industrial land. The outcome of this policy can be characterized as follows: as a matter of principle, land is owned by the state; users obtain time-limited rights through auctions and long-term leases. Singapore's public Housing Development Board (HDB) has authority over 80 percent of the housing stock.

According to Haila, the property state enables land use in the sense of guaranteeing property acquisition, allocation, and ownership, while directly exploiting it – in other words, it is the main actor in land use.[15] And at the same time, it regulates third parties' access: «The developmental state of Singapore owns land and leases it to developers in public auctions, appropriates land for private developers, makes private developers compete, provides public housing and industrial space, intervenes in the real estate market and promotes ‹good values›.»[16] In this sense, the classic dilemma of accessing land in federal systems has been solved: as a rule, local decision makers are too close to individual business interests to make decisions in the public interest, whereas the state is too far removed to articulate an interest; what is more, the state generally has no legal competence to enforce such an interest. In a city-state, land is allocated for municipal uses and services, especially public housing, in theory independently of social class, ethnic origin, and particular business interests.[17]

Haila argues in her case study that this system enables questions of distribution to attain the same standing as aspects concerning the efficiency of markets, and that

14
Geoffrey Baldaccino,
Island Enclaves. Offshoring
Strategies, Creative
Governance, and Subnational
Island Jurisdictions,
Montreal 2010.
15
Haila 2000 (see note 12).
16
Haila 2016 (see note 12),
p. 113.
17
Ibid., p. 116.

Markus Hesse / «Property States» and the Financialization of Urban Development

this provides an alternative to the doctrine of private ownership of land. Recognizing this does not necessarily mean blocking out the downsides of Singapore's political model, which is considered autocratic.[18] Also, a political price must be paid for the extraordinarily active role of the state in politics, the economy and society. The fact that the state provides welfare and social control constitutes a functional mechanisms that may doubtless run counter to generalizing from this case.[19]

This caveat may also apply to the property state of the other small country we are concerned with here: the Grand Duchy of Luxembourg. Luxembourg, too, has been characterized in recent decades by its small size and by rapid growth of the economy and the population; per capita economic figures are exceptionally high.[20] The country is de facto a kind of city-state formation, and with its recent development trajectory of finances, economics, and technology, it is more like Asian or Arabic city-states than cities in larger central European countries. With numerous international holding companies and head-quarters, Luxembourg is among the top 10 European and the top 15 global financial centers. The home ownership rate is roughly 73 percent, the share of land held privately is about 92 percent. Rentals play only a minor role. On average, rents and real estate prices are twice as high as in locations just across the border in Belgium, Germany, or France.

Land is a key factor in this country's success story: it is a resource that cannot be increased – that is, it is both an absolutely and relatively scarce resource whose profit-oriented management yields maximized returns. On the one hand, the actions taken are very liberalistic, decidedly unideological. On the other, the state is ubiquitous here, too: the political community and public administration act in a more or less recognizable coalition with private land owners and secure their generation of surplus value by making and keeping land scarce in a calculated, if not cultivated, way. Multiple factors contribute to the financialization of land: first, private households hold their own land reserves as a family savings bank, thereby contributing to land scarcity; second, most market trans-actions take place via commercial brokers and developers;

18
See Sock Yong Phang, «The Singapore Model of Housing and the Welfare State,» in: Rick Groves, Alan Murie, Alan and Christopher Watson (eds.), Housing and the New Welfare State: Perspectives from East Asia and Europe, Aldershot 2007, pp. 15–44.
19
See, for example, Chua Beng Huat, «Public Housing Residents as Clients of the State,» in: Housing Studies, No. 1/2000, pp. 45–60.
20
See Christmann, Hesse, Schulz 2016 (see note 11).

third, investments in land are made strategically to further develop Luxembourg as a business location. Finally, developers play a major role in this system, as they purchase developable land strategically and have excellent contacts with the political community; besides, they exert far-reaching control over the value-added chain in the country's construction industry.

The growth of business-related services and the financial center has triggered strong demand for land (especially for office space), but housing construction is lagging far behind: as a result, the gap between the number of jobs and the residential population is widening. Far more than 4,000 additional units per year would be necessary to keep pace with population growth; the actual number is about half that figure. Even though the planning processes for office space and residential space are separate, the two categories do compete in effect, not least because the municipalities' incentive structures have rewarded job creation much more than housing construction. Social housing is the responsibility of two state-owned companies; however, they are far from able to fill the gap between supply and demand.

The vigorous promotion of economic development, the liberalist policy approach that has traditionally been cultivated in Luxembourg and what could be perceived as the culture of speculation both in the commercial and the private milieus have exacerbated spiraling land exploitation. Exorbitant land prices as well as the corresponding processes of displacement on the real estate and housing markets result directly from this development. The lack of housing may limit further economic growth, and it is also fueling the exodus from the country of the autochthonous part of its population that can no longer afford the eye-watering real estate prices.

A Future for the Land Question?
It seems to be an irony of recent history that what is perceived as the dominance of market- and profit-oriented governance of land is in fact heavily determined by the type and extent of state action. Property states can deepen and cultivate the problem, as the example of Luxembourg shows. Under certain conditions, they can also point to

Markus Hesse / «Property States» and the Financialization of Urban Development

possible alternatives, as can be seen in Singapore – recognizing the historical specifics of the case. In this respect, the two cases outlined here indicate the broad range of possible political solutions.

Pragmatic, if by no means uncontroversial, approaches to solving the problem were formulated in 2016 by the sociologist David Madden and the urban planner Peter Marcuse: definancialization, vigorous promotion of social housing, and granting the local population priority over real estate interests.[21] The call for a new land policy, which is doubtless in the tradition of the approaches of the seventies, goes even further.[22] It assigns cities a key role, through long-term land policy, municipal right of pre-emption, and stronger cooperation between municipalities. Such instruments have recently been given increased attention in the Grand Duchy of Luxembourg too. A socially responsible, active property state imposing a tax on land would massively support them. However, as long as dealing in real estate is a golden business opportunity for commercial actors and private households alike, one should not foster illusions about the prospects for fundamental reforms.

21
David Madden, Peter Marcuse, *In Defense of Housing. The Politics of Crisis,* London / Brooklyn 2016.
22
Difu, vhw (eds.), *Bodenpolitische Agenda 2020–2030. Warum wir für eine nachhaltige und sozial gerechte Stadtentwicklungs- und Wohnungspolitik eine andere Bodenpolitik brauchen,* Berlin 2017; see also the contribution by Florian Hertweck in this volume on the positions on land policy held by the SPD at the time, pp. 100–109.

Markus Hesse / «Property States» and the Financialization of Urban Development

Christian Schulz
<u>Land for Post-Growth</u>

It was only recently that the IPCC, the Intergovernmental Panel on Climate Change, called for radical rethinking of how to manage land as a resource.[1] Even though debates in the media and the political community focus on the increasing scarcity of fertile land and the climate-relevant dimension of land use by agriculture and forestry, the IPCC explicitly addressed questions of land use in built-up areas as well. And in this context, it addressed not only aspects of settled land spreading at the expense of areas that can be used for agriculture or are ecologically relevant, but also the question of how to manage land as a resource in already built-up areas. This chapter seeks to link this question to increasingly urgent demands for urban and regional planning to adopt a post-growth orientation.[2]

Planning and (Post-)Growth

Urban and regional planning has traditionally been confronted with the problem of scarcity of land, landscapes, habitats, and resources, and accordingly aspires to channel or limit land consumption sensibly. It seems all the more astonishing that the prevailing concepts, models, and theoretical approaches for spatial planning remain in the grip of a growth paradigm that is not called into question. Systems of indicators (for example, GDP, regional development statistics), and guiding principles (for example, specialization and competitiveness) commonly used in regional development are based on the assumption that quantitative growth must be considered the most important motor of any positive development. Although the problems of negative «externalities» of growth are discussed, approaches to solving them tend to focus more on reduction (of, for example, environmental impacts) and management (for example, by designating development corridors) than on remedying the causes of the problems. Hardly anyone asks whether continuous growth makes sense. People accept the neoliberal growth imperative «grow or go!» as if it were a law of nature.

Bizarrely, this is also true of much of the debate about shrinking cities and demographic change in rural areas. Ways of returning to growth trajectories and the problems arising from change are discussed much more

1
IPCC – Intergovernmental Panel on Climate Change, *Climate Change and Land. An IPCC Special Report on Climate Change, Desertification, Land Degradation, Sustainable Land Management, Food Security, and Greenhouse Gas Fluxes in Terrestrial Ecosystems. Summary for Policymakers.* https://www.ipcc.ch/site/assets/uploads/2019/08/4.-SPM_Approved_Microsite_FINAL.pdf.
2
See, e.g., Yvonne Rydin, *Future of Planning: Beyond Growth Dependence,* Bristol 2013; Christian Lamker, Viola Schulze Dieckhoff, «Mit oder gegen den Strom? Postwachstumsplanung in der Fishbowl,» in: *RaumPlanung,* No. 2/2019, pp. 48–54; Christian Schulz, «Postwachstum in den Raumwissenschaften,» in: *Nachrichten der ARL,* No. 4/2018, pp. 11–14.

Christian Schulz / Land for Post-Growth

Post-growth is about turning away from the illusory notion that present-day production systems and consumption patterns could grow globally over the long term, provided resource consumption can be continuously reduced through technological innovations and increased efficiency.

Christian Schulz / Land for Post-Growth

often than the opportunities that transformation opens up. To rule out a potential misunderstanding: post-growth is not the same as shrinking, say, in terms of population losses or economic recession. Instead, it is about turning away from believing in growth – that is, from the illusory notion that present-day production systems and consumption patterns could grow globally over the long term, provided resource consumption can be continuously reduced through technological innovations and increased efficiency. This expectation that economic growth and global resource consumption would become «decoupled» has not been confirmed empirically in more than 20 years of «ecological modernization» (the «myth of decoupling»).[3] On the contrary, relative gains in resource productivity are countered by more rapidly growing consumption of natural resources and energy (the rebound effect).[4]

Yet post-growth does not mean that material growth should no longer be possible as a matter of principle. Instead, the starting point for most approaches to post-growth is that spatial differentiations are necessary and that disadvantaged regions in the Global South, for example, must be allowed to have strong material growth to enable the general population to enjoy food security and participation (pro-poor growth). Post-growth is essentially about reassessing growth and reviewing whether certain developments make sense in the long term, and seeking alternatives. I mean «make sense» not only in terms of being ecologically sound but also in terms of individual and societal needs: orientation toward the common good having priority over economic profitability for individuals. An expanded concept of «the economy» comes into play here: besides formally established companies whose actions follow market principles, it includes forms of economic activities that follow social goals and practice solidarity as well as other private activities, such as home nursing care, and communitarian activities and networks, such as neighborly help and barter exchanges. This is not to suggest that the latter should be commodified and follow the logics of the market in the future. Quite the contrary: their key contribution to societal prosperity should receive greater recognition, even if they are not included in GDP.

3
See Niko Paech, «Eine Alternative zum Entkopplungsmythos. Die Postwachstumsökonomie,» in: Humane Wirtschaft, No. 5/2010, pp. 12–14.
4
For information about the data currently available, see surveys by the Research Group Sustainable Resource Use, Vienna University of Economics and Business: www.resourcepanel.org/global-material-flows-database and www.materialflows.net.

Christian Schulz / Land for Post-Growth

Land As a Resource

Besides its ecological and food security functions, land as a resource is primarily discussed as a scarce economic good, especially in urban contexts, as a good whose price has seen dynamic development in many cities due to increasing privatization (such as municipal housing stocks), and financialization (residential and commercial real estate as speculative investment properties). Current debates about land ownership and the opportunities for the state to shape policy are therefore especially motivated by social policy; a reevaluation of ownership rights and usage rights is overdue.[5] The *Bodenpolitische Agenda 2020– 2030* (Land Policy Agenda 2020–2030) of the German Institute of Urban Affairs (Difu) and the Federal Association for Housing and Urban Development (vhw) recently set forth remarkable ideas.[6]

Questions about urban development being resistant to governance in times of sweeping privatization and commercialization are closely linked to the question about the type of growth desired – for example, which kind of housing is created for whom. Besides social and design aspects, including sustainable building standards, the question is also how forms of housing can be enabled and promoted that provide space for post-growth lifestyles and forms of production. One option could be to combine relatively small private residential units with jointly used spaces such as offices, workshops, playgrounds, sports facilities, or gardens. It is also about forms of collaborative planning, investing, and living in cooperatives and other co-housing ventures (e.g., *Baugruppen*).

The debate is currently focused on housing, for understandable reasons. But the question should also be discussed of whether and how changes to land policy can promote or enable post-growth commercial activities. By this I mean far more than what is practiced in many municipalities, which is usually limited to individual cases and often only temporary: making (abandoned) land available for community-supported agriculture, co-working spaces, or socially oriented housing developments. Instead, a fundamental debate is necessary about creating prosperity and thus about the question of what we consider to be «economic activity.» The scope of municipal business

5
Markus Hesse, «In Grund und Boden. Wie die Finanzialisierung von Bodenmärkten und Flächennutzung Städte unter Druck setzt,» in: *ARCH+*, No. 231/2018, pp. 78–83.
6
Difu/vhw, *Bodenpolitische Agenda 2020–2030. Warum wir für eine nachhaltige und sozial gerechte Stadtentwicklungs- und Wohnungspolitik eine andere Bodenpolitik brauchen*, Berlin 2017.

«Hobbyhimmel» («Hobby Heaven») in Stuttgart. People come together regularly in the repair café, an open workshop, to fix broken things either by themselves or working with experts.

development and land policy increases if activities are included that are not oriented toward the market, but toward the common good: an economy of solidarity, neighborly help, child care, family care, volunteering, etc. Not only is this discussion inextricably connected with the question of how we measure prosperity and development – that is, which indicators are used to assess individual well-being and socioeconomic stability – it is also about breaking open established notions of the functional-spatial division of labor from a planning point of view, making up-to-date infrastructures and configurations of buildings available, and enabling new forms of urban production. Besides urban agriculture, this includes open workshops or maker spaces, forms of joint or temporary use of offices (co-working – increasingly in combination with childcare and eateries) as well as a large number of other shared or hybrid uses.

Planners should also critically examine the very diverse varieties of the «sharing economy.» Despite what is commonly claimed, the «sharing economy» is by no means post-growth-oriented per se; nor is it necessarily more sustainable than other forms of use. On the contrary, quite a few commercial services that form the «online platform economy» are only ostensibly about sharing – for example large commercial car-sharing providers and vacation rental platforms – and are increasingly subject to critical examination[7] as «pseudo-sharing.»[8]

Planning as Enabling
New forms of linking gainful and non-gainful work, the debate around new models of working hours and lifetime working hours, orientation toward the common good, and participation in society generate hybridity and diversity that cannot be grasped using the traditional dichotomies of time spent at home and time spent at work. Urban planning, building design, and infrastructure planning are challenged to respond to new, often multifunctional, demands placed on land, which often change over the long term. Aspects of post-growth can be taken into account more or less explicitly at all levels of planning. Especially in urban planning and architecture, approaches can increasingly be seen that promote the design and infra-

7
Chris J. Martin, «The Sharing Economy: A Pathway to Sustainability or a Nightmarish Form of Neoliberal Capitalism?,» in: Ecological Economics, No. 121/2016, pp. 149–159.
8
Russell Belk, «Sharing Versus Pseudo-Sharing in Web 2.0,» in: The Anthropologist, No. 1/2017, pp. 7–23.

structure prerequisites for activities oriented toward post-growth, or that make such activities possible in the first place. For example, the design of residential or commercial buildings and concepts for public spaces can proactively create spaces for sharing, like co-working spaces or community gardens, and essential infrastructures such as workshops, car sharing and bike sharing. They can also create new spaces for creative collaboration as in the «third place,»[9] – in other words, spaces that cannot be allocated to any of the established spheres of residential, commercial, recreational, or cultural uses, and that intentionally invite people to encounter and engage with each other in the most varied activities. They give life to spaces for experimentation while seeking post-growth-oriented forms of economic activity and communal life.

Since fundamental reform of land ownership law is hardly to be expected in the near future, it is worth examining alternative projects that attempt to gain the power to design urban spaces and real estate with an orientation toward the common good under the prevailing underlying conditions. One of the best-known examples in German-speaking countries is the *Mietshäuser Syndikat* (roughly: apartment building trust or apartment building syndicate).[10] It has also served as a model for comparable initiatives in the Netherlands and France. It functions as an umbrella network for individual, similarly named residential projects whose goal is to purchase, as a group, abandoned real estate or housing already rented by the members, and to make it inaccessible to the mechanisms of the real estate market.[11] This is guaranteed by using a model of self-managed cooperatives that gives a voice both to the local shareholders and to the syndicate as an umbrella, thus preventing either of the partners from selling the real estate.

These initiatives and comparable ones – for example, community land trusts in the US – are, not least, democratic projects in which decisions about the configuration and use of populated spaces are made in collaborative processes. Through their practical work, they call attention to concrete and practicable alternatives to market-based development models grounded on the prevailing logics of ownership. In so doing, they form a counternarrative to the neoliberal

9
Olivier Cléach, Valérie Deruelle, Jean-Luc Metzger, «Les ‹tiers lieux›, des micro-cultures innovantes?,» in: *Recherches sociologiques et anthropologiques,* No. 2/2015, pp. 67–85.
10
See www.syndikat.org/en.
11
Ivo Balmer, Tobias Bernet, «Selbstverwaltet bezahlbar wohnen? Potentiale und Herausforderungen genossenschaftlicher Wohnprojekte,» in: Barbara Schönig, Justin Kadi, Sebastian Schipper (eds.), *Wohnraum für alle?! Perspektiven auf Planung, Politik und Architektur,* Bielefeld 2017, pp. 259–280.

rhetoric of exploitation and constant growth. They demand guiding principles for municipal policies oriented toward the common good, and they should be regarded as complementary to progressive public strategies such as «concept procurement» (*Konzeptvergabe*), where municipalities procure bids from investors for housing projects and choose those that best meet social, ecological or urban-planning criteria. And this reorientation is obviously not only about social-policy aspects of housing but also about the fundamental question of how to deal with land as a scarce resource, which has not received sufficient attention in the debate about forms of post-growth economic activity.

Laura Weißmüller
<u>The Value of Land</u>

The outcry is getting louder. More and more people do not want to accept the constantly rising rents in their cities. In Berlin alone, 25,000 protested this development in spring 2018; 10,000 marched under the banner of #ausspekuliert (speculation over) in Munich; and there was a major demonstration against #Mietenwahnsinn-Hessen (rent frenzy in Hesse) before the election in Frankfurt. This shows that the fight for affordable housing has finally made it to the broad public. Now the middle class shares the worries of more vulnerable groups that they soon will no longer be able to afford their homes. There is hardly a tenant in the more attractive cities of this country who is not concerned about their future housing situation. However: all of these protests, large-scale demonstrations, and information events on tenant protections and gentrification will come to naught unless the Germans' relationship with land undergoes fundamental change. For while the protest posters are painted and the banners hoisted, the battle has long since been decided. Already, there is a building people have to move out of because they can no longer afford their rent. Already, the ownership status of the real estate has been clarified and the land irretrievably lost for society.

Yet to the majority of the population it is not at all clear what role land plays in the battle against displacement raging in our cities. And not only there: In fact, the way that real estate is dealt with stipulates how a country, and thus its entire society, develops. Whether farmland and fields are sealed and new development areas earmarked, or whether climate protection is taken seriously. Whether there are attractive public spaces that are well looked after, where people can encounter each other without having to consume anything, or whether the most beautiful areas in town are available only to those who can afford to pay admission. Whether buildings are built whose apartments can be rented even by people without much money, or only those with prices per square meter as expensive as the marble in the foyer. In short: the way that land is dealt with is the key issue of our future. The decision is made not at the borders of this country but right here: whether social harmony in Germany is preserved – or whether society is ripped ever further apart into landlords and tenants, rich

Laura Weißmüller / The Value of Land

and poor, ancestral inhabitants and new arrivals, no matter what their nationality.

Land is of the same elementary importance for people's lives as water and air. In spite of this, it is treated like any other good, like a sofa set or a car. Even worse: land is an object of speculation. For far too long, even the state sold its own property to the highest bidder. Just as if it could simply order more once it ran out. But land is not a good for the simple reason that it is not renewable and cannot be replaced.

And ever-more municipalities are noticing. They hardly have any more properties on which they can create affordable housing. The reason for this is as simple as it is alarming. In recent decades the public sector engaged in a sell-off of its properties so gigantic that it seemed as if the point was to get rid of troublesome remaining stock as quickly as possible. The municipalities themselves undertook to sell properties. Their financial authorities kept a keen watch on these sales because they wanted to refurbish their budgets. Even the city of Munich, which had to fight a housing shortage and high rents back before other towns had heard of these problems, continued selling its properties until 2016. The fallacy that the private sector could deal with these properties better than the public sector made them a favorite target for resourceful bargain hunters all over the country. Yet what was sold at bargain-basement prices in this case was not T-shirts and electronic devices but precious land.

The free-market fallacy of this sell-off was especially clear in Berlin. The properties that were sold by the city in the last decade alone have multiplied in value. The official valuation of some of the land in the capital has risen by 1,000 percent since 2008.[1] The new private owners can rejoice in the fact that their properties and the buildings on them are worth much more, but it had absolutely nothing to do with them. The extent of this kind of unproductive profit was documented by a study at the University of Bonn in June 2019, according to which owners of residential buildings in Germany became up to three billion euros richer through price increases between 2011 and 2018 alone. That is pretty much equivalent to the annual German gross domestic product.[2]

1
Michael Hörz, «Zehn-Jahres-Analyse der Bodenpreise. So teuer sind Grundstücke in Ihrem Berliner Kiez geworden,» published on rbb|24 on March 13, 2018 at https://www.rbb24.de/wirtschaft/beitrag/2018/03/bodenrichtwerte-berlin-grundstueckspreise.html.
2
Till Baldenius, Sebastian Kohl, Moritz Schularick, «Die neue Wohnungsfrage. Gewinner und Verlierer des deutschen Immobilien-booms,» Macrofinance Lab, Universität Bonn, at http://www.macrohistory.net/wp-content/uploads/2019/06/Die-neue-Wohnungsfrage-.pdf.

The rising rent prices are like new city walls. They decide who may come into the city and who must remain outside.

The rising rent prices are like new city walls. They decide who may come into the city and who must remain outside. The public sector gains practically nothing from appreciating land values – aside from the infrastructure costs. If investors adhere to the speculation period and do not resell a property for 10 years, they do not even have to pay taxes on their profits.[3] Only with real estate can profits be made in Germany so simply and with so little risk. Yet it is not enough to blame all this on private investors and denounce them as evil gentrifiers. Aside from wealth philanthropists, anyone who pays such high property prices has to erect a building with expensive rental apartments and condominiums in order to recoup their investment.[4] Demonizing this does no good at all unless the whole system is challenged.

No matter how complicated every attempt to fundamentally change how we deal with land may be, the question behind the issue is simple: Who is allowed to decide how society will live in the future? Private investors who have shown in recent years how little interest they have in the common good? Or should it be society, meaning all of us?

Perhaps it is a coincidence, but this question was once answered quite clearly, over 40 years ago in Munich. It was a brief essay just four pages long, back in 1972 that gave us the answer about who should decide how society should live in the future. «Land Law and Urban Development» was the sober title that Hans-Jochen Vogel, who had been elected Mayor of Munich just months before, selected for his article in the *Neue Juristische Wochenschrift*.[5] Yet this short title belied the explosive power of the essay's message. For the land is what decides how the city built upon it develops.

Vogel's critique concentrated on two points. First: «The rapidly increasing appreciation of land values and the equally rapidly increasing returns on ground rent are concentrated in just a few hands.» In other words, the real-estate business creates wealth for very few. Nothing about this has changed since 1972; on the contrary, only a few landowners benefit from the explosion in real estate prices in more and more cities. The public gains nothing. But what did the owner, the private investor do to make the area around their real estate more attractive? Generally, nothing

3
German Income Tax Act (EStG) §23.
4
The spring 2019 Assessment Report of the Real Estate Industry by the Council of Real Estate Experts calculates the amount by which an investor who buys a rental apartment has to raise rents in order to yield a gross return of 4 percent. Such rent hikes can be enormous, particularly in magnet cities. In Frankfurt am Main, for instance, the current rents have to be increased by 63.9 percent, in Munich by 70.4 percent, and in Berlin by a whopping 90.4 percent. At https://www.zia-deutschland.de/fileadmin/Redaktion/Meta_Service/PDF/Immoweisen_2019_web.pdf.
5
Hans-Jochen Vogel, «Bodenrecht und Stadtentwicklung,» offprint from *Neue Juristische Wochenschrift,* No. 35/1972, pp. 1544ff.

at all. The attractively designed plaza with a fountain, the theater around the corner, the new park and the museums, not to mention the schools or the hospital, let alone the public transport, buses and trains – all of this is paid for by the public sector.

A good location is what determines how much real estate is worth. It is no accident that every realtor's battle cry is «location, location, location!» Yet, the quality of the location and thus its market value are improved by the community, not by the individual. And that is why the community should partake in this profit. Anything else is unjust. This was obvious even to Winston Churchill, who wrote that «[the landowner] contributes nothing even to the process from which his own enrichment is derived.»[6]

There was a solution for all of these undesirable developments, Vogel's essay continued: land must be taxed according to an appropriate valuation basis. Such a levy would be an intervention into private property. And that gets difficult. For the Germans cultivate an intimate relationship with their homes. This probably outranks even the German passion for automobiles. For precisely this reason, when Vogel made the case for a tax on land, home and property associations were able to induce panic among their members, who were convinced that they would no longer be able to afford property after the introduction of a tax on land. The fears of ordinary people blocked Vogel's initiative at the time. Apparently, they are still haunted by the prospect. This is probably why no party has recommended – or at least, not out loud – a program for fundamental land reform.[7] But this will not work without intervention into private property. Article 14, Paragraph 2 of the Basic Law, which states, «Property entails obligations. Its use shall also serve the public good,» has been ignored for far too long. What is going on in German cities today is precisely the opposite. Waiting any longer to change this would endanger social harmony.

There are certainly plans for a tax on real estate that would do justice to the importance of land. For instance, from the initiative Grundsteuer: zeitgemäß.[8] Today's «real estate tax B» imposes a tax on land as well as the buildings erected upon it. The signatories to the appeal find this system unjust, cumbersome to administer and a

6
Winston Churchill,
The People's Land, 1909,
accessed at: http://www.
wealthandwant.com/docs/
Churchill_TPL.html.
7
The results the Building Land
Commission presented in July
2019 document this lacuna
in the political discourse.
Rather than deliberating over
steps toward more just land
management, the expert
commission concentrated
on the issue of how to obtain
building land more quickly.
Laura Weißmüller,
«Mehr Bauland allein wird die
Wohnungsnot nicht lindern,»
in: *Süddeutsche Zeitung,*
July 3, 2019, at www.sz.de/
1.4507981.
8
www.grundsteuerreform.net.

catastrophe for the environment. For this reason, they demand equal treatment of developed and undeveloped properties. The real estate tax should be transformed into a land tax that excludes the buildings built on it. This model is supported by the environmental NGO Bund für Umwelt und Naturschutz (BUND) as well as the German Economic Institute and the urban development association Bundesverband für Wohnen und Stadtentwicklung. And also by many mayors: A tax of this kind would restore to municipalities the ability to pursue an active land policy, with the opportunity to purchase buildings and real estate. At the same time, this tax would ensure that undeveloped properties that are ready for construction no longer lie fallow while speculators wait for prices to multiply. In an interview with *Spiegel* magazine in mid-January 2018, former Federal Minister for Building Barbara Hendricks advocated this pure land tax, declaring that, «in the future, only the value of land should count, and not the kind of building.»[9] The current government is not pursuing this course. Real estate tax reform does not have what it takes to shift the direction of policy. The supporters of Grundsteuer: zeitgemäß reject the reforms proposed by Federal Minister of Finance Olaf Scholz, «because they would, in part, lead to considerably higher taxation of tenant households,» explained Lukas Siebenkotten, federal director of the tenants' organization Deutscher Mieterbund in a press release of the initative in late November 2018. He continued, «Only with a pure land tax can we ensure that the majority of tenants would in fact experience no additional burdens; for many, the tax load would even be reduced.»[10]

By instituting a pure land tax, Germany could pick up where it was once a pioneer: In the period between the wars, the country imposed what was called a *Hauszinssteuer* to finance housing construction so exemplary that it attracted the crème de la crème of international architecture to Frankfurt am Main in 1929. The topic of the International Conference that year: The Minimum Dwelling. The participants were able to see for themselves how such housing could be both sophisticated and functional in the housing developments in «New Frankfurt.» In Berlin and Magdeburg, too, the state came onto the scene as a

9
Anne Seith, Gerald Traufetter, «Grundstücksmangel. Bauministerin Hendricks will Bodenspekulanten ausbremsen,» in: *Spiegel Online*, January 19, 2018, at: www.spiegel.de/wirtschaft/soziales/immobilien-barbara-hendricks-fordert-strafsteuer-gegen-bodenspekulanten-a-1188741.html.
10
Press release: «Grundsteuer: Nur Bodenwertmodell entlastet das Wohnen für die Mehrzahl der Haushalte,» published on November 29, 2018 at www.grundsteuerreform.net/wp-content/uploads/2018/11/181129_PM.pdf.

It is true: Germany needs thousands of new, affordable apartments, especially in cities like Munich. But no matter how frightening these numbers sound, there is no debate about quality at all.

visionary master of housing construction – for instance, in the Hufeisensiedlung by Bruno Taut in Berlin. These «Golden Twenties» of public housing construction seem light years away from the way in which the public sector behaves as a builder today. Contemporary architects who design public housing must be marveled for their endurance. Only those who fight like a lion for their ideas are able to prevent their design from being pruned down to an unimaginative shoebox. No wonder so many people visualize only piles of concrete and tower blocks like the ones in Berlin-Marzahn when they hear the term «social housing.» But there are other examples, as Vienna demonstrates. More than half of Vienna's population lives in publicly owned housing, with rents that are moderate to low.[11] How can the city afford this? Ever since the 1920s – the «Red Vienna» years – the city has believed firmly in building housing with public funds, and has erected buildings that look nothing like a poor ghetto; on the contrary, some of them are quite sophisticated, like the terraced houses, built in the seventies by architect Harry Glück at Wohnpark Alt-Erlaa, which feature very deep balconies and even a few rooftop pools. And they are located not in a chic downtown area but way out to the southwest in the 23rd district. Polls have repeatedly established that residents of Glück's buildings are among the happiest people in Vienna.[12]

With the money from a fair tax on land, it would once again be possible to finance a housing contruction program in Germany that deserves to be called public and social. It is true: Germany needs thousands of new, affordable apartments, especially in cities like Munich. But no matter how frightening these numbers sound, there is no debate about quality at all. What should the 1.5 million apartments promised by the coalition agreements look like?[13] There is no mention of this in the documents. Yet, just as in education and training, in architecture quality is decisive. In the long term this is what determines whether a new development becomes a bleak neighborhood where everyone rushes home behind closed doors, or a vibrant quarter where the residents enjoy gathering together. So what do our houses have to look like in order to fit into our lives, so that we can once again encounter each other as a community?

11
Peter Münch, "So geht Wohnen," in: *Süddeutsche Zeitung,* September 19, 2018.
12
Reinhard Seiß: «Am Menschen orientiert,» in: *Bauwelt,* No. 5/2017. www.bauwelt.de/themen/betrifft/Am-Menschen-orientiert-Harry-Glueck-2772190.html.
13
Coalition agreement of 2018, p.109, www.bundesregierung.de/resource/blob/975226/847984/5b8bc23590d4cb2892b31c987ad672b7/2018-03-14-koalitionsvertrag-data.pdf?download=1.

Terraced towers in
Vienna-Alterlaa, 1973–1985.
Architect: Harry Glück

And this brings us to Vogel's second point: «In case of competition for a single property for several uses, generally that use prevails which extracts from the property the highest yield for the private owner, and thus can pay the highest purchasing price.»[14] In short, whoever can put the most money on the table gets the property. And this has not changed either, although today strong financial investors from all over the world are competing for land. So far, even the federal government has sold almost all of its properties to the highest bidder. Only gradually can signs of a policy shift be seen. For instance, Minister of Finance Olaf Scholz directed the Bundesanstalt für Immobilienaufgaben – BImA (Institute for Federal Real Estate) to prioritize cities and municipalities in the allocation of federally owned properties, not only through a simplified procedure but also at a discount.[15] Still, even now most cities and municipalities are obligated to sell their real estate to whomever pays most. And even when they are allowed to be satisifed with the commercial value – which federal building code stipulates must be equal to the market value – after the steep increase in land prices, the property is far too expensive for most cooperatives or smaller builders. Yet, the financial authorities supervise properties and keep close watch to ensure that nothing is sold «below value.» But the highest offer is worth nothing if it generates just another dead piece of town.

There is only one solution: like water and air, land must remain a public good. This sounds so simple, and so logical as well, but it's a lot to ask. Architect Christian Schöningh of Berlin, one of the founders of Berlin's Initiative Stadt Neudenken (Rethinking the City), compares the change in awareness this would require with the «condemnation of slavery.»[16] But nevertheless: it can happen.

It can do so by allocating public properties only as ground leases. For Rolf Novy-Huy, the founder of Stiftung trias, which has been promoting a different way of dealing with land since 2002, this is the vehicle for a more sustainable way of treating land. For if a municipality grants a ground lease for a property, it is still the owner and can stipulate a certain use. «Often, a professor who writes about land policy is astonished that it can be implemented this way as well,» says Novy-Huy, a banker by training.[17] He gets

14
Vogel 1972 (see footnote 5).
15
www.bundesimmobilien.de/7948394/erstzugriff-und-verbilligung.
16
Laura Weißmüller, «Mit Füßen getreten,» in: *Süddeutsche Zeitung,* September 2, 2017.
17
Laura Weißmüller, «Die Bodenfrage,» in: *Bauwelt,* No. 6/2018. www.bauwelt.de/themen/betrifft/Die-Bodenfrage-laura-weissmueller-bodenpolitik-wohnungsbau-3137405.html.

invited to events because he is not «like the blind speaking of color.» The managing director can indeed rhapsodize about the ground lease as if it were a Bach sonata performed by a virtuoso. The problem is that most city administrations and municipalities do not share Novy-Huy's passion for ground leases. Pleasure in handling ground leases is entirely lacking there, with drastic consequences: either they are not used at all, or they are botched. «It's as if they are playing the piano with two fingers.» In some places, this is starting to change. Since the coalition of Social Democrats, the Left Party and the Greens took power in Berlin in 2016, nearly all publicly owned properties have been allocated as ground leases. The problem: after selling off so much of its real estate in the past few years, it has hardly any more properties to allocate.

This is why an initiative like Stadt Neudenken, which made a decisive contribution to establishing ground leases on Berlin's River Spree, is now concentrating on *Konzept-verfahren* (concept processes) to change the way in which land is treated. «This is currently our favorite work in progress,» says Florian Schmidt, one of the initiators of Stadt Neudenken, and since late 2016 also a member of the District Council for Construction, Development and Facility Management in the district of Friedrichshain-Kreuzberg.[18] The question is which criteria are used to allocate a property – and who is allowed to participate in the process at all? The answer to this should actually be clear: in Germany, real estate should be allocated only to those who can prove how their plans for the property will create added value for the community.

Of course, allocating real estate in line with the common good means that a municipality has to check building applications much more closely, and thus: Will rents really remain more affordable in the long term? Can the playgrounds in the new development be accessed by the neighbors as well? Are free spaces being created that are open to everyone, and that everybody will like to use? Are there common rooms for the residents, like work-shops or music rooms? But this sounds more complicated than it is. Even now there are exemplary new developments: the Kreativquartier Südliche Friedrichstrasse on the site of the former wholesale flower market in Berlin, where

18
Ibid.

the real estate was allocated according to a sophisticated *Konzeptverfahren,* a process designed to create not only new housing, but also space for studios, industry, and social projects. At the award-winning Domagkpark in Munich, residents have an ingenious mobility concept with many attractive alternatives to driving, and social spaces like workshops and roof gardens. The «More than Housing» cooperative development in Zurich shows how an entire neighborhood can bustle all day and all night. Innovative cooperative projects in Switzerland have been especially successful in showing how housing that is socially sustainable, but also innovative and architecturally ambitious, is possible even in cities as expensive as Zurich and Basel. This is no mere coincidence. The city of Zurich has not sold any publicly owned properties for decades, and since a referendum in 2016, Basel has banned the practice as well.[19]

Speaking of architecturally ambitious: although the land issue can be resolved only through policy, every architectural design must also address the question of how society can meet on its land. There are certainly convincing historical examples – for instance, the São Paulo Museum of Art by Lina Bo Bardi, completed in 1968. The Italian-Brazilian architect elevated the actual exhibition floor to create a public space under the museum. Bo Bardi's desire to create places where society can meet is the reason her work has been rediscovered in recent years. Or Norman Foster's building for the HSBC bank in Hong Kong. In 1979 Foster created a public space by lifting a 183-meter sky-scraper several meters off the ground. This is fascinating to see and experience – especially every Sunday, when the city's large Filipino community, most of them domestic workers and nannies, meet to picnic there. Since 2014, the trick of creating public space by elevating buildings can be studied in Los Angeles as well. For his Star Apartments there, architect Michael Maltzan heaved an entire block of houses into the air, generating a free space below.

Yet the world of architecture has actually been slow to address the land issue. Many citizens have been faster. One example is the Netzwerk «Immovielien» – a play on the German words for «real estate» and «many,» founded in February 2017. It represents 4,000 initiatives that

19
http://www.neue-bodeninitiative.ch.

Laura Weißmüller / The Value of Land

advocate nationwide for the idea of neighborhood-development projects oriented toward the common good.[20] These initiatives vary as widely as their locations in Germany. Dessau has to find a solution for its empty properties and a shrinking population. Munich, Cologne and Hamburg are facing the opposite problems. What all the initiatives have in common is the desire to understand urban development as the work of many for many. Profit-oriented real estate companies and builders cannot tolerate such an approach. Just as they have little interest in long-term affordable rents and social interaction in their developments. There is no need to criticize them for this; the point is that it makes private entities thoroughly inappropriate as partners in public housing construction. There are enough cooperatives, publicly owned residential building companies and owner-occupiers who can do a better job of this in terms of the general interest.

Ground leases, *Konzeptverfahren* – municipalities and their public housing associations can use such instruments effectively. That is why the Münchner Initiative für ein soziales Bodenrecht has set a primary goal: it wants to bring together those cities that are suffering most from housing shortages, high land prices and scarcity of space.[21] The city where the initiative emerged in 2017 provides the best example. Supporters of the Munich initiative include the Alliance for Affordable Housing, the German Academy for Urban and Regional Planning (DASL), the Hans Sauer Foundation, the Lutheran City Academy of Munich, and former Mayor Christian Ude. At the initiative's first public appearance in fall 2017, he managed to present himself as prosecutor and defendant at the same time. As prosecutor, because he had followed the rising land prices in Munich «for 50 years with great anger.» As defendant, because of his response to the question as to what he had achieved against this development during his term as mayor – namely, «Nothing at all.»

This is precisely what is to be changed by networking municipalities. Christian Stupka, founding member of the Wogeno housing cooperative in Munich, who is now developing concepts for sustainable housing and development projects for Stattbau München, prepared the «Münchner Ratschlag zur Bodenpolitik» (Munich Proposal

20
https://www.netzwerk-immovielien.de.
21
http://www.initiative-bodenrecht.de.

for Land Policy). In summer 2018 the initiative brought stakeholders from large cities together with experts, civil-society initiatives and state and federal parliamentary representatives in order to work out a shared agenda. «The chance to achieve something in Berlin is simply greater if we join forces,» Stupka explains. Many of the proposals for dealing with land in a new way, such as the real estate tax, can only be implemented by the federal government.

The Deutsche Institut für Urbanistik, Difu (German Institute of Urban Affairs) demonstrates how many adjustments must be made to these parameters. Difu drafted a «Bodenpolitische Agenda 2020–2030,» which presents a nine-point plan that should be printed out, framed, and hung for display in every local building authority – and another in every finance department.[22] The plan effectively pools all of the ideas from the various initiatives. «The point is not to develop a single instrument that will save the world. Something must be done all over the place,» says Ricarda Pätzold of Difu. The roadmap developed by her institute is much more concrete than the position paper by the Deutscher Städtetag (Association of Germany Cities), which also demands a «reorientation of housing and building land policy»: «The way public sectors deal with their real estate and housing property must change fundamentally.»[23] Real estate properties must no longer be allocated to the highest bidders; instead, land policy must be oriented to the common good.

What precisely this means can be understood best in the Difu's nine-point plan. It begins with a public-welfare-oriented allocation of public real estate that is to take place not according to the highest offer but in a *Konzept-verfahren* and in the form of a ground lease. Next, it demands that a land fund be set up in the form of a federal land foundation, as also suggested by Frauke Burgdorff, Jochen Lang and Stefan Rettich; and further, municipal land banking, so that municipalities can once again dispose over their own properties. The Difu also advocates strengthening the right of preemption for municipalities and taking into consideration public policy objectives for building in accordance with Paragraph 34 – namely, on empty sites. Moreover, the «interior development program,» with which municipalities are allowed to dictate

22
https://difu.de/publikationen/2017/bodenpolitische-agenda-2020-2030.html.
23
www.staedtetag.de/imperia/md/content/dst/veroeffentlichungen/mat/positionspapier_neuausrichtung_wohnungs-_und_baulandpolitik_verlinkt.pdf.

an obligation to build on undeveloped or largely under-used properties, should be introduced in a timely manner, as should a tax on real estate and land area. And finally, the land transfer tax must be lowered and cooperation between municipalities strengthened. The Difu agenda makes clear that land policy entails more than just technical solutions: «It is becoming clear that a functional, ‹technical› debate about the effects of urban development or the housing market does not do the subject justice. On the contrary, what is needed is a values debate, for justice, solidarity, the common good and sustainability are at stake – values that constitute the foundation of a demo-cratic, open society capable of a rational reconciliation of interests.»

A clear nine points, plus unambiguous words about why dealing with land in a socially sustainable way is a basic requirement for a democratic and open society – actually, the perfect guidelines for the required course change. Yet, apparently many have yet to recognize this fact. Although all politicians demand affordable housing – even Bavarian Premier Markus Söder, who sold 33,000 units of public housing while he was minister of finance[24] – no one fundamentally questions the existing system. Nobody opposes a reform of real estate tax which could lead to a tax levied only on the land, exclusive of buildings. Nobody is against better protections for tenants, if they were truly effective, rather than merely providing a bit of relief here and there. But there are certainly reasons to oppose absurdly counterproductive measures such as a support scheme to buy new property (*Baukindergeld*) or increased housing benefits. Such steps merely feed a system that is currently driving thousands of people out onto the streets. Subsidizing the private contruction sector follows the logic that the market will fix everything if it is given enough power. Recent years have shown that this is not the case. Rolf Novy-Huy gets angry when he hears these vows of confidence in the market: «The market is a predator. It eats as much as it can get.»[25] This is why Novy-Huy, long before the initiative was launched for a referendum in Berlin to expropriate the private housing company Deutsche Wohnen,[26] prompting discussions about expropriation all over the country, wanted to expropriate and buy back the

24
Roman Deininger, Klaus Ott, Nicolas Richter und Wolfgang Wittl, «Deal weiß-blau,» *Süddeutsche Zeitung,* July 21, 2018.
25
Weißmüller 2018 (see note 17).
26
www.dwenteignen.de/ aktuelles /.

Laura Weißmüller / The Value of Land

large housing stock which many municipalities and federal states – including Bavaria – had sold in recent years in order to consolidate their budgets. «We must dare to say things like this; otherwise we'll always be left playing with those few blocks in the toy box they leave behind.» This sounds radical. But anyone who continues reading about property in Article 14, Paragraph 2, finds: «Expropriation shall only be permissible for the public good.» In the struggle by residents for the right to their city, the Basic Law is on their side.

However, they can only take advantage of this fact if society undergoes a shift in values. For anyone who seriously wants more affordable housing, who wants the battle against displacement in our cities to not intensify, and perhaps even to stop, and, last but not least, who wants our country to be able to offer nature to our children and our children's children, instead of only surfaces covered with concrete and industrialized landscapes – anyone who wants all this must do everything they can to ensure that land becomes common property.

The concept for this, common land, expresses the idea that land is shared by society. Only society should be able to decide what happens on land, whether buildings are constructed there and who may do so, what buildings and places are created, and what kind of people live and work there. Especially in a country with 80 million inhabitants, where 62 hectares are covered with concrete each day,[27] land must be used in the public interest. Or does anyone have an idea how else we can plausibly explain to coming generations why we were so wasteful with this precious good? Why we covered it with so many superfluous and bloated single-family housing developments and industrial parks? Why we squeezed out the last speck of dust to plant monocultures?

There are the tools mentioned above which allow land to be dealt with in the public interest. And there are people who advocate dealing with land in a way oriented to the common good. Yet, their efforts can only truly take root if the public finally recognizes the value of land – not for the wealth of the individual, but for the development of society. This requires a tremendous change in thinking, for grasping this value means understanding that the

27
https://www. umweltbundesamt.de/ daten/flaeche-boden-land-oekosysteme/flaeche/ siedlungs-verkehrsflaeche#-das-tempo-des-flachen-neuverbrauchs-geht-zuruck.

Laura Weißmüller / The Value of Land

public sector must have much greater influence on land in the future. Some individuals will suffer. But there are things that are much greater: the welfare of an entire country.

«Property is a Myth»

Interview with Berlin architects Arno Brandlhuber and Christian Schöningh by Florian Hertweck and Nikolaus Kuhnert on options for addressing the land question

Nikolaus Kuhnert

I would like to start by formulating the following thesis: The decisive transformation in urban development in West Germany took place in 1977 in Frankfurt am Main. After street fighting between squatters and police had turned the mood in the population against the occupation movement, SPD Mayor Rudi Arndt lost the election. Walter Wallmann, whose CDU won by a landslide, came to power. Along with his personal assistant and office manager Alexander Gauland, he placed the return of the bourgeoisie to the city center on his agenda. In order to achieve this goal, Wallmann and Gauland pushed the rebuilding of the Alte Oper, which Arndt had rejected, and of the half-timbered houses on the Römerberg square, as well as the restoration of the station district. With these projects the CDU attempted to bring the city back under control, in the truest sense of the word, initially facing resistance from the leftists headed by Joschka Fischer and Daniel Cohn-Bendit. Gradually, a tacit collation of the right and the left bourgeoisie emerged.

Florian Hertweck

So the CDU pushed into the inner city in the period when cities like West Berlin and Frankfurt, known also as «Krankfurt» (from the German word krank for sick) at the time, had hit rock bottom. By the time Wallmann was elected, Frankfurt had lost 5 percent of its population, and West Berlin a whopping 10 percent. Was there a connection between the return of the bourgeoisie to the city and the neoliberal turn?

Nikolaus Kuhnert

Certainly. What must also be taken into consideration here is post-modernism, which was not only an architectural phenomenon but also a cultural movement. With the neoliberal turn, which began in Frankfurt a few years earlier than in the US and Great Britain, where, as we know, it was driven by Ronald Reagan and Margaret Thatcher, Frankfurt experienced a cultural and political turnaround in urban policy. With Walter Wallmann and Alexander Gauland, a kind of bourgeois urban policy emerged, which was not only open for architects like Oswald Mathias Ungers but also directly sought the cultural standards for architecture and urbanity embodied by his work.

Arno Brandlhuber

If this thesis of the bourgeoisie returning to the city is still valid today, this finding contradicts activists on the left, who always speak only of international capital gentrifying the city. In my opinion it is an error to zero in on this bogeyman. Eighty percent of the total investments in Berlin's real estate market are made not by inter-national companies, but by groups that invest between 10 and 30 million euros. This is quite classic upper middle class: family groups, albeit often organized

Walter Wallmann (front),
Alexander Gauland
(background), and Head
of Cultural Affairs Hilmar
Hoffmann, mid-1980s

«Property is a Myth» / Interview

into company structures. All these family offices are not anonymous international capital. In the 1990s Hans Stimmann also spoke of the bourgeoisie returning to the city, in the context of the townhouses in Friedrichswerder, which only millionaires could afford. The advertising agency Jung von Matt apparently bought an entire block here on Brunnenstrasse in Berlin-Mitte. However, I find the term «bourgeoisie» quite difficult in this context because the German term *Bürger* carries the meaning of bourgeoisie in the economic sense of middle class, but also «citizenship.»

Christian Schöningh

The *neoliberal turn* you just mentioned also triggered veritable brainwashing. I remember how the first bids for a public bus line in Berlin were advertised by the public transport authority, the BVG, in the nineties, and were then actually granted to a private operator. Before then I could never have imagined that a bus line could be operated by a private company. The entire debate about urban development has a great deal to do with this power of imagination: What city do I live in, and do I have enough fantasy to imagine a different kind of world? To put it in the most basic terms: property is a myth. The ownership of land, in particular, is merely a right granted to someone. This right is created in legislative bodies, applied by administrations, reviewed and developed further by courts. Yet everything is in constant flux, and this absolute right to do whatever one wishes with possessions – that is how property is defined – is potentially restricted, especially for land. The problem is that politics and administrative authorities do not apply the laws, regulations or their options for implementation to the land, and thus, indirectly to housing; that they have, in a sense, forgotten how to do so. Councilor Florian Schmidt of Berlin's Friedrichshain-Kreuzberg district is one of the few who applies the legal situation in the sense of social urban development. Indeed, his utilization of preemptive rights to purchase is quite a harmless intervention into property rights. Actually, it only intervenes in the rights of the buyer, not those of the seller. The sellers receive their due: they transfer their property, only they can no longer specify who their successors will be. Germany's federal town planning law alone thus offers many possibilities for the city to develop in different ways. And other new regulations can also be introduced, which could be a step-by-step path toward land expropriation. Land expropriation is *the* battle cry, of course. But it is truly astonishing how this once so scorned word is used so naturally and unemotionally in the broad circles participating in the debate these days.

Arno Brandlhuber

With urban development programs, obligations to build, and capped preemptive rights to purchase, today there are already far-reaching instruments at our disposal – but they are hardly used, aside from a few exceptions like in Munich. This is because politicians do not believe their application in a five-year term to be opportune with regard to potential reelection. Indeed, experience has shown that these measures tend to trigger influential countermovements. Back in the seventies Hans-Jochen Vogel learned that the fear of land expropriation could be mobilized specifically. He himself speaks of a sort of cross-party consensus to avoid using the term or even mentioning the topic, knowing full well that it would ultimately help only his political opponents. And this is true not only for land expropriation but also for a multitude of inconvenient measures and truths that everyone keeps quiet about when elections are looming – for as we know, after this election means before the next. We have to keep this in mind when speaking about trust in politicians and their capacity to act.

Christian Schöningh

Perhaps we first need measures other than land expropriation. For example, owners of real property could be banned from selling their land. They would only be allowed to grant ground leases. This would be a sudden change to the system that would not affect the substance of the property issue but could curb speculation with land.

Florian Hertweck

The ancient Greeks actually used that kind of system when they founded new towns. Every citizen was supposed to receive a piece of land that was more or less the same size, which they were not allowed to sell. The consequence was that there was initially no market for real estate. As a result, the inhabitants, and especially new arrivals, had to engage in other activities. A whole host of outstanding traders of goods other than buildings as well as craftsmen emerged – for houses still had to be built as well. Curbing trade in land today would similarly cause the money that flooded the real estate market after the global financial crisis to flow back into more productive sectors. Thus, suppression of trade in land also makes economic sense. But I would like to go back to Christian Schöningh's thesis that land ownership is a myth. Could you please elaborate on that some more?

Christian Schöningh

I see property as a right that is granted. Why are apartments in the very same house regularly assessed at different monetary values, although the concrete above and below is identical and was purchased for the same price? Because what is rented or purchased is not the concrete but the right to live next to that strut up there and not next to the strut down here. Property is not a thing but a right to a thing or a space, and this right can be regulated just like any other […] the law is changed through legislation or adjudication; it is a generally recognized convention that subsequently became legally binding. Tenancy law, for example, could also be expanded toward the direction of property. We have to do more than merely protect tenancy law, we must strengthen it. This unconditional control or ruling over things, especially over land, must be further restricted.

Florian Hertweck

But doesn't the question of property today solve itself in a sense? After all, our parents' themes – my house, my car, my yard – are no longer so attractive for the younger generations, who are sharing more and more – their apartments, their cars, even their yard: *the* new form of community space.

Christian Schöningh

If Nikolaus calls the situation in Frankfurt in the late seventies a tacit coalition of left radicals and right conservatives, then today we may end up with a new coalition between, on the one hand, vagrant funds ultimately bundled in capital, for the sole purpose of transforming money into stone and then leaving as more money, and on the other, people who no longer endeavor to own a part of the city. Those who share and lease everything: here today, gone tomorrow. The two actually work together wonderfully if there is no interest in the connections between property as right of control, investment and its refinancing through rents.

Florian Hertweck

The so-called creative class that economist Ottmar Edenhofer calls «superstars,» very well-trained people who earn extremely good money, the cosmopolitans on the go. New nomads who always want to be at the center of town, but never for very long.

Christian Schöningh

Who are truly no longer interested in the question of who the land belongs to. The practical conclusion of such disinterest being shared by everyone would be, of course, that the land then no longer belongs to anyone.

Florian Hertweck

But we are still interested, of course. In Luxembourg, hardly anyone who comes into the city can afford to live there. These days, not even the upper middle class. People live ever further out of town and commute ever-greater distances to get to their workplaces in the city. This is a social and an ecological problem. How can we make it possible for people – and not just the global elite and the superrich – to live in the city?

Nikolaus Kuhnert

That is in fact the decisive question that resonates with the land issue. Who lives where and how in the city? Of course, it is a political issue…. In my view, halfway balanced conditions can only be produced the way the SPD demonstrated in the 1920s: Back then the Social Democrats joined forces with bourgeois circles to push through state-funded housing construction. But because the state was bankrupt, they financed this housing construction through the *Hauszinssteuer* and, from 1924, with the *Rentenmark.* In other words, they mortgaged the existing land in order to obtain funds for their housing construction.

Arno Brandlhuber

Yet at the time you're talking about here, it was still possible to organize housing construction on the national level, be it in Austria, Germany, or France. This is practically inconceivable today, however, after the turn to neo-liberalism – also because there is hardly any land left, or because the land that is left is too expensive for public, cooperative, or collective housing. For in purely arithmetical terms, the only possibilities remaining for architects today are to reduce construction costs and/or the size of housing units. We see this in cities like London, Paris, and even Beijing, and read about how the middle class is being forced out of the city center. One alternative would be to collectivize the available land, if necessary by buying it back on the free market, and for the municipalities to then amend building laws to make the completed housing affordable.

Florian Hertweck

Maybe this is no longer possible on the national level, but there is still plenty that could be done in this regard on the municipal level. Indeed, there certainly are some progressive municipalities, such as the City of Vienna; communities in Switzerland; and even certain cities in Germany like Munich, Ulm, Lübeck, Tübingen, and Freiburg. Unfortunately, they are up against their limits, especially regarding questions that concern land, be it in terms of legal measures, which can only be stipulated by legislators, or their budgets, which could only be balanced by a land fund on the national or European level. If we recognize the state's inability to take action on these issues, as well as the difficulties that this presents for municipalities,

does that mean we have to be content with initiatives from co-housing groups and cooperatives? Is promoting such associations the route municipalities should concentrate their efforts on?

Christian Schöningh

Certainly not. Such individual projects can always show only one possibility. Their importance is always marginal. A more effective measure would be to not only motivate housing societies to start building again but also to direct them to do so in other ways: other floor plans, other rules, municipal and self-governing – in short, a different form of property. Where issues of housing and land are concerned, we must strengthen the public sector wherever possible.

Arno Brandlhuber

Well, politics has not really done any-thing, at least here in Berlin, to counter this negative development. What is the balance after all these years? Three or four competitive procurement processes – that is, competitive procurement according to the best concept (*Konzeptverfahren*) and five or six ground lease contracts. Absolutely ridiculous numbers.

Nikolaus Kuhnert

You have to argue more politically. It has to be reiterated: The appropriation of the city by the bourgeoisie is so complete that it has yielded the same exclusive conditions as prevail in Luxembourg. The same is true in London and Paris, and soon in Berlin as well…

Christian Schöningh

Berlin is still far from those conditions…

Nikolaus Kuhnert

Maybe not yet in Berlin, but here, too, things are at the tipping point. Frankfurt is at the tipping point. In Munich and Hamburg conditions are, for the most part, already like those in London and Paris. Who can still afford to live in the city? That is the decisive question. If not even the middle class can live in the city, if the nurses and the firefighters we need in the city have to drive an hour and a half or two to get to work, then it will collapse. In 1977 it rolled over in the one direction, and soon we will be back at the point where it rolls in the other direction. Where the majority of the city population says: This is no longer my city.

Florian Hertweck

By now there is at least a consensus that no more public land should be sold, though, isn't there?

Arno Brandlhuber

In Berlin, yes, although this attitude shift took a long time. This does not necessarily mean that there is an active land policy, however.

Christian Schöningh

Both the city-state of Berlin and the housing associations state that they are not currently allowed to stockpile any land without an indication of a specific need. I am certain, however, that these statements are mere

claims, or that the situation could be changed easily with the commensurate political will.

Arno Brandlhuber

At all events their business objectives do not include any obligation to not stockpile land. When the housing associations buy land, they could purchase undeveloped land in order to transform it into residential land at a later point in time. Then all of it would belong to a city-owned subsidiary. The same applies to the rezoning of existing estates and the collectivization of the profits they yield. This takes us back to Hans-Jochen Vogel, who insisted: profits are privatized, construction and infrastructure costs collectivized. This should not and must not be allowed! The legislators could sequester these zoning profits and through targeted zoning of industrial areas, for instance, the cities could valorize their own properties. All of the zoning profits could flow into the public treasury if it were to pursue active land policy. Then the question would no longer even arise.

Christian Schöningh

Ulm is a city that has done this for over 100 years. First it purchases, and then it starts planning. The profits from new planning regulations are not generated until the land is municipal property.

Arno Brandlhuber

This certainly does not exclude private partners, as the Freiburg model shows. Private investments can happen after rezoning, and planning and construction on city-owned real estate can take place under a ground lease. Zoning profits and increases in value remain in public ownership, and transformation into property is preempted.

Florian Hertweck

That's how the Netherlands handled land up until the neoliberal turn. Well, assume that the municipalities were able to build back up their reservoir of land. What should they do with these properties then?

Christian Schöningh

Allocate them as ground leases until the property issue changes in general. With ground leases the public sector finds the right partner, using simple means, legally and free of any discrimination whatsoever. When today's Governing Mayor of Berlin, Michael Müller, was Senator for Urban Development, he posed the interesting question as to the right partners. Of course, we usually think of public, state-owned housing authorities. But that is not enough. If a city grants ground leases and formulates the political goal of organizing an equitable city, the right partners will be found. You simply write what you want in the mission statement clauses of the ground lease, like a supplier, and find whomever has demand for the same ideas. It is really much easier to achieve one's goals with more or less like-minded partners than to dissuade those who are actually scheming toward different ends, with dubious methods and maturities that are much too short.

Arno Brandlhuber

That is the great positive aspect of ground leases. However, with today's minimal-interest-rate policies, ground-lease fees are much too high. When even Swiss foundations demand over 3 percent interest, but the construction can be financed with more or less zero percent, one has to ask: Why doesn't the public sector do the construction itself? Simply because there are still too many people in the administration who believe the neoliberalist dogma that the private sector can do it better.

Christian Schöningh

Yes, but you can't just flip a switch to change that. The housing associations were pure housing-administration associations, which had downright forgotten how to build. They no longer had any construction and planning departments. This is gradually improving. Here in Berlin they have now acquired good people, who are gradually realizing good projects.

Arno Brandlhuber

That's what's so perfidious about the *neoliberal turn,* that the administration had two legs and two arms cut off, and then stood there without their precious instruments and had to reach an agreement with the privately organized developers on new instruments and procedural roles. Another problem with ground leases is regression after the agreement expires. In the next 5 to 10 years, all lease contracts that the cooperatives granted in the 1920s will expire, and it is completely clear that the government will not dare to tell them: We will compensate you for 60 percent of the current market value, as defined by law, and then take over the properties and concentrate housing there, because you are not doing so yourselves. That would be a further active policy instrument: the purchase of large-scale housing – according to preemptive purchase rights with a price limit – and its reorganization with regard to urban development programs like redensification, social desegregation, etc. Then we would have a preemptive purchase right that would apply to the earning value rather than the market value.

Everyone: nodding in agreement

Nikolaus Kuhnert
Your ideas are good. But they will not be enough to get the tanker back into the right channel. You have to act more systemically. Everything that is moving to the right these days must be picked up and turned to the left, just as Chantal Mouffe calls for.

Arno Brandlhuber
So, like her, you would advocate a populism of the left?

Nikolaus Kuhnert
There is no other way!

Florian Hertweck
If companies that are located in the city centers can no longer acquire qualified personnel, because they all say: The high salary does not compensate for the effort involved in commuting from my suburban estate to the inner city – then that is a symptom of collapse. Several companies in Munich have brought back the practice of building company housing.

Christian Schöningh
That's back in Berlin as well.

Florian Hertweck
And even those who benefit from this problematic development of the cities are often caught in traffic jams and bored with the social and commercial homogeneity in the thoroughly gentrified city centers, in which all the same chain stores offer all the same products. The inner cities have become mock-ups for these global players, for whom a reconstructed half-timbered or Wilhelminian-style façade presents the best fit for their self-image. Just as shopping malls used to simulate urbanity, the inner cities are doing so today. Many second stories in the city center of Luxemburg are now empty: stairs have been knocked out from the ground floor to create double-story properties worth even more than the previous ground floor plus the floor above.

Nikolaus Kuhnert
That's crazy! Such a broad issue has to be taken up again in order to get the left more involved.

Florian Hertweck
And how can we manage that?

Nikolaus Kuhnert
Yes, I don't really know…

Everyone: laughs

Florian Hertweck

There is another aspect of the land issue I would like to discuss as well: Nikolaus Kuhnert just described the collapse in Frankfurt and said he thought that Ungers' architecture was best able to give shape to this shift from a socially to a culturally configured city. Now, a question that concerns me a great deal: Do you believe that a socially equitable treatment of land also generates a particular architecture? Does it allow other typologies to emerge? And what narrative do we need?

Arno Brandlhuber

First of all, it must be stated that the largest architectural agencies in Europe, most of which are located between England and Scandinavia and have three letters in their names, produce a great deal of housing but have nothing to do with the idea of a socially integrative city. There is no progressive architecture scene that is anything close to relevant. Lacaton & Vassal is one of the few exceptions that proves the rule.

Florian Hertweck

But try to speculate for a moment: What kind of a narrative would we have to develop?

Arno Brandlhuber

Nikolaus just spoke of a populism of the left. This can emerge in architecture if it functions as argumentation – which is the case per se for a cooperative, for

instance. Your housing is secure. In which arguments can we embed architecture and then stabilize housing? Here in Berlin, there is a single interesting model at the whole-sale flower market, with cross-financing between condominiums above and a cooperative below – but this is not inscribed in the architecture. The architecture is not able to communicate this as an argument. But it should have to do so.

Florian Hertweck

But if new communities now emerge – which organize themselves in cooperatives and formulate new, more hybrid, programs – then more hybrid structural typologies would also emerge. We have to extract these as a stronger narrative.

Arno Brandlhuber

That was our aspiration with the terraced building in the Wedding district of Berlin – to typologically embed the heterogeneity of usage, because you have rooms 10 to 30 meters long, which allow for different types of living and working. But what happens in the operational model, when a small English investor allocates leases there to only the best creative-class start-ups? The heterogeneity of usage should thus have to be inscribed in the architecture so that the operational model is implied.

Christian Schöningh

This is where you lose me. For me, architecture and its structural shape –

where such issues are concerned –
are totally overrated.

Arno Brandlhuber

I have the counterargument: Take the
Berlin City Palace, which it was possible
to rebuild only because it stands for
a pictorial argument for a certain kind
of thinking and model of society.
Architecture becomes the tool used
for a kind of reformatting, and yields a
shift in our conceptual orientation.
Or take the eco-houses by Frei Otto,
which are a pictorial argumentation for
a legal and societal model. If we now
retreat and say that architecture
cannot solve anything – «You can't fix
it in the detail» – then we haven't
played all our cards. We have to make
image politics as well.

Christian Schöningh

Yes, but in that sense our project is
totally populistic. Like the most
wonderful experience I had at River
Spreefeld. One Sunday morning in the
spring, blue sky, beautiful atmosphere,
a 75-year-old man comes onto
our lot with a rickety bike – I had the
impression he had just come out
of a basement apartment in Kreuzberg,
stood there and said in broad Berlin
dialect: «It's really beautiful here.»
I found that so touching.

Arno Brandlhuber

As an architect, you cannot be scared
of such emotional reactions. On
the contrary: You should take it even
further. You should actually say, if
I employ an architect who coordinates
all of the trades, then I also need an

architect who merely designs the
narrative. Who embeds this new
populism Nikolaus is talking about in
the manifestation of the architecture
itself.

Nikolaus Kuhnert

Exactly, like Ungers used to do
for the other side, when he attempted
to build a bridge between real estate
and architecture in Frankfurt.
He opened doors and was welcomed –
but by the wrong audience.
Today the «Dortmunder Vorträge zur
Stadtbaukunst» (Dortmund lectures
on urban architecture) are trying
to achieve this. You have to counter
these with something substantial, in
addition to political activism.

«Property is a Myth» / Interview

ExRotaprint, Berlin
since 2007

ExRotaprint, Berlin

The concept of having the resident tenants take over the former Rotaprint site emerged out of self-defense. The property policy of the State of Berlin in the first decade of the 2000s, which aspired to achieve the short-term exploitation of publicly owned properties by selling them to the highest bidder in order to pay off debt, would have affected «our» site as well. Only the proceeds raised – the most money, no concept, no urban development policy consideration – were decisive for the allocation of real-estate properties. In the Wedding district of Berlin, the location of the former Rotaprint factory and a classic arrival district, production sites had dried up back in the 1980s and 90s, followed by the loss of workplaces, prospects and identity. Places that are characterized by neighborhoods facing so many challenges must not be sold for the highest possible price but rather appraised in terms of their potential for consolidation and chances for further development «from within» the district and neighborhood, and thus potential benefits for their residents. In retrospect, the years of selling off real-estate properties that were «non-essential» did grave harm to urban development, social and fiscal policy. Now these properties are needed for the growing city, for housing, schools, daycare centers, inner city businesses, for social and cultural infrastructure. The risk of selling over 5,000 properties under pressure over a narrowly limited period was realized to its fullest

negative effect in Berlin. The low purchase prices in the first decade of the 2000s allowed investors to reap 10, in some cases even 20 times their original investment. Today the city is buying buildings and real estate back at inflated market prices.

How can speculation be avoided?
Like many other «investors» at the time, after tough negotiations, in 2007 we, the ExRotaprint tenants' initiative, were able to acquire the 10,000 square meter property for a very reasonable price. Conflicts about individual ownership and profit in the early, founding phase of the initiative alerted us to the risk that this bargain presented: the lower the price, the higher the future expected profits – and thus the danger of the project collapsing. In a heterogeneous group of tenants that materialized out of necessity, and not out of commitment or similar views, with different fields of work like workshops and production, social institutions, ateliers, and creative studios, different expectations for potential future ownership are present from the outset. We faced the challenge of developing an ownership model for ExRota-print that permanently ruled out the possibility of it disintegrating into particular interests, and committed the profits earned from managing the property to the realization of our shared goals. The prospect of purchasing and renovating an archi-tectural monument that had been neglected for years, and then adapting it to the needs of contemporary uses,

with all of the risks and uncertainties about financing that this entailed, ultimately resolved the conflicts. The negotiation process led to the development of a nonprofit, anti-speculative project, for which we are solely responsible. The goal is to offer affordable rents, long-term prospects for existing and future uses, and an inclusive location that is useful to the surrounding district of Wedding. In order to secure the project's development in the long term, we decided on a legal structure combining nonprofit status and ground lease agreements. In order to acquire the property, 10 tenants who intended to participate actively in developing the project founded the nonprofit limited liability company ExRotaprint. Transparency and direct access to the company's decisions was guaranteed by the eleventh share-holder, Rota-Club e.V., the tenants' association. The shareholders do not profit from the company's revenues and, should they leave the company, do not receive any share of profits from appreciation of the real estate. The revenues from rentals, after deduction of all costs, flow into the public benefit objectives of ExRotaprint, preservation of the architectural monument, and the promotion of art and culture. For 12 years now, ExRotaprint has been investing the surpluses from rentals into renovating the architectural monument, paying interest and repaying the building loan borrowed in 2009. In spite of the affordable rents, averaging 4.20 euros «cold» (without heating and utilities), ExRota- print has invested nearly five million euros in the renovation and preservation of the architectural monument. The management is so efficient thanks to our solidarity as tenants, the planning team's precise concepts for renovation, and the architects who actively engage in socially oriented real estate development. The decision to permanently preclude resale and future speculation with the real estate is the foundation for ensuring ExRotaprint's beneficial development. It is the prerequisite for a change in perspective: from making profits with real estate to using real estate.

Since the State of Berlin did not want to grant us a ground lease in 2007, we inserted the Stiftung trias and the Edith Maryon Foundation in the purchase contract that we negotiated, in order to close a 99-year ground lease contract with them immediately after closing. The ground lease separates the land from the buildings; the foundations own the land, and ExRotaprint owns the buildings. In return for payment of an annual fee to the foundations, Ex-Rotaprint has the land at its disposal for the entire duration of the agree-ment and is solely responsible for all aspects of project development: for financing, renting, renovating, and maintenance. Selling the real estate is the only thing we are not allowed to do. The foundations that own the land have the declared goal of taking land off the market permanently. Through the ground lease, we secured the initially affordable land price for the project and «froze» it. The market price of the site today is many times what we paid, but the cycle has been broken: because of the joint ownership structure and the rules in the ground lease, the property cannot be liquidated for profit. ExRotaprint pays the foundations 5.5 percent interest on the land value at time of purchase, but always at least 10 percent of the basic rent revenues. A 10 percent share of the rent to cover the value of the land has become inconceivable today; in new rent contracts in Berlin, 50 percent or more of the basic rent goes to cover the value of the land. Increases in land prices cause rent hikes, an effect that we have precluded through our legal construct. The contract is also profitable for the foundations as the ground lessors. Over the years, after having refinanced the invested capital, the foundations will earn many times the original land price through the interest on the ground lease.

A Site for Everyone?

In addition to the land policy and economic aspects, we used the ground lease contract to specify our long-term, binding target uses. From the outset, we were a heterogeneous group of people coincidentally working on the same site, with different backgrounds and professions, with perspectives and attitudes that were just as different. We perpetuated and broadened the mixture of local businesses, social institutions, and creative users. This creates facilities for the district, integrates the neighborhood, strengthens the local economic fabric, and brings new energy to a location that was marked by job losses and poor prospects. Besides the commitment to public benefit, in our ground lease contract we defined our rental concept as «Work, Art, Community,» meaning that we split the space equally, renting one third each to businesses, social institutions and creative uses.

A major advantage of a ground lease is the cooperative contract, in which stipulations about the use of the location can be secured for a very long period – going beyond the founding generation. Our tenants today include the local electrician, carpentry workshops, and small factories, all of which provide workplaces and apprenticeships; social institutions such as a school that teaches German to immigrants, an educational project for school dropouts and centers offering advice to people who are new to Berlin, refugees and the unemployed; and creative tenants in ateliers, rehearsal rooms for musicians, and design firms and film agencies. Each of these leaves its mark on the site with its unique combination of participants and guests. What the specified combination of «Work, Art, Community» will look like in 30 years is up to the next stakeholders in ExRotaprint. We believe that the heterogeneity of uses and people on site presents a great opportunity to counter the segregation of the financialized city. It provides a level playing field for people of all kinds of specific worlds and constructs to meet with people who have other life plans. A place for everyone. Renting becomes curation in its literal sense, «care,» and the site becomes a social sculpture. New rentals are to be granted not to our own clientele or to low-maintenance tenants; we do not want to give in to the pushiest candidates. Considering instead what the site is missing, what would be the most useful addition to the current uses, is a discipline in itself. Heterogeneity also entails moderation, conversation and negotiation in order to keep the structure balanced. Many of these negotiation processes are informal. ExRotaprint is like a village with a multitude of protagonists. The main contours of the project are defined by the shareholders, nearly all of whom are on-site tenants themselves, who have consciously chosen to share responsibility. There is no obligation to participate, there is no pledge, no price of admission, tenants can simply be tenants – they do not even have to understand the construct they are joining.

ExRotaprint is a model for a different kind of land policy, bound to a perspective on society as a whole, in order to make space available to people and uses that are being displaced by the usual processes of appreciation and commercialization for the sake of profit. Our neighborhood can find space here – to realize its goals and take advantage of offerings for further training and getting settled. The city's sellout in the first decade of the 2000s – and the resulting limitations that the government faces due to the lack of

properties for housing, schools, and communal uses – must force cities like Berlin to shift course radically in the long term. The future focus in urban development is not on real estate as an investment; the goal must be utility for society as a whole.

Daniela Brahm, Les Schliesser

ExRotaprint, Berlin

Models for the City

Models for the City

«May Land be Sold like Shares in a Company?»

Interview with Elisabeth Merk (urban planning commissioner of Munich) and her predecessor Christiane Thalgott by Andreas Garkisch and Florian Hertweck on Munich's model for Socially Just Land Use (SoBoN)

Florian Hertweck

Ms. Thalgott, the view that urban land has considerable social significance and must thus be defended in city policy as a public good has a tradition in Munich – from the measures and proposals of Hans-Jochen Vogel (SPD), mayor from 1960 to 1970, which are currently once again the subject of lively discussion, to the so-called «Munich Model» of Socially Just Land Use (SoBoN) implemented in 1994 during your term of office. How did this approach come into existence and to what extent did this tradition play a role in your model?

Christiane Thalgott

The extent to which the public sector is able to protect public interests in land use is in fact an age-old topic in Munich, which began well before the initiatives by Hans-Jochen Vogel. By the nineteenth century, prices for developed land had already risen so much that the city, poor as it was then, could not compete in the land market. Thus, while urban development was driven by the private sector, the city sought to represent the public interest – and not always with elegant methods. According to nineteenth-century contracts, the land needed for infrastructure, i.e., for the construction of roads, had to be provided by the land companies (*Terraingesellschaften*). Actually, it was the city that was responsible for the construction costs of infrastructure. But it simply waited until the investor, i.e., the land companies, had been softened up and constructed at least the foundations of the streets, because the new houses could not be accessed in any other way. The city itself only began to build on a large scale after World War I, mainly because the private developers had gone bankrupt at the turn of the century. This is the way the urban housing authorities such as the GWG came into existence. Industrial companies founded cooperatives for their employees, who were advised by the municipal housing authority. In the 1920s, development of large areas by the two municipal housing authorities began. As was the case in the nineteenth century, after World War II there was a return to private companies, which developed large areas such as Hasenbergl and Neuperlach. And, there, too, Munich asserted municipal interests over private interests through town planning agreements; in other words, it made about one third of apartments available to lower-income groups and always resolved any questions about site development. When Lord Mayor Georg Kronawitter (SPD) promoted urban development in the 1980s, he shifted these social issues back into the center of discussions. He wanted to award private building rights only if it was guaranteed that at least 40 percent of housing was subsidized. This led to the near

«May Land be Sold like Shares in a Company?» / Interview

Baugenossenschaft 1898, cooperative housing project Camerloherstrasse, Munich. The municipality or the state should be reliable partners in ground leases.

On June 17, 2018, Anna Hoben wrote in the daily *Süddeutsche Zeitung:* «In the coming years, the ground leases for numerous plots [owned by the predecessor of today's Deutsche Bahn, the German rail service] will run out. The plots are still owned by the public sector, but there are plans to sell them to the highest bidder.... The Green Party faction in the *Bundestag* [the German parliament] posed a parliamentary question about this matter. A petition by the tenants' initiative in [Munich-] Neuhausen urges the federal government to put the *Wohnraumoffensive* [a housing program of the federal government, the states and the municipalities] into practice by changing the Federal Budget Code. Then it would no longer be mandatory to sell the property to the highest bidder. Another option would be to enable extending the ground leases under the previous conditions.»

stagnation of housing construction, because it was no longer perceived by the private sector as worthwhile. The «local residents» model frequently practiced in Bavaria, which was repeatedly questioned by the EU, was a form of town planning agreement: with exorbitant and ever-rising land prices, local interest in affordable land for the local population was imposed on contracts for land sales with, for example, a 30 percent share. When urban development contracts were incorporated into the Planning Code to promote diverse development after German reunification, Munich immediately seized the opportunity to design urban development contracts in accordance with the new Section 11 of the Planning Code so that they could be applied in all cases – to larger projects such as the residential development of former army barracks, as well as to small projects by private landowners. Instead of negotiating individual contracts, they were now subject to a regulatory code.

Florian Hertweck
What exactly does this «Munich Model» of socially just land use involve?

Christiane Thalgott
The urban development contract on socially just land use specifies that one third of the increase in value when a greenfield site is developed into building land goes to the landowner. The developer must finance development of the site and provide at least 30 percent subsidized housing in the form of rental accommodation from the remaining two thirds. To the extent permitted, the developer must also bear the cost of financing infrastructure. At the same time, and it is important to say this, Munich has entered into a large number of more comprehensive contracts, which are intended to appear as development measures, with the railway and the German government (for army barracks), which encompass more extensive contributions to infra-structure, such as the S-Bahn station Hirschgarten. With all these contracts, a particular difficulty for investors lies not in the infrastructure costs or in the establishment of roadways and parks but in the construction of subsidized housing. The effect of subsidized housing construction is not restricted to reductions in the value of the building lots, because only a price that is high enough to finance the subsidized housing is accepted. When we started, this involved rents of 300 to 500 euros. Today we are at 300 to 900 euros, whereas rents are up to 3,000 euros and more on the open market. Thus, this intervention by the city really means a loss in value. However, even more difficult is the fact that residents now have tenants of subsidized apartments in their neighborhood. To a property developer whose clients are millionaires, these neighbors lower the value of even the most luxurious housing. This model, in which social housing in the city is evenly distributed like a parsley garnish sprinkled on soup, has been accepted in the city only because the alternative to such a model would have been to

use all urban land for only subsidized housing. This would have created a mono-structure of subsidized housing, which nobody wanted. And we never approved the transfer of subsidized housing from point A to point B – everyone had to follow this rule.

Andreas Garkisch

In comparison with other cities in Europe, and this must really be emphasized, the social mix *within* city districts is a special characteristic of Munich.

Elisabeth Merk

The Stuttgart urban researcher Tilman Harlander has shown in a study that, despite the high costs found in Munich and despite the gentrification problem, with which we are also confronted, over a period of more than 20 years socially just land use has actually led to a lower segregation factor in Munich than in other major German cities. Despite the problems we have discussed, we are doing so well because this policy has been applied so rigorously for such a long time. I can only say that it is still a topic of negotiation. Although everyone has to comply with the SoBoN, there is hardly a developer who does not try to make it plain to us at some point how good it would be if the subsidized housing were provided on a different piece of land. I agree with Ms. Thalgott's view that in Munich there is a long tradition of urban development contracts for larger areas. But the new quality of SoBoN was that it is transparent and the same for everyone.

Andreas Garkisch

During your term of office you developed the «Munich Model» further.

Elisabeth Merk

First of all, a further 10 percent for housing with capped rents procured based on the best concept – including consideration of social criteria – has been added to the 30 percent. In this way, the state capital city of Munich avoids price competition in the sale of building land and sells land at whatever current market rate that can be obtained. The bidder with the most convincing concept in the tendering process is awarded the contract. A binding contractual provision is the capping of rents for the initial tenants and the way increases in rent are regulated. We have also expanded our housing program by requiring that 50 percent of municipal land designated for housing be used for subsidized housing and 40 percent for concept-based rental housing, with 20 to 40 percent of the entire housing program assigned to housing cooperatives. The decisive factor is always what can be demanded from private buyers. We recently had a discussion with the lord mayor and the major companies about some kind of «commercial SoBoN.» In response to this the mayor appealed to the companies: If you generate new business space, which we certainly support, because we, too, want to keep business in the city, then we also need apartments. Workers' housing is an old-fashioned term, but it is simply a matter of the willing-ness of those who create jobs to go beyond the present housing policy requirements, beyond the 30 percent, perhaps even if they are not otherwise involved in housing at all.

Florian Hertweck

By doing so, the model would thus be further developed in the direction of bringing work and living together again. What challenges does the city administration still face?

Christiane Thalgott

In the future, there will be an increasing focus on how we respond to new patterns of social development, for example, that there are fewer and fewer families because more and more of us are becoming loners. We have to boost models like building collectives and cooperatives, which are quite different from what they were 40 years ago. Cooperatives are generally better because they are more enduring.

Florian Hertweck

But to make building cooperatives possible – and here we are dealing with land issues – we have to have land available.

Elisabeth Merk

You must always distinguish between privately owned land and city-owned areas such as the army barracks, almost all of which have already been converted into residential areas. In principle SoBoN is identical for both types of land, and we now have 50 per-cent subsidized residential construction on city-owned land, as well as concept-based rental housing construction already mentioned with cooperatives accounting for 20 to 40 percent. There is no longer any free-market financing of private property on city-owned land – only building associations, also called co-housing groups (*Bau-gruppen*). We now approve only projects based on the ground lease system. Another factor is that we are no longer promoting the cooperative model as such with a counseling center or similar approaches in the competitive concept-based tenders already mentioned, but rather the idea of a neighborhood. But we also have instruments for influencing what happens even where the land does not belong to us: there we consider generating more building rights if the land is used sensibly and sustainably. I would like to explain this with an example: if a developer provides us with a good mobility concept, we are prepared to reduce the required parking space provisions. If we are presented with a good concept for a vibrant neighborhood, we can handle the building rights extension differently – which can, however, become a very touchy issue in legal terms. In cases like these, lawyers emphasize that existing building law must not be bound by new criteria. Currently we have reached an interesting juncture in this regard. In the case of commercial development plans, we usually have existing *Bebau-ungspläne* (as defined in the German Real Estate Valuation Ordinance Section 6, Paragraph 1, *ImmoWertV*). We do not always develop new plans. Then we grant certain specific exemptions. And these exemptions can be coupled with conditions, which in turn require a different form of contract that follows a similar rationale to SoBoN. This way we can develop various concepts. We are also considering how we can increase density in the Section 34 areas, where there are no *Bebauungspläne* and no new ones are being developed.

Andreas Garkisch

Section 34 you mention permits a minor expansion of building rights without a *Bebauungsplan.* That sounds marginal, but in reality it affects about half of all permits in *all* German cities, not just in Munich, and thus half of all apartments in Germany. On the one hand, apartments are created so easily and quickly; on the other hand, it is difficult to absorb added value without a *Bebauungsplan* and an urban development contract.

Elisabeth Merk

There should be a special urban planning law that covers not everything, but three important goals. Then, in a certain sense, I would be able to intervene to control the land, but we are still in the phase of legal invention in that regard. We are already realizing that we really need to target the Section 34 areas, because they are greatly heating up the land price machine and we are going to have major problems there, for example with infrastructure. It would be desirable for Section 34 of the Building Code to also provide a legal opportunity to require reasonable contributions to social infrastructure and public green spaces. However,

Munich is different from cities like Hamburg and Berlin. In inner city neighborhoods there are areas that have been in the hands of particular property owners for 100 years, such as breweries that pursue local interests, meaning that they have a long-term business commitment to Munich. Although we have large financial organizations that sit somewhere behind them, most of the ones we are dealing with here still have a name and a face. As a result, there is a certain willingness to abide by such rules. The SoBoN has even become an export hit in the region. Finally, the surrounding area is also growing, and local communities are finding that they lack the financial resources for kindergartens and social infrastructure when it comes to building large amounts of housing. And so project developers who have become acquainted with SoBoN through us propose a SoBoN model to the municipalities when they work in the surrounding region. On the other hand, the implementation of SoBoN is very strongly influenced by legal issues, which has an impact on planning and processes. In comparison with cities that do not have this type of contract, we sometimes need a year longer. That is why we keep thinking about where we can exert control while reducing the amount of regulation. But one point is currently worrying me the most when I think about Hans-Jochen Vogel: despite all these measures, I am always lagging behind the price of land. Although I can control goals with the SoBoN, I cannot control the price of land. Although it has a dampening effect over a long period of time, I cannot get to the heart of the problem. We were recently reminded of this once again, when we advertised land for cooperatives with land prices that are much too high, on the basis of which other city council decisions were drafted to reduce these valuations. This works for a specific project, but nine months later it is already outdated again. At the moment we cannot break out of the spiral without regulating prices on a higher level.

Christiane Thalgott

I see the key problem in the Federal Real Estate Valuation Ordinance (*Wertermittlungsverordnung*), which underlies all real estate transactions in Germany, being based only on the fair-market-value method or going rate for the land. Actually, an income capitalization valuation method (*Ertragswertverfahren*) needs to be incorporated into this procedure carried out by expert committees formed to determine the value of real estate. This would mean that a kindergarten does not pay what an international real estate developer pays for land, because the developer compares the price with housing prices in New York or somewhere else. The kindergarten has no income and social housing produces low yields, whereas housing construction produces high yields on the open market. We will not break out of the spiral if, as stipulated today in our Federal Real Estate Valuation Ordinance, land value assessments are tied only to the fair-market-value method.

Elisabeth Merk

Again and again land value is reassessed as a cross-sectional value, which poses the question as to why I must set a price for the city plots which Hans-Jochen Vogel as mayor acquired in Freiham for a specific purpose in 1963, the year I was born, that is based on current standard land values in Munich. I do not understand that. It cannot be that urban plots, which the city developed for its own purposes, are valued in the same way as the cross section. They should not be treated this way, because we do not generate this level of income at all – and are not seeking to realize income on that scale. In shrinking areas, there is exactly the opposite, no less problematic effect. I worked for six years in Halle on the Saale, where we could actually do no urban development because the land was in reality worth nothing because there was no demand, but was appraised as being worth insane sums. In both cases, during strong growth as well as economic downturns, determining the value of land creates problems. Not all companies strive to achieve the highest prices; for example, the Bayerische Versorgungskammer and Munich Re, which invest funds for pension funds and are subject to very strict regulation. Because of their orientation, in some cases they cannot determine the value of properties in any other way and are caught up in the same spiral. Valuation is even stranger for our own city-owned companies. Depending on how and when land became private property, it is entered in the books with different valuations, so that one and the same measure, regardless of the actual construction costs, looks completely different because of varying land appraisal values. These are factors that have nothing to do with value in use or real value at all. Here we are once again with Hans-Jochen Vogel and the decisive question, which we always come back to: May land be sold like shares in a company?

Christiane Thalgott

In my view, research has not sufficiently taken into account the emergence of the ideological view that land must be treated like any other private possession, that freedom of construction applies, and that restriction by obligations to the common good is nothing other than communism. An influential apologist for this thesis in the postwar period was Theodor Maunz, a professor and judge with a Nazi past. Not only did he formulate his view of the land issue in this way, he also indoctrinated his students with it, including several generations of judges.

Florian Hertweck

When Vogel was mayor of Munich, he hosted a conference entitled «Initiative for a Reorganization of Land Law,» which the constitutional judge Gerhard Leibholz also attended. Leibholz himself considered the division into *Verfügungseigentum* and *Nutzungseigentum,* – meaning that each individual plot of land has two aspects regulating it: its ownership by the municipality and its use by a private individual or

entity under a ground lease or similar arrangement – to be consistent with the constitution. Unfortunately, the CSU, to which Maunz also belonged at that time, carried on a polemic against the idea so successfully that the project came to nothing. Nevertheless, a CSU grandee said at the 1970 party congress, «Profits from land, which are largely generated by the efforts of the general population, must be taxed like other income. This is again one of the priorities of the tax reform. Land prices in the Federal Republic of Germany are rising to such an extent that it is irresponsible to permit these profits to flow into the pockets of just a few without taxing them. For example, the city of Munich purchased land for roughly 650 million DM between 1957 and 1967. If it had bought all of it in 1957, that is, in the first year of this 10-year period, it would have paid just 148 million DM. Therefore, a few people have earned half a billion, and haven't even had to pay taxes on it, because of public services – the costs of infrastructure development.»

Elisabeth Merk

That was Franz Josef Strauß.

Florian Hertweck

This quotation not only illustrates how the fact that land is a commodity that can be bought and sold impacts public coffers. The further developments of the last decades remind us, above all, that politicians have learned nothing from them and have continued to diligently sell publicly owned property. They do not do so any longer today, but – as you said – only grant land on the basis of leasehold contracts and concept-based tendering, as Vogel and the SPD had called for back in the early 1970s. The question today is instead how the sparse land resources of the municipalities can be replenished. As in the example described by Strauß, by buying back expensive plots of land or, an issue in Munich, by acquiring public land based on SEMs (*städtebauliche Entwicklungsmassnahmen*)?

Christiane Thalgott

First of all, there is a right of preemption. But this usually fails in practice because the prices are too high for the city. Consequently, we believe that the right of preemption should be limited in terms of price and the price determined by the income capitalization rather than the going rate on the free market. The other instrument is in fact the development measures, whose price limitation at the time when the land was acquired by the city opens up the possibility of developing larger areas on favorable terms, including for low-cost housing.

Andreas Garkisch

In this context, the accusation is often made that the municipalities enrich themselves excessively by means of such SEMs.

Christiane Thalgott

In my view, criticism like that is idiotic. The development of large projects costs much more than what can be achieved from the difference in value between undeveloped and developed land.

SEMs are also an instrument with which, for example, agricultural exchange areas can be carried out – that is, an instrument that involves not only financing but, above all, the planning of future development, which is completely ignored in the public debate.

Elisabeth Merk

SEMs are not primarily undertaken to gain access to the land. The motivation is based on two aspects. First of all, we see many landowners who want to achieve something through project developers. But these areas cannot be developed individually. Integrated planning is needed in order to implement urban planning, social and environmental goals. In addition, regardless of the cost breakdown, such large investments made by the public sector and financed by the tax-payer must be justified. The outlay is justified only if it ends up creating something useful for the general public – for example, affordable housing. According to the latest projections, measures such as those in Freiham have produced a deficit of 800 million euros, because we are building schools and other facilities necessary for the neighborhood. Compared with the Neuperlach development area from the seventies, the difference lies in the fact that on the one hand we are dealing with many more individual players and, on the other, we are confronted with the logic of the financial sector. An example: for the Freiham areas there is a standard agricultural land value guide, but for years the banks have been granting loans to owners and farmers on the basis of appraising the land as land for building development. Thus, if a farmer wants to continue farming but needs a new shed and five new machines, and needs a loan to pay for them, a land charge based on its value as building land is registered on the land, without any sale of land actually occurring. In practice, this establishes a gray market valuation of real estate as the benchmark. Of course, landowners rightly say, How can that be: At the bank, we expected that I would get a certain amount of money for my land based on the land charge and you do not even want to give me a tenth of that amount? And these are the players who are reasonable and still have their feet on the ground. But then there are those whose only interest is in achieving maximum profit from the transaction. And then again there are those who do not want anything at all, are at the mercy of this dynamic, and cannot escape it. Consequently, we adopt the attitude that SEMs should not dispossess anyone. Instead, we manage the process so that it is transparent and everyone is treated equally, unlike individual contracts. Of course, we have to keep in mind that Germany has a difficult history regarding rights of preemption and expropriations. There were pernicious expropriations under the Nazi dictatorship – with consequences that are still noticeable today in some places. And there was a second wave of expropriating land as public property of the GDR, the consequences of which I was actively involved with in Halle. There were, for example, *Bebauungspläne* without plots of land, on which the public property was marked in yellow felt-tip pen. These were – even if not at the same level – two principles of injustice that have burned into the collective memory in a way that should not be underestimated. Another aspect enters into the picture, too, which our former Town Planning Director, Stephan Reiß-Schmidt, called *land banking* or *land fracking.* This involves compensatory or «impact mitigation» land swaps based on areas that are actually cow paddocks. Building committees of relatively remote municipalities are reporting that more and more land is being sold without their initially becoming aware of it, with compensatory or «impact mitigation» areas being declared there which are not guaranteed by the state. If the municipality then decides to develop land, this proves to be impossible because somebody has placed the land in a land impact mitigation pool in connection with another region.

Andreas Garkisch

Some sellers have specialized in it. Some of these areas have even been used in this way twice.

Elisabeth Merk

Such area certificates and quotas are quite controversial in the spatial development discourse. I do not regard area certificates and quotas as the right instrument for tackling land price development. In addition, I see new conflicts regarding the planning powers of the municipalities. This is linked directly to a question which is even more difficult to answer: how this affects urban planning typologies – i.e., which city comes out on top when applying procedures like these. That's a question that underlies the basic question as to what urban development would occur if every square meter of land in Germany cost the same? That would be an interesting simulation game. Would we then have the same growth in Munich? We are also interesting as a city because of these banking concepts. The financial crisis has made it much more interesting to deposit money with us. For example, Credit Suisse bought blocks here, which it is now developing. They do not need any loans at all, but just park their money here. They do so because they can and because it's attractive. The land not only retains its value, but also increases it significantly.

Andreas Garkisch
When the market is deregulated, excesses – both positive and negative – become stronger and stronger. Volatility simply increases. But I would like to return to the topic of expropriations in Germany. These multiple expropriations have led to a situation where anyone who intends to interfere with land tenure in a major planning move in the public interest is immediately labeled a communist.

Christiane Thalgott
In my experience that is a variant of a thought-terminating cliché.

Elisabeth Merk
Regarding the emotional nature of the debate, although serious newspapers like the *Süddeutsche* and the *Frankfurter Allgemeine Zeitung* publish critical reports on the land issue, the popular press publishes huge headlines such as «now even humble homeowners are having their land taken from them.» This has no truth to it whatsoever, but has the desired effect on the public. Unfortunately, these publications did not publish interviews with Hans-Jochen Vogel, who was quite capable of responding to the whole business, emotionally as well.

Florian Hertweck
Recently, even the *Frankfurter Allgemeine Zeitung* published an extremely polemical editorial which immediately used the ugly word «expropriation.» In fact, in the 1970s, Hans-Jochen Vogel's concept of *Verfügungseigentum* (with each individual plot of land having two aspects regulating them, one that it's owned by the municipality and the other that it is used by a private individual or entity under a ground lease or similar arrangement), failed largely because the CDU was able to trigger the fear of the homeowners.

Christiane Thalgott
But the resistance was successfully imported into Vogel's own party, the SPD: rumor has it that the housing association Neue Heimat devoted a great deal of energy against it internally, because it was perceived as as a risk to their real estate business.

Florian Hertweck

And of course, the FDP did not play along, although their program at the time, the 1971 «Freiburg theses,» was so liberal in social terms that they would have gone along with the land value increment tax and the land capture tax. But there were fears among the liberals at the time that the SPD might achieve an absolute majority in the next federal election… How would it be possible today to tackle the land issue without emphasizing ideologies?

Christiane Thalgott

That's precisely why it's so difficult, because the topic is so emotionally charged. It is interesting that since the emergence of the initiative for the expropriation of Deutsche Wohnen in Berlin, for the first time the real estate industry has begun to discuss that they could have a problem if they overstep the socio-political limits. In real estate newspapers, it is always stated that Germany is so attractive as a business location because it is so stable economically and as a democracy. And if an eruption is suddenly threatening at Deutsche Wohnen, the real estate industry has to respond.

Elisabeth Merk

But you also have to say that the public sector has not always done everything right. It has sold land to the highest bidder instead of dealing responsibly with its own stocks. When I started with the Munich city administration, public land from the city utilities was still being sold…

Christiane Thalgott

…in the face of massive resistance by this department…

Elisabeth Merk

Or in connection with the railway land, which was the property of the federal government. It was quite controversial that, when these properties were no longer needed for railways, they, too, were sold on the market to the highest bidder. Perhaps we can find a different way other than expropriation. There is currently talk of an unconditional basic income, something about which I am very skeptical. However, if you treat land as a stock, why not treat all land in public ownership as the people's share? If everyone had a real share in this national wealth, many things could be discussed differently. The general aim is to make tax money more tangible as a collective good.

Andreas Garkisch

The status quo of discussions on this topic in Switzerland seems very interesting to me. Referenda are likely to make citizens aware of the state as their property. This makes the sense of responsibility for the community much greater.

Florian Hertweck

As a result, the referendum being held in Basel is a special event. In it, the decision was made that the public sector could no longer sell its own public land. This has given much more weight to this decision, which is now being adopted by many municipalities.

Christiane Thalgott

The concept of a land bank (*Boden-fonds*) is a move in the same direction – namely, that the public sector must use its land for the public good.

Andreas Garkisch

In tax legislation, too, property owners are significantly favored by depreciation. To date, there has been far too little public awareness of the extent to which taxation favors income from ownership over income from personal labor.

Florian Hertweck

That brings us to Henry George and the question of tax justice: What kind of a society do we wish to live in? In a society where profits made on land without any effort are taxed, or one in which work is taxed?

«A Lethal Cocktail for the City»

Interview with Carolien Schippers (Head of the Department of Urban Development of the Municipality of Amsterdam) and Reinier de Graaf (Partner at OMA) by Florian Hertweck and Stefan Rettich on the land question in the Netherlands and the ground lease (*erfpacht*) system in Amsterdam

Florian Hertweck

About 85 percent of the built-up area in Amsterdam consists of public property. How can this large proportion be explained? Especially given the small size and special geography of the Netherlands, where (because of the specific history of land reclamation) land is regarded as a more valuable good than in other countries.

Reinier de Graaf

Land is not a given in the Netherlands. Its presence is the result of a public effort, sometimes in the form of land reclamation. But even the land that wasn't reclaimed needs constant public effort to keep it dry. Since it is regarded as the result of constant public investment, profiting from the land is less acceptable here than in countries where it is more abundant.

Carolien Schippers

Given that the city of Amsterdam has always and continues to invest in its land – in its infrastructure for example – the public sector should expect to receive revenue from the value of that land in return.

Florian Hertweck

But there are different instruments for treating land as a commons. One is taxation, and another is by using ground leases. Why did the ground lease system become so firmly established in Amsterdam? How was the decision reached not to sell the land itself but to separate it legally from buildings which can be bought and sold?

Reinier de Graaf

If the public sector invests in the land, and the land increases in value, it is only fair that the public sector benefits from that increase. Otherwise public effort results in private gain.
This was also the argument used by Hans-Jochen Vogel in the seventies. In order to carry out any public project in Munich, the municipality had to buy back the land for much more than it had been originally sold.
This was perceived as extremely unfair, since the increase in the value of the land had resulted from public investment.

Florian Hertweck

That's right, but Vogel pleaded for a package of measures, from fiscal measures to distinguishing between public land and private buildings. Why does the culture of ground leases predominate so strongly in the Netherlands?

Reinier de Graaf

Property taxes are very low in the Netherlands. The idea of the public sector earning more money through higher taxes on individuals and private companies would meet with more resistance than simply retaining ownership of the land in public hands.

Florian Hertweck

Does the Amsterdam ground lease system generate, or necessitate, a specific kind of urban development?

Carolien Schippers

Yes, definitely. If the owners of a building want to change it, for example, to transform residential into office space or to increase its footprint, they have to deal with the city in order to change the ground lease agreement. As a result, we have significant influence on city development because we are continuously in close contact with the people involved. Of course, we have instruments regulating construction. Such as the *Bestemmingsplan,* which is similar to the German *Bebauungsplan* (a legally binding urban development plan), except that it also regulates land use and a number of other things. But these are not as strong as the ground lease agreement.

Reinier de Graaf

How does the private sector deal with the ground lease system? Do developers in Amsterdam have a different attitude to the ownership of land? Or would they still prefer to buy the land?

Carolien Schippers

Yes, of course they would still prefer to buy the land. I am not familiar with every case of the 15 percent that is not publicly owned, but as far as I know

people are very happy with what they own. Perhaps they won a legal case against the city, or they had an option to purchase the land.

Florian Hertweck

Does this 15 percent share of privately owned landholdings consist of smaller properties or larger plots?

Carolien Schippers

In general, smaller properties which are widely distributed across the city.

Florian Hertweck

I ask, because in many countries – such as England or Luxembourg, for instance, the land is very unequally distributed.

Carolien Schippers

That's not the case in Amsterdam. Most of the important bankers and investors also have ground lease contracts for the land they use.

Florian Hertweck

If the traditional ground lease system is such a meaningful tool for urban regulation, why was such a momentous change recently made? The change from limited-term to a perpetual ground lease eliminates the advantages of ground lease you mentioned.

Carolien Schippers

Liberal politicians here in Amsterdam were the ones who wanted to change the ground lease agreements for their own benefit, in order to make more private ownership possible.

They wanted to give the owners of buildings more certainty about what was happening with the land. This decision has presented us with a huge challenge, as we have to change about 120,000 ground lease agreements – many of which only exist in written form.

Stefan Rettich

How will this change in the ground lease system affect urban development? Especially if a buyout clause is added – in which case the holders of a ground lease can pay out the whole lease as a lump sum, creating the opportunity for land speculation.

Carolien Schippers

We can't estimate the special effects of the perpetual ground lease agreement yet, because we are still working with the traditional ground lease agreements. However, we are already seeing a great deal of speculation with buildings in good locations, and no doubt people will also speculate with land if they can. But today we still have traditional ground lease agreements, through which we can absorb land rents and reinvest them in urban development. Perhaps we will simply have less money for urban development in 10 to 15 years. Nevertheless, if developers want to change a ground lease agreement, they will still have to deal with the city.

Florian Hertweck

The income from land rent makes up a substantial portion of the municipal budget, after all. So the ground lease system is very important for the development and governance of the city. And it has always been constant. Fresh income flows into the public coffers every year.

Carolien Schippers

It's extremely important. Especially if we have to make major investments in infrastructure – building bridges or expanding the public transport system for example.

Reinier de Graaf

I fear that changing the ground lease system, coupled with rising housing prices, will have a mutually reinforcing effect, becoming a lethal cocktail for the livability and the character of the city as a whole.

Stefan Rettich

If lump sums are paid for the buyout of ground leases, what will the city do with all the money that can be expected? Will you reinvest it in urban development or (as has already happened in other cities) finance other indebted areas?

Carolien Schippers

We have a fund into which all the money from the buyout of ground leases will flow.

Florian Hertweck

Is it a fund with which you will buy land?

Carolien Schippers

That's possible, but most of it will go into urban development. Most projects achieve a surplus. I'll give an example. We are currently building a new island (Strandeiland) and investing 100 million euros, which we are taking from the fund. And even if we produce a lot of social housing, we will still make a profit, which will go back into the fund. Right now, we are making a lot of money with it. And sometimes leaseholders buy the land in their ground lease agreement, and the proceeds go into the fund.

Florian Hertweck

Is it still customary in the Netherlands for the public sector to buy agricultural and uncultivated land (for a maximum of twice its value), before transforming it into «building land» and, after developing the infrastructure, selling it at a profit? Much as the *Terraingesell-schaften* did in Berlin at the beginning of the twentieth century, except that here in Holland the public sector is involved in the business.

Carolien Schippers

It still happens sometimes, but today it is mainly by private developers. They buy land from the farmers in antic-ipation of future urban development in those areas. But in Amsterdam this is not an issue, because we are now only pursuing development within city boundaries.

Reinier de Graaf

This already happened with the VINEX program in the nineties. One million homes were built from 1995 to 2005. When developers became aware of the locations of these developments

they began buying the land from the farmers so that they could then sell it to the municipalities at a substantial profit. It was like insider trading.

Carolien Schippers

Until 2008 both the public and the private sectors made substantial profits. There were cities which made a lot of money by rezoning the land: sometimes it was private developers making a lot of money, and the farmers made money on it as well. But prices fell after the financial crisis in 2008. The building lots were heavily mortgaged, and at the same time hardly any building was being done. Many went bankrupt, even municipalities. It was no different in Amsterdam, because the city had bought a lot of land that was difficult to develop. For example, we bought a large site from Shell with office buildings and so on. And then the crisis came and everything collapsed. We thought we had a lot of money, but in two years everything vanished into thin air.

Stefan Rettich

As a reaction to the financial crisis, the City of Rotterdam discontinued ground leases. They hoped that they would stimulate the real estate market by opening up the sale of land.

Reinier de Graaf

The City of Almere still owns a lot of land. Before the financial crisis many major developers were on the market in the city. Then, with the financial crisis, self-building boomed. It kept

the construction industry going, even when a lot of property developers were in trouble and had to struggle through the crisis. Then, as the economy recovered, the big developers moved into the market again and the whole self-building initiative was relegated to the sidelines. Self-building was not about ground leases, it was about the owner-occupied acquisition of land. It is interesting to observe that in one state of the economy the possibility of buying land leads to the emancipation of citizens, whereas in another it strengthens the monopoly of the real estate developers.
The same thing happened with the conservative revolution, first in England and then in other parts of Europe. The first generation of middle class people went from being tenants to being homeowners, thus experiencing financial emancipation. As house prices increased faster than their salaries, the next generation no longer had the same access to the market. If I look at my friends in Amsterdam, people all roughly my age and with the same education and background, the financial divide runs exactly along the line between those who decided to buy a home in the nineties and those who continued to rent.

Florian Hertweck
And some of them started to speculate themselves?

Reinier de Graaf
We never bought a house in order to speculate, but simply to house the family.

Florian Hertweck
Ms. Schippers, to whom do you lease land in Amsterdam when you develop new areas? Do you proceed like Munich and many other communities, where they now only grant ground leases to cooperatives?

Carolien Schippers
When we own the land, we have a 40/40/20 rule: 40 percent for social housing or cooperatives, 40 percent for the middle sector, and 20 percent for private ownership. The Liberal mayor who changed the ground lease system is no longer in office. Since we have had a left-wing politician as mayor, there has been a debate about who owns the housing and who should develop the city. Nowadays city politicians want to invest more in cooperatives and social housing organizations. Families who want to build, especially in collaboration with cooperatives, are coming to the fore. We went to Zurich to seek inspiration from the housing cooperatives there.

Florian Hertweck
Has this become a trend in the Netherlands, which seems from the outside to be very individualistic?

Reinier de Graaf
In Germany the culture of cooperatives has existed for a long time, and now it's under discussion here too. More and more municipalities are making excursions to Germany and Switzerland. It is a form of social urban development for left-leaning

people, without completely turning against the capitalist system.

Florian Hertweck

But cooperatives can only emerge if they are given access to land under favorable conditions.

Carolien Schippers

That's right. That's why we are now thinking about buying back the land from private investors, in order to support cooperatives.

Florian Hertweck

But under what conditions? How do you negotiate with investors? Is expropriation an issue in the Netherlands?

Carolien Schippers

It's very difficult. But sometimes it can have the effect of a threat.

Florian Hertweck

But I would like to know from you, Reinier. Have you, as a global player in architecture, ever worked for a client who held a ground lease? And if so, did it change anything for you as a planner?

Reinier de Graaf

I have an anecdote about this. We have often worked for developers who didn't own the land, for instance the Holland Green project in London. The land, the Ilchester Estates, was owned outright by old aristocracy who had employed a property developer to redevelop it in order to increase its value. The former Commonwealth Institute was located on the estate, and was to be converted into a museum. In England, under Section 106 developers receive development approval when there is a clear benefit for the city. This usually entails the provision of a certain percentage of affordable housing. The Holland Green project was approved because it involved the restoration of a listed building and the creation of a museum, which was to have been financed through the sale of the housing units. The project started in 2009, and at first profits looked very good. But then converting the existing building seemed more expensive than originally estimated, and for this reason the whole project was put on hold. Precisely at that moment, the museum and the property developer entered into a very favorable agreement because the developer was able to claim financial hardship. Consequently, prices for apartments escalated rapidly again to a level much higher than before. There were three blocks of apartments, and the profit made on the smallest alone paid for the museum. I think it would have been a much better deal for us if we had asked to be paid with a single apartment, instead of fees. Most of those apartments are like furniture showrooms. They were bought furnished and are scarcely used. But to return to your question, I don't know to what extent the availability of land can prevent people from buying real estate they don't need, and then don't occupy.

Florian Hertweck

If the ground leaseholder is a public

institution, the heritable building right system prevents land speculation. And if the owner of the land has social goals, appropriate conditions can be stipulated in the ground lease agreement, such as a certain range of uses or a limit on rents. The problem after 2008 was that the real estate market had been flooded with so much money, and at the same time many municipalities like Berlin had to sell their land stocks in order to balance their budgets. In good locations private interests jumped in, in order to build luxury apartments on the land. And very often, as you have described in London, many of these apartments remain empty. They are just an investment asset, as many say nowadays. The investors don't want to have the nuisance of people living in them. Two years ago, I invited the sociologist Saskia Sassen to give a lecture in Luxembourg. She showed this collage of London, with all the high-rise apartments financed by funds from China, Russia, and the Middle East. The yellow spots showed the occupied flats and the black spots the empty ones. It was a sea of black with a few isolated yellow dots.

Reinier de Graaf
You see the same in New York, where many of the new residential skyscrapers are as good as empty.

Florian Hertweck
Or look at Paris. In the sixties, three million people lived in the city, and six million in the outer suburbs. Today a little more than two million live in the

city, but 10 million in the outer suburbs. There has been a significant migration of the less privileged from the city to the periphery, as is well known. But it is quite perverse that the inner city, where the number of buildings is not less than it used to be, is simultaneously emptying out because fewer people require more and more space.

Stefan Rettich
Have you studied the impact of the low interest-rate policy of the European Central Bank on the real estate market?

Reinier de Graaf
The interest rate was rather high until 2007–2008. Borrowing was expensive, and that sparked the mortgage crisis. Then, to help the banks out, they were flooded with money. Interest rates had to be lowered to keep the economy ticking over. The fact that there are low interest rates means that, with all the cost of banking, you become poorer *de facto* by keeping your savings in the bank. So what we are currently seeing is that much of the real estate activity involving global capital is not happening because people are looking for a home, but because money is looking for a home – money that would otherwise rot away in the bank at a minuscule interest rate. So the real estate sector has become a form of banking.

Carolien Schippers
You can observe this here in Amsterdam too. There are a lot of apartment buildings we would like to buy from private owners, but we are competing

with numerous real estate companies which are buying everything they can get their hands on. That drives rents up, and poorer to medium-income population groups are being driven further and further out of the city. Through this we are getting more and more commuters, more and more traffic jams, more and more CO_2 emissions, and more and more stress. Isn't the ground lease system a good way to prevent this?

Reinier de Graaf

I'm not sure that it would have a major effect. You only have to read Thomas Piketty, when he compares revenue from labor with revenue from capital. We all assume that people ought to make more money from working than from having money. However, the historical period in which that really was the case was an exception. It was the «short twentieth century.» And it was the case then because the natural tendency of the system was constantly disrupted by strikes, labor unions, world wars, and so on. To keep the system in check, you need a fundamental form of instability. I would be astonished if the instrument of ground lease proved to be enough to keep the system running.

Florian Hertweck

But Piketty was accused by Joseph Stiglitz and other prominent economists of neglecting land in his work. And that's when it becomes interesting. Economists like Ottmar Edenhofer, the director of the Potsdam Institute for Climate Impact Research, shows us that avoiding land speculation would have an extremely positive effect on the political economy. Often 50 percent of the overall cost of a real estate project is for the acquisition of the land. This money is actually frozen. Now imagine this huge amount of money flowing into more productive fields.

Carolien Schippers

Amsterdam is a very highly rated city, not because of the land but because of the buildings. You need a lot of money to carry out projects in this city. And that can only be done by big real estate developers. And they simply buy the building with the ground lease agreement connected to it. We then check how much the ground lease agreement is worth. As I said, with the ground lease you have a power-ful regulatory instrument, but extreme speculation is happening with the buildings. And if you want to stop that, you need other instruments.

Reinier de Graaf

Amsterdam is definitely becoming more and more expensive. I know of developers who want to acquire development rights here. The city is aware of its desirability, and is able to make good deals. And the developers complain about it!

General laughter

Carolien Schippers

They complain a lot. We frequently talk with our colleagues in Rotterdam, the second-biggest city in the Netherlands.

They obtain far less money from private developers.

Florian Hertweck

What role do housing associations play in the Netherlands today, especially in Amsterdam? Are they still as powerful as they used to be?

Reinier de Graaf

They were privatized. They are still active in social housing, but they are now allowed to build housing for profit as well.

Carolien Schippers

The discussion is very difficult in the Netherlands. The housing associations earn a lot of money from social housing, but they argue that these profits are locked into the bricks the houses are built from. So they don't have any access to it. Meanwhile, the national government demands high rents and uses the profits for other national projects, while at the same time saying «We don't have enough money left to invest.» It's a complicated discussion.

Reinier de Graaf

You said that Rotterdam isn't as successful as Amsterdam in absorbing tax income from real estate development. Do you think that is related to the system of ground lease agreements that Rotterdam does not have?

Carolien Schippers

That's one reason. Another is that Amsterdam is still more attractive than Rotterdam. In Rotterdam they have about 70 percent social housing.

We, by contrast, have far more privately owned buildings. And we have politicians who are very aware of what we value, and what we want in return. So when I meet developers who usually work or negotiate with the City of Rotterdam, they are really amazed by what we demand from them in connection with sustainability, the quality of architecture, and social housing.

Stefan Rettich

But isn't this paradoxical?
The cities that have the best land policy and the best urban planning are faced with the highest rates of speculation. You can also see that in Munich or Hamburg. So how to escape from this paradox?

Reinier de Graaf

All private success has a public component. Even somebody like Donald Trump, who disparages the public sector, owes his fortune to his father, who got his start building government-subsidized housing for veterans. The same is true for the VINEX program, where developers bought land solely to sell it to the municipalities while earning hefty profits. The Netherlands is a strange country. We have very high income taxes, but one of the lowest corporate taxes in the world. For some, we are a tax haven… On the one hand it's extremely mercantile, yet on the other it's really a wretched little country.

The Homeruskwartier, Almere. An Example of Owner-Occupied Housing on Public Land

The introduction to this volume cites Jean-Jacques Rousseau's *Discourse on Inequality* of 1755. In this treatise the French philosopher argues that the ownership of land was a ploy on the part of the rich to secure their property by supposedly protecting the poor.

Rousseau's moral appeal seems to have had little effect. Over 250 years later, the private ownership of land is generally accepted as the cornerstone of modern capitalist economics – idly accumulating value and generating income for its owners. The further civilization progresses, the more people appear to feel justified in exercising a general right to seize land for their own needs. And the state upholds the right to property ownership, allowing expropriation only under extreme circumstances and so long as the owner receives generous compensation.

Building Rights through Property Ownership

In the Netherlands, building rights are usually closely linked with the ownership of the land to be built on. In order to ensure that sufficient housing is built, many cities depend on professional real estate developers who strategically purchased attractive land in advance. Because no normal citizen or group of citizens can afford to «stockpile» land, corporate landowners retain a monopoly over the housing market. Even today, a mere 10 percent of all housing in the Netherlands was built by its occupants, most of which is located in rural areas. Only those municipalities that happen to own large, obsolete railway properties, or who have reclaimed land from the sea, are fortunate enough to be able to sell land directly to prospective residents. The city of Almere, built on reclaimed land starting in the 1970s, enjoys the unique position of monopoly ownership. Its development of the Homeruskwartier and the semi-agrarian community of Oosterwold has made it the Netherlands' pioneering municipality for self-building.

The Homeruskwartier

With 1,400 properties, the Homeruskwartier is the largest self-built district housing in the Netherlands since 1945. In 2006, the city administration of Almere deliberately decided to sell land directly to its citizens, reflecting its critical attitude toward the collusion between municipal authorities and professional real estate developers. The amount of housing constructed as a consequence indicates how eager ordinary residents are to build their own housing without intermediaries. The great diversity of building types demonstrates what can happen when people can make truly free housing decisions. A rich mix of living concepts has been realized on a variety of properties, alternating between large and small, tall and ranch style, and townhouses and detached homes.

In late 2007, 350 properties were sold, followed by another 300 in 2009. Ultimately, the city sold a total

The Homeruskwartier, Almere

The Homeruskwartier, Almere

of 1,400. A crucial factor was the absence of any aesthetic specifications. The builders, who were the future occupants of the home, enjoyed complete freedom to design their homes. No resident was obliged to work with any particular architects. The only thing specified by the regulations was the dimensions of the structure to be erected on each property – namely, the maximum width, depth and height. Within this «envelope,» each owner-occupant could design their building of choice. The result is a collage of canal houses, townhouses, multi-generation homes and summer houses. The smallest occupies less than 50 square meters, while the largest has 1,000 square meters of floor space. A three-story house was built on the smallest property, covering just 17 square meters. The amounts invested by the owner-occupiers ranged from 100,000 to 1.5 million euros.

What makes Homeruskwartier so special is that it depicts a cross section of society: low, middle, and higher incomes; singles, families and multi-generational households; young people and the elderly – all of them live here, despite the fact that hardly any of them has a background in construction or architecture. The diversity of the population also accounts for the aesthetic variety of the neighborhood. For elderly residents, security, well-being, and independence were the decisive motives for building and living here; accordingly, they built «smart homes» in which they can grow old

comfortably. Some residents scoured all of Europe to find a certain stove for their home, while others wanted a perfect model house, or even a home without windows. Seemingly irrational preferences became a matter of individual design rationale.

Oosterwold

In the owner-occupied area of Oosterwold, a 4,300-hectare development in Almere, the residents not only build their homes but also take charge of the entire urban development concept. They can determine the shape and size of the plots for building, and work together with their neighbors to build and manage their streets, water and energy supply, and trash removal. The main task remaining to the municipality is to check that building permits comply with hygiene and construction standards and uphold the specifications on security and sustainability.

The focus in Oosterwold is on low-density urban agriculture: More than half of each property must be used agriculturally; construction may take place on only 12.5 percent of the area. The low density this yields hardly offers a solution that can be adapted more generally, as most of the world is facing a general trend of increasing urbanization. Further, this experiment has shown that not everyone is equally willing to debate and cooperate at this level. However, with 600 properties sold, and a waiting list of 9,000 more potential residents, this community will offer many people great freedom to design their living environment.

Freedom or Choice?

In today's urban planning, it is widely accepted that governments have a role to manage free trade when it comes to the allocation of land. Yet it is also understood that not everyone will enjoy the opportunity to purchase land. Although the neoliberal land policies were designed to accommodate the freedom of choice to acquire property, very little of this plan has been realized. Owner-occupiers generally come up short when development rights are allocated, losing concessions to better-organized investors and developers. When just a handful of investors are able to secure ownership and use rights preemptively, as is generally the case today, this raises questions about the moral authority of disposing over land without any intention of using it oneself.

Just imagine a truly free market for land: Hundreds of thousands of individuals, collectives, architects, small, customer-oriented companies, and so on would have an equal chance to acquire property. Imagine a property market in which every-one can participate. The result would be an unprecedented variety of housing construction – in line with actual demand and the real needs of residents.

Jacqueline Tellinga

The Homeruskwartier, Almere

The Homeruskwartier, Almere

«Urban Development Based on the Ground Lease is Related to Negotiating Processes»

Interview with Martin Weis (Christoph Merian Stiftung, Basel) by Simon Frommenwiler, Tanja Herdt, and Florian Hertweck on the Swiss ground lease (*Baurecht*) and dynamic urban development

Florian Hertweck

Mr. Weis, you represent the Christoph Merian Stiftung (CMS), one of the largest landowners in Basel. The special feature of your foundation is that you only grant ground leases. What does the ground lease system mean to you and how do you apply it?

Martin Weis

If you have a house on a piece of land, the house belongs to the land parcel. This is called the «accession principle.» In Switzerland, this principle is suspended for a period of at least 30 years, up to a maximum of 100 by the ground lease (*Baurecht*). During this period, the house belongs to the leaseholder and this person can use and develop it in any way, provided that doing so is allowed by the provisions of the ground lease contract. As part of this process, a lease parcel is created, and a separate object sheet is entered for the parcel in the land register as property. The ground lease is negotiable and can be alienated. According to Swiss civil law the owner of the land has the right of preemption. The following applies for the property owned by the foundation Christoph Merian Stiftung Basel: leaseholders cannot buy the land. Only the foundation can repurchase the ground lease parcels and, by extension, also the buildings. As landowners, we have stipulated this and it generally functions well. However, the special ground lease arrangement also introduces some difficulties. Problems often arise when the landowner and the leaseholder want to implement a project together, because they are usually pursuing different interests. One party is strongly focused on daily business, whereas the party granting the ground lease has long-term ambitions. This issue doesn't exist when the traditional «quick and dirty» approach of buying land, developing it, and reselling it is followed; but that is not our objective. The goal of the CMS is to retain its land in order to use income gained from these land-holdings to promote social and cultural projects as well as projects related to nature and urban living space. So, basically, we do not sell any land. Now and again the rumor is spread that this is not legal, which is not true. We want to generate solid, long-term returns. The ground lease contract is key in this regard, because we do not want to and are not able to develop everything ourselves.

Florian Hertweck

How did the CMS acquire so much land?

Martin Weis

Christoph Merian (1800–1858), who was born into an aristocratic Basel family, was given a 56-hectare summer estate as a wedding present. Because of his interest in farming, he defied the family tradition and studied agronomy instead, and successfully increased his landholdings. Since he believed in the power of land, he acquired land over a period of 30 years, with the result that at the end of his life, he could call over 325 hectares of land his own. After the death of his wife, he made the city of Basel his main heir and the Christoph Merian Foundation was founded to manage his assets. This is how the foundation became owner of the land. However, the reverse question also needs to be asked: How does the foundation relinquish land? For it has had to accept enormous land expropriations. For example, until the first half of the twentieth century, the Wolf freight yard in Basel was expropriated in two stages. It is currently being developed by SBB Real Estate.

Simon Frommenwiler

Is the foundation still buying more land?

Martin Weis

Of course, when we have the opportunity to do so. Look how the population is growing. Christoph Merian was born in 1800. The first census was carried out in 1850 and at that time Switzerland had a population of 2.5 million. Today, we have 8.4 million inhabitants. The demographic factor is immense and, as a result, pressure on land is also growing. That is a simplified conclusion we all have only become aware of in the last few years. You may be familiar with *Bodenmarktpolitik* (Land Market Policy) by Daniel Wachter, a book published in 1993 about land from an economic

point of view, which already states that land is a non-elastic good. Another book on the same topic, *Die Stadt und ihr Boden* (The City and Its Land) by Hans Bernoulli, is also noteworthy. In it, Bernoulli calls for land to be kept in public ownership and building kept in private hands. Doing so would guarantee a balance between public and overriding interests as compared with private ones. He sees the ground lease system in the Swiss sense of the term as the appropriate instrument for achieving this.

Florian Hertweck

How do you draft ground lease contracts and how do you determine the fee to be paid?

Martin Weis

The models used are widely different. The basic model simply charges Swiss francs per square meter per year. The transaction model multiplies the market value of the land by the current mortgage interest rate (for a variable mortgage). However, this model is not appropriate for the current situation, because land prices have risen considerably over the past few years, whereas capital scarcely earns any interest anymore. The model also fails to function in the reverse situation, when inflation is rising sharply but land prices are stagnating. Finally, there is the partnership ground lease model developed by finance experts in the late eighties, with the goal of making it possible for everyone to share in the earnings as a partner. In principle, this is a good way of acting because

Aerial photograph of the
industrial area near Dreispitz;
view toward the northern
corner and the Wolf freight
yard in the background,
1924

On the Swiss Ground Lease and Dynamic Urban Development / Interview

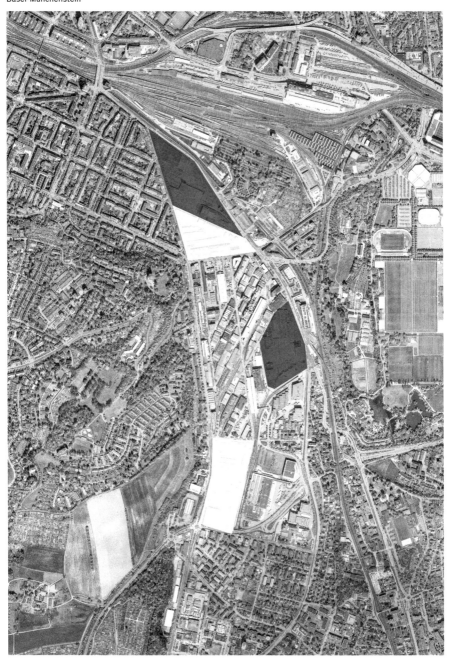

with a ground lease system the contractual relationship extends over a long period. We apply a similar model – also a revenue model – that starts by calculating the revenue that can be achieved with a piece of real estate and then subtracts a portion in the form of fees paid by the leaseholder. How this works can be seen in the CMS's Dreispitz area in Basel-Münchenstein (Canton of Basel-Landschaft), a former freight yard which is currently a commercial zone. While the property is huge and includes a number of infrastructure items, such as railway tracks and a tunnel, the leaseholders only have their footprint as a ground lease. Despite this, they are required to contribute to the costs of development and maintenance of a commons. Of course, this raises the general question as to what this commons is – namely, land that must be paid for through earnings derived from ground leases. The regular fee paid to the lessor is vital, but the adjustment mechanism is just as important. Usually, five-year adjustments apply. After 10 years the fees are reviewed to ensure that they match the development of land prices reasonably well. Some ground lease fees paid are adjusted only every 20 years. Compensation for reversion (*Heimfallentschädigung*) is also very important in this regard. If the ground lease ends after 70 or 90 years, the key question is the value of the house standing on the property. Most of the CMS's ground leases in the Dreispitz area were granted from 1955 to 2053, without any compensation for reversion.

No investor would take on a project with a ground lease valid for another 30 years if the real estate is no longer of any value. The attraction then would involve changing the model so that the real estate would still be assessed at 70 or 80 percent of its market value. As long as there is a residual value, the investor still has an interest in investing, even in the last 10 years of the term of the contract. This approach avoids downgrading. Central to this legal structure is whether the leaseholder is an owner-occupier or an investor. The Dreispitz area involves owner-occupiers. If you have 50 different building owners, as is the case there, you will never achieve a single, universal development model. There are always two leaseholders who have a different opinion. In one case – the grounds of the Freilager AG – we were able to buy both the land *and* the building. As a result, we had control of everything we needed to develop the whole project. We then divested again, certain buildings, a school, etc. In the case of ground leases, it always depends on when the building was built and what its use has become. For example, in the Basel-Bruderholz neighborhood, the foundation owns several single-family housing developments. Ground leases and single-family homes are not a good fit. If the residents are also the owners, they have to declare some kind of rental value because the revenues yielded by the real estate matter in most ground lease models. However, in the case of owners of single-family dwellings, they all say,

On the Swiss Ground Lease and Dynamic Urban Development / Interview

«I live here for nothing, I don't pay anything.» Disagreements are inevitable. Combining condominiums with ground leases is even more difficult, and actually poses the biggest challenge.

Simon Frommenwiler

Your remarks on ground leases make it clear that the development strategy is highly dependent on the existing parceling of the land. The smaller the parcels of land, the more difficult an overall development model is?

Martin Weis

Yes, of course, parceling is long-term, as Aldo Rossi already showed. Of course, that also applies to ground leases, where, interestingly, it proves to be especially persistent.

Florian Hertweck

For Hans Bernoulli, the small parcels of land in the old city were a nightmare for modern urban development. Bernoulli – like many modern postwar urban developers – wanted to municipalize urban land in order to facilitate cohesive and coherent urban development, which he saw impeded by historical parcels of land. We refer to Bernoulli today in connection with his understanding of land, but we long for small land parcels again because they generate a certain degree of heterogeneity and user density.

Martin Weis

Of course, a certain diversification or robustness is enormously important to us, also because the buildings must remain tradeable assets. We have to avoid any constructs from which we cannot divest. The question now is whether I am doing this with one leaseholder who has a large contiguous area, or with many different leaseholders with small parcels of land. In the southern part of the Dreispitz, we own undeveloped land that used to be an industrial zone but was scaled back. That is the usual structural change. There are very large plots of land of 27,000 square meters. Now the question is: How do we want to dispose of this in order to achieve the right level of marketability? Parcels of land that are too small? Here we concur with Bernoulli: it won't work. Parcels of land that are too large? Then we have the clumping risk associated with having only a single investor. Until recently, ground leases were also severely frowned upon in Switzerland. Whenever possible, people wanted to buy. There is an unwritten rule for ground leases: they are only suitable for premium («A») locations. Ground leases are not advisable for lower categories («B» and «C» locations). Poor locations are simply unsuitable for ground leases. That is a basic premise. And, of course, this location here in Dreispitz is excellent. It offers the opportunity for investors to develop something without having to buy the land.

Tanja Herdt

Because what they save on the purchase price can be invested.

Martin Weis

That is right. And that is precisely why

it depends on the model whether an interested person has an incentive to invest, or whether to participate either proportionately or cooperatively. It is very important to achieve this balance.

Florian Hertweck

Why have ground leases experienced a renaissance in Switzerland?

Martin Weis

It was the result of the pressure on land, on the one hand because of the demographic growth described above and on the other because of the incredible pressure from investors. Suddenly, an incredible amount of money was being invested in real estate because there was no other way to achieve returns of that kind.

Simon Frommenwiler

I find it difficult to imagine, especially with different terms, that it is possible to develop the city by means of ground leases and manage active urban development this way. Who can, or should, manage it? It seems to be a very pragmatic procedure that offers scarcely any opportunities for intervention.

Martin Weis

Yes, in day-to-day practice, pragmatism hits the nail on the head. But, of course we also have a kind of guideline plan, meaning strategies for deciding where we want to do what. We also know exactly where and who is involved down to the individual parcels of land. Ground leases offer the benefit of actually being in constant dialog with

the leaseholder and you know who is willing to be flexible. There is very direct contact with the leaseholders. And, as I said, the law gives us the right of preemption, which we exercise on a regular basis because it makes sense to buy strategically important parcels of land with the aim of either developing them ourselves or granting the ground lease to an investor. There are key parcels of land that are vital to an upgrade or the overall development of a neighborhood.

Tanja Herdt

I find it very interesting that ground leases lead to far more dynamic urban development than a conventional master plan.

Martin Weis

That is right. The fact that the contracts expire at different times, that you are in contact with the leaseholders and negotiate with them before the agreement expires, enables urban development to be guided in a way quite differently than when land is sold and urban development is only regulated by the ground lease. We deliberately do not make master plans with absolute goals, as these are never achieved anyway. Ground leases require a different approach when dealing with the city and its players. You need to get a certain amount of pleasure out of interacting with people and offering them perspectives on how to proceed after the ground lease expires. You see each other at least every five years; you know each other. And, of course, you ask yourself: What are their needs?

On the Swiss Ground Lease and Dynamic Urban Development / Interview

And very often urban development issues that affect the neighborhood emerge from this dynamic interaction.

And work and life may also be brought together again, which does not happen with outdated land use plans.

Tanja Herdt

But whether you like it or not, you play an extremely important role in a kind of urban development in which civic commitment and identification by the players with the city are significant factors. Even if in the first analysis, ground lease contracts are only a form of investment for you, the way in which the provisions of this instrument are formulated means that you act as an intermediary in urban development.

Martin Weis

Yes, my work is often that of a mediator. Urban development based on a ground lease system has a lot to do with negotiating processes rather than with planning authority.

Simon Frommenwiler

But all the same, there is no way to do this without an overarching idea of what you are trying to achieve.

Martin Weis

Of course, it calls for ideas; it requires clarity and also expert knowledge. However, I believe that it is much more dynamic than traditional, rigid, overall planning, or even master plans that are already outdated by the time they are revised for the third time.

Florian Hertweck

This kind of dynamic urban development is likely to result in much more intensive land use and higher density.

Martin Weis

That's right. Incidentally, the foundation still holds five agricultural sites, which cost a lot of money. But, of course, we do not want to develop them. This inevitably forces us to adopt a holistic view of land as a resource.

Florian Hertweck

Also because farming is always a «D» location.

Martin Weis

Yes, farming is always a «D» location [laughs]. But seriously, we have a social obligation to retain this land and not convert it into land earmarked for development. A basic policy of the foundation is to develop only where the land has already been sealed for urban use.

Tanja Herdt

However, when the ground lease contracts for the Dreispitz area expire in 2053, development will have to start quickly.

Martin Weis

I do not see it that way. It has nothing to do with the actual date.
Of course, the closer to the end of the contract, the greater the incentive to sit down together. Discussions happen more frequently. At the same time, the leaseholders have to recognize structural changes: the city has come closer, the surroundings have changed,

and, as a result, shared perspectives have to be developed. Many have specified purposes in their old ground lease contracts. When this is the case, new ground lease contracts have to be concluded that may, if necessary, change how the land may be used. All of that shows how dynamic the ground lease model is and the tremendous potential it offers.

«We Want Buildings to Stay in the Hands of the People who Use Them»

Interview with Klaus Hubmann
(Stiftung Habitat, Basel) and Tanja
Herdt (Metron planning firm) on
the role that foundations play in urban
development and the Lysbüchel Süd
project

Florian Hertweck

Mr. Hubmann, you represent the
Stiftung Habitat, which is the owner
of, among others, two areas in Basel
that are currently being developed:
Erlenmatt Ost and Lysbüchel Süd.
Instead of granting ground leases to
developers for real estate in whole
or in part, you have decided on a far
more rigorous approach by developing
urban development concepts for
both – in Erlenmatt with Atelier 5 and
in Lysbüchel with Metron and Tanja
Herdt. What were the reasons for this?

Klaus Hubmann

As a not-for-profit foundation, we have
purchased the areas with the aim of
creating livable urban neighborhoods
and providing affordable housing.
This motivation emerged after
dissatisfaction with a previous urban
development measure at Erlenmatt.
There was a building code there
that foresaw large – investor-friendly –
structures, which were then developed
by profit-oriented investors in a
completely monotonous way. We feared
that if this continued, Erlenmatt as
a neighborhood would be dead.
As a result, we sought to have smaller
urban structures, not least to have
smaller cooperatives move in. Many
cooperatives are no longer able to
acquire building land in Basel today, so
we wanted to make projects possible
for a few of them.

Florian Hertweck

What conditions did you impose on
ground leaseholders?

Klaus Hubmann

At Erlenmatt Ost – due mostly to
the situation at hand – an enormous
number. First of all, we defined a central
plot of land that cannot and should
not be developed. Various small
building plots of the cooperatives are
grouped around this. We subsequently
stipulated that the entrances to
the buildings around the park should
not be from the outside but from the
courtyard, in order to keep this
communal area vibrant. Other requirements were aimed at sustainable
mobility, such as our requirement that
space for parking bicycles should
be established for each room that was
built. Because 40 percent of the
bicycle parking spots are housed in the
underground car park, there is only
room for 70 cars there, which means
that – in addition to commercial
spots – there is only one parking spot
for every 10 cars. We forbade the
construction of another underground
car park. The residents have to
organize themselves.

Florian Hertweck

In Germany, this requirement would
clash with the building and related
parking space, which are still based on
the idea of the car-friendly city and
can be circumvented only by making
compensation payments.

Klaus Hubmann

In Basel – unlike in the surrounding region of Baselland, for example – only the maximum number of parking spots is specified. This means we are in compliance with regulations. Another central requirement was the amount of space per person: by considering the heated area per resident and imposing specific requirements, we achieved a density of 45 square meters of heated area per ground lease unit – not living space – which is well below the average and not easy to accept for some people. This was resolved architecturally, for example, by creating an arcade. We make every effort to ensure that this requirement is met.

Simon Frommenwiler

How do you deal with the situation when the structure of a family changes?

Klaus Hubmann

We handle this through an internal swap. When an apartment becomes available, we start by offering it within the cooperative. As a rule, this is dealt with in the bylaws of the cooperative. Our sustainability concept includes a pioneer measure: a central energy concept. The groundwater is cooled and made available to industry by means of a channel for cooling their production facilities. The thermal energy obtained in this way is used to heat the entire building complex and to heat water for domestic use – all done via a large, centrally controlled solar power system. All ground lease-holders have committed to obtaining electricity from us or from the energy cooperative ADEV that operates the plant, because otherwise the concept would not be financially viable. With one exception: Heinrich Degelo, the architect for one of the developers, was of the opinion that his building would not require any heating. We accepted that. We've already won an award for the energy concept, because it is regarded as a showcase project. I can only say that it cost us a great deal of effort to get that accepted.

Simon Frommenwiler

Was the open space defined in this process?

Klaus Hubmann

The open space is secured via the central plot of land, which may not be built on. It accounts for about 50 percent of the total area. In practical terms, the plots with ground leases have an area no greater than the footprint of the building plus 3 meters (for the transition area facing the front). Since the open areas of the building plots were transferred to the central plot of land, this has led to quite extensive regulation regarding transit rights, escape routes, fire service access routes and the like. The special situation in Erlenmatt resulted in a comprehensive set of rules based on which all situations are regulated.

Florian Hertweck

Why didn't you build there yourselves?

Klaus Hubmann

There were various reasons. Based on

Basel Erlenmatt Ost.
Urban design: Atelier 5, Bern.
Client: Stiftung Habitat,
Basel

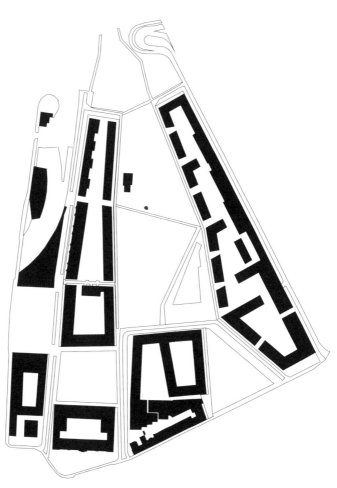

«We Want Buildings to Stay in the Hands of the People who Use Them» / Interview

the dimensions alone, we would not have been able to complete 10 such buildings in this period, or nine plus the garage. And if we had done so in such a restricted time period, the architecture would inevitably have been monotonous. We wanted to give the cooperatives – communities that come together in different ways – the chance to plan something within our set of rules and thus to achieve diversity in the neighborhood. Indeed, very different houses have emerged.

Florian Hertweck

What do you mean by «diversity»?

Klaus Hubmann

Working and living are shaped by the zoning laws. There is a certain pro-portion of commercial premises, which are important but difficult to rent. In this regard, we are still faced with a massive vacancy rate. An important aspect of diversity – regarding both rules and the sustainability concept – was the variety of living arrangements and housing sizes, which generate varying mixes of residents.

Florian Hertweck

At Lysbüchel Süd you wanted to establish the same small-scale system, but with a less extensive set of rules?

Tanja Herdt

That was a new challenge for us planners, because we usually receive commissions for building on the largest possible plots of land and are required to develop appropriate urban development typologies. Here it was the other way around. The smallest possible plots of land were required, with the widest possible variety of use.

Klaus Hubmann

Unlike in Erlenmatt Ost, urban planning and all other regulations had to be clarified before the cooperatives came on board. In addition, we did not have to and did not want to specify as many rules. We specified four key additional principles and only launched the bidding process after that: first, we wanted to prevent speculation, second, offer affordable rents, third, achieve good density, and fourth, enable energy-efficient, ecological, and healthy building. The cooperatives had to have a concept of social coexistence that they wanted to base their buildings on. And we made it clear that we only wanted owner-occupiers, meaning they had to live there, thus ruling out investment properties designed to generate profits. Of the 14 plots, we initially advertised 10, and received 32 bids. Of these, we eliminated the clearly identifiable investment projects right away. We would have liked to include two or three cooperatives we were interested in, but were forced to reject them. The groups selected are now all working on their construction projects.

Florian Hertweck

And now, with the important principles all adhered to and the cooperatives developing their architectural design with their architects, have you stopped supervising them?

Klaus Hubmann

Some thought that design coordination would be needed, as in Erlenmatt Ost. Even the new canton director of urban planning was a bit taken aback given the potential heterogeneity of the projects. For us it is sufficient if the people take their projects to the housing inspector or the city building commissioner for assessment. We ourselves did not want to take over design coordination; we do not see that as our task.

Tanja Herdt

The canton's director of urban planning initially had reservations about our proposal, because he had imagined a common overall architectural design using block-edge buildings. However, our small-scale plots result in buildings that vary in their design. One owner might build a fully glazed house, the neighbor may plan wood paneling, and a third might build a brick house.

Florian Hertweck

That's a question which ties into the land issue that I consider as an architect. Does the treatment of land as a commons or, as in this case, splitting up ownership of land from ownership of buildings bring about a different form of architecture?

Simon Frommenwiler

That's a question that automatically comes to mind with the requirement of 45 square meters of heated floor space per resident and the change in social (family) structures that takes place over time. For example, rooms that can be split off from apartment floor plans can be integrated into other apartments or turned into ateliers or something similar. Naturally, that has a direct influence on the apartment floor plan.

Tanja Herdt

Because we assume that everybody will take advantage of every possibility, we have to try out different variants in urban development planning in order to ensure that high-quality urban development will occur even without additional regulations, for example, concerning the size and use of open spaces, the creation of access lanes, or the configuration of ground floors in each building. All of these aspects must be tried out from the very beginning by subdividing land into parcels, and then established in such a way that they ensure good outcomes. We have tried to define how urban development will be designed in advance by using planning techniques. Subdividing land into plots makes only one particular urban development typology possible, but on the other hand it ensures a certain degree of freedom if building regulation instruments are applied. To achieve this, we have made use of a trick by specifying public access lanes as a commons running through the private plot of land. This made it possible to plan the area in accordance with the specifications of the building regulations and with the required density. Both the owners and the city had to make various concessions

«We Want Buildings to Stay in the Hands of the People who Use Them» / Interview

in connection with the construction and the maintenance of the access lanes. The street promoted pedestrian networking in the neighborhood, because in the future it will link a newly planned park with the St. Johann neighborhood. Dense and fine-grained development of the area was possible for the cooperative. The result was that both sides made concessions.

Simon Frommenwiler
Who finances this public space?

Klaus Hubmann
It is treated as a commons.
We proposed that we would build the street and the city would maintain it and carry out modernization at some point in the future. The sewer system would be installed by the canton and we would pay sewer installation fees, in the same way as when an area is newly developed.

Florian Hertweck
What I ask myself is: you have gone to mind-boggling lengths – both externally and internally – to promote this project. Has it paid off at all?

Klaus Hubmann
Building site A at Erlenmatt, next to our part of the area, has probably changed owners four times in the last 10 years. Millions in development funds have been invested in a number of different building projects. Ultimately something is emerging from which probably everybody has earned something, at least by selling something off. When drafting the ground lease contract for Erlenmatt Ost we took the plot area (which essentially corresponds to the building footprint) multiplied by the current estimated price of the land as the basis for calculating the annual ground lease fee subject to a moderate long-term interest rate. This is the formula for calculating the interest on ground leases in Erlenmatt Ost. And where we did that, the average land value was 1,300 Swiss francs and five years later 2,600 Swiss francs. If we wanted to sell we would definitely make a big profit. And this is why we said we wanted to preserve the land. We don't have to pay out this profit or invest in exaggerated salaries, but want above all to make it possible for people to continue to have affordable living space and so we are holding onto the land. We don't have to make a profit simply because the land has developed in this way. If we wanted to trade in land, we would also achieve the same amount.

Florian Hertweck
How many years does the ground lease run?

Klaus Hubmann
Ground lease contracts run for a maximum of 100 years, in the case of Erlenmatt Ost with extension options of 50 years plus 30 plus 20 years. In the case of Lysbüchel Süd we simply adopted the cooperative standard contract that the canton uses for 600 properties and adapted by adding a few provisions, particularly related to sustainability. It was important to us to include a restriction on the right of

preemption for selling buildings based on a ground lease contract, so that a cooperative could not sell its holdings at a high price and divide the profits up among themselves. Legally, however, this is only valid for 25 years, so that it does not extend over the entire ground lease term of 100 years. What's also important to us – and we copied this from Zurich – was to offer the residents affordable rents: the cost-based rent model. This prevents a cooperative from demanding high rents that can be applied for other purposes, and ensures that rents simply remain affordable. As a result, all commercial investor-developers are automatically excluded. We wanted the buildings to remain in the hands of their users. Those are the main differences from the usual ground lease contracts.

Tanja Herdt

What I find most interesting about the projects is the issue of the size of the plots of land. How big should these be in the context of a ground lease approach? In the Lysbüchel project they tended to be at the lower end, oriented toward the smallest plot size. It would be interesting for future projects to find out a bit more about the relationship between the sizes of plots, social diversity, and variety of use. Perhaps both large and small plots could be combined in other projects while still generating a certain degree of diversity. That is a question for researchers.

Klaus Hubmann

From the point of view of urban planning, the small plots of land in Lysbüchel are incompatible with sustainability. Diversity is an argument for smaller scale, but sustainability is not. Building smaller buildings is less efficient and less sustainable than building large structures in a single building process. We simply said, «Build what you want.» Some are building in a small format, others involve four families sharing the building. And we made sure that this didn't just involve 25- to 35-year-old architect couples who wanted to build their own house. There are «only» four of those. Thus, the awarding of contracts to 11 external groups and three projects of our own has led to a varied structure.

Tanja Herdt

What I find so interesting about the Lysbüchel project is that, based only on planning measures and the way contracts were awarded, a diverse neighborhood was promoted. Of course, the foundation's tendering process allows it to influence the mixture of those involved. However, when architects design a mixture of uses, doing so usually has a homogenizing effect. As far as the misgivings about planning are concerned, I feel Basel has enough capable architects to be able to build 14 buildings that are contextually linked in some way.

Simon Frommenwiler

That's also a question of the procedure. Is there some kind of coordination or workshop procedure where one person can see what the others are doing?

Klaus Hubmann

In Erlenmatt Ost we had overall coordination in the sense of construction logistics; it would not have been possible in any other way. In the case of the Lysbüchel area, we believed that coordination was necessary. People joined an informal group. The communities set up a *jour fixe* that meets every two months. The initiative did not come from us. Of course, we offered support where it was necessary. But we were merely participants through our own construction projects; we were neither the organizer nor a mediator. At these meetings core topics were discussed, such as «Shouldn't we have common construction logistics?» Then we said, «We're prepared to join in, but we're not willing to organize it. You'll have to get together and then we can ensure that everyone pays a fair share.»

Tanja Herdt

This also applied to the way in which we shaped the commons. The idea was not to leave shared areas untouched but to leave their design up to the community. Of course, this requires a certain sense of responsibility and commitment on the part of the people involved, who, after all, are not required to take on this task. Organizing the *jour fixe* meetings is based on a key principle of Swiss culture: people get together and sort things out together.

Klaus Hubmann

At the last *jour fixe* they discussed planting flowers in the courtyard and

said, «What do we want as the least common denominator?» It wasn't the Stiftung Habitat that then specified this or that kind of plant. Instead, it was the residents who agreed on it together. That was our goal, that future residents sit down together, discuss the situation and work out joint solutions. If I were to take stock now, I would have to say that it is working very well. I'm very pleased. We haven't had a single point yet where anyone thought that it basically doesn't work. No one has been able to show that our requirements cannot be met. And everything to do with the law has now been sorted out.

Florian Hertweck

Can we now speak of a Swiss model or even of a Basel-based model of ground lease law? After all, it is remarkable that in Basel, through popular vote, it has been decided that publicly owned land can no longer be sold. And it's unlikely that any other city has so many active foundations that are carrying out the socially oriented urban development for which city politicians and administration are actually responsible.

Simon Frommenwiler

The initiative was a reaction to what has happened in Basel in recent years. The city had sold several central properties and placed them on the free market.

Klaus Hubmann

That was what really set off the land initiative, because we were all annoyed that Novartis had bought and expropriated the Hüningerstrasse, that the canton had sold Münsterplatz 2, and that it had sold the Markthalle – several instances of choice pieces of land and real estate being sold off. At the same time, there was a change in the Pension Fund Investment Act in 2012 according to which valuations of pension fund landholdings, which are subject to similar investment pressure as real estate funds, are calculated in the same way in ground lease law as in property law. In this way, ground lease law was given new significance, which makes it even more effective as an instrument. The mood had thus shifted to the opinion that the canton should only allow property to be used based on ground leases. Over several years this led to the initiative being held in 2016, with 67 percent voting in favor of it. People have come to grasp that it isn't good for the community of Basel if the public sector sells off its land.

Florian Hertweck
Does the canton have much reserve land?

Klaus Hubmann
It depends on how you calculate it. The canton owns about 27 percent of its surface area directly as building land. Now add the streets, and when you also add all non-building land it comes to about 40 percent.

Simon Frommenwiler
The canton also owns building land outside its own borders, even outside Switzerland.

Klaus Hubmann
But it's allowed to sell that.

Everyone laughs

Florian Hertweck
The referendum has now forbidden the canton to sell its public land. But does that also mean that it has to develop it with affordable housing or at least see to it that leaseholders build enough affordable housing?

Klaus Hubmann
The shortage of affordable housing is a major issue here. The pressure on the canton as the main landowner has now become a political issue, with regard to what it does with its financial assets – not its administrative assets. With the initiative we had intended to start by securing the land in public ownership, and not addressing the question of what is to be done with it until a later stage. If we had combined the two, we would have been unsuccessful. Now there is a new initiative with the goal of rezoning commercial and industrial land into residential land with 50 percent not-for-profit housing, genuinely guaranteeing participatory decision-making, and operating the area with a verifiable net-zero carbon footprint. Admittedly, this has less to do with land owned by the canton, but it will still have some kind of effect on the canton. With the initiative we want to break out of the price spiral. We need more players on the market who demand less money for housing, because they extract fewer profits from it. If this works right, it will exert

pressure on real estate prices, in other words on land prices.

Florian Hertweck

This would mean that more money would flow into more productive areas, which would make economic sense.

Tanja Herdt

That's right. Investments in housing are frozen capital that is not available for more productive purposes for long periods of time.

Florian Hertweck

Isn't it a fiasco when foundations take over the functions of the public authorities? And isn't it also problematic when foundations accumulate so much land?

Klaus Hubmann

It's true that the Stiftung Habitat is present for now because we are developing new projects. But as land-owners we continue to be of minor significance from the point of view of how much land we own: at Erlenmatt Ost it is 22,000 square meters, at Lysbüchel Süd 12,000 square meters. By comparison, the Klybeck area in Basel, which has just been sold, encompasses 300,000 square meters. It is true that the public purse is acquiring large areas, but this doesn't often happen the way it did with the Klybeck area. Precisely because of the economic power of major real estate funds, we have to find other ways to proceed. In view of the unequal financial resources that are available, otherwise we scarcely stand

a chance. As already mentioned, a new initiative is being started that will have consequences for the areas being converted to residential property: When a commercial and industrial area is released for housing construction, at least 50 percent of the usable area of each *Bebauungsplan* must be run as not-for-profit housing. A law like that gives the city leverage regarding large-scale investment projects, so that not all building projects are focused solely on achieving profits. This would decisively affect the entire Klybeck area, for one! I am looking forward to it, and hope that we will continue to make good progress with this initiative.

Lysbüchel Süd, Basel.
A New Piece of the City as
a Socioeconomic Experiment

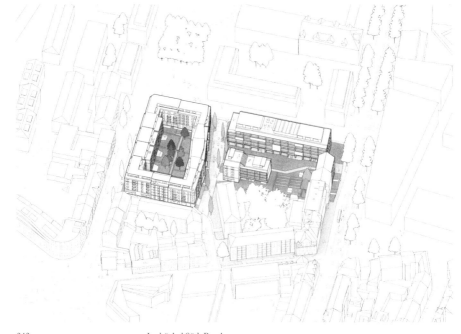

As one of around 850 foundations in the city of Basel, the Stiftung Habitat has dedicated itself to the promotion of affordable housing. It does so by pursuing a clear approach that places the needs of urban residents at the center of their development plans.

When the foundation purchased the 12,400 square meter industrial site Lysbüchel Süd in Basel in 2013, the focus was not only on securing the area for the provision of urban housing but also on developing a socially diverse and ecologically sustainable district.

Questions about the urban qualities of the new district were thus at the heart of the urban planning concept:[1] What are the characteristics of a good neighborhood? How does a lively district emerge with a socially diverse population, good environmental conditions, and attractive public spaces? And how can these qualities be realized so that the district remains affordable for the majority of the population?

For this reason, the urban planning design of the district dispensed with the usual instruments used in site development plans. Instead, it worked with relatively small subdivisions and urban planning typologies that generated the highest possible building density. The site was divided into 15 plots, which were handed over by the foundation as ground leases and developed by small investors in accordance with the existing building code. This guaranteed a wide variety of uses and high-quality urban architecture in the overall concept.

While the individual ground lease-holders were granted free rein over the development of their projects, the foundation secured (via the instrument of the ground-lease agreement) the central objectives of the district's development – such as compliance with criteria of sustainable construction and energy supply, the stipulated cost rent, and the adherence to a maximum floor area per person.

This generic city planning approach produces an urban design scheme that interprets the area not as a self-contained development, but as an expansion of the St. Jakob district built in the early twentieth century. The high density (floor-space index: 2.8) thus contributes to the district's attractiveness in two ways. It ensures living space for more than 500 inhabitants while also producing a high density of use and events.

To realize these goals, the creation of a commons plays a key role in the urban planning concept. It not only serves as a shared free space that offers the possibility for neighborly interaction but also creates a pedestrian and bicycle connection to the St. Jakob district and the future park in the newly emerging Volta-Nord district. The commons also assumes a planning function, without which the design's diversity and density could not have been achieved. By drawing new street lines, it succeeds in integrating the site into the existing structure of the district and provides access to all plots. As a result, the individual plots can be developed in parallel, reducing planning time and construction costs. This is a significant benefit for the realization of projects, especially for small ground lease-holders.

With this urban planning approach, four different building typologies are planned on the plots, enabling a broad spectrum of housing types. The closed building block typology will have five- to-seven–story townhouses, offering various models ranging from a residence for musicians all the way to multigenerational homes. The concrete skeleton of the former wine warehouse is to be converted by the foundation into a place for experimental forms of living and working. Compacted townhouse typologies in the courtyard help replicate the feeling of «living in the countryside.» Residents can also move into smaller apartments in the existing buildings on Elsässerstrasse, which have been designated historical monuments.

Depending on the house typology and location, the urban planning concept also offers different configurations for the ground floor. From living on the mezzanine above the corner shop and the bicycle repair shop in the former wine warehouse, to the two-story loft for office space and medical practices, the ground leaseholders can fill the various use concepts with contents. Since 2018, more than 100 individuals have organized cooperatives and associations to build on the site's first 11 plots. The first buildings will be ready for occupation in 2021.

The Lysbüchel Süd project deliberately weights objectives that promise to develop a diverse district more strongly than a homogeneous overall design. Ensuring homogeneity would certainly have been possible through a supplementary design statute, but would have required higher-level coordination and implementation, without creating any detectable added value for the foundation as regards the realization of its development goals.

However, it is already becoming apparent that the ground leaseholders have also recognized the benefit of coordinating their individual projects. In workshops they are coordinating their building plans and working together to draft shared design proposals for the public space. Now it is up to their involvement to make another contribution to a high-quality architectural design of this new piece of the city.

Tanja Herdt

1
Projekt Lysbüchel Süd,
Planning office: Metron
Raumentwicklung AG, Brugg;
Project Director: Dr. Tanja
Herdt; team: Josip Jerkovic,
Marc Knellwolf.

«No Substitute for Social Housing»

Florian Hertweck

On the European continent, ground leases are viewed as an instrument for social urban development. In Britain they are quite widespread, but there the leasehold is seldom granted by the public authorities, right?

Anthony Engi Meacock

The ground lease in Britain is not a social concept. It was used by the nobility in order to preserve their land. If you grow up in an aristocratic family in the seventeenth century, then you think that your dynasty will continue to exist indefinitely. And if you would like to secure this continuity, you quickly arrive at the solution of leasing the houses, while retaining ownership of the land, well knowing that they will revert to your family after 99 years. The ground lease is thus deeply anchored in the British psyche. It is an instrument that appears to sell some-thing without really doing so, because the land, at least, continues to remain your property.

Florian Hertweck

So what role does the public sector play in the issue of housing and land?

Anthony Engi Meacock

In recent years, British city adminis-trations have been encouraged to sell their land. According to estimates, the public reservoir of land has been reduced by half in the last 20 years.

Florian Hertweck

Did the municipalities sell their land in order to consolidate their budgets, or to finance special projects?

Anthony Engi Meacock

Sometimes it was also possible to finance large-scale projects, but above all the sales had to do with the conviction that the state sector should be reduced. The state, so it has been argued for decades, was not supposed to own significant assets – a position which I by no means share. In the framework of austerity policies, many local councils needed additional capital to balance their books. And since most of them actually were in debt, great pressure was exerted upon them to sell their land and housing property.

Florian Hertweck

Did this begin with Margaret Thatcher?

Anthony Engi Meacock

Yes, especially where public housing stock was concerned. Thatcher's politics was the start. Well into the 1980s there was a substantial social housing construction program in England. A considerable share of the housing stock was public property and, accordingly, affordable. Thatcher introduced the «right to buy.» That allowed all tenants of publicly owned housing to purchase their own homes at a preferential price. This did allow those who already belonged to the middle class, or were close to it, to take ownership of their homes. But it certainly did not help the poorest segments of the population, who relied most on public housing. Consequently, the poorest faced strongly reduced housing options. A truly perverse situation arose: while the buildings remained the property of the municipalities, the individual apartments became private property. Many of the apartments were no longer used by their owners themselves, but rented. What is more, subsequent governments expanded the right to purchase: now even the housing associations – by now largely privatized – were required to sell their apartments under the right to buy, with devastating consequences: the housing associations were forced to sell off their housing stock at below market rate, but there was no government investment to replace it. This was, in fact, a fundamental attack on the idea of affordable living space. This policy triggered major criticism, of course. It ultimately also explains why community land trusts (CLT) and cooperatives were greeted with growing interest. After the wave of privatization in Great Britain, they are the only models that were exempt from the right to buy.

Florian Hertweck

Can you explain what CLTs are in general, and what role they played for Granby Four Streets in Liverpool?

Anthony Engi Meacock

I believe the community land trust originally comes from the US. It was rural in origin and cooperative in principle. In Great Britain, the first CLTs were founded in order to provide for communal ownership of village shops and pubs – the type of things that were recognized as community assets.

Florian Hertweck

So what is the difference between this and the commons?

Anthony Engi Meacock

The primary difference is that the commons is owned by an entire community, but the CLT is owned by a group of people who are members, although membership is open to all. In principle, the CLT is like a fund, but without shares. In contrast to an entity with shareholders, the purpose is not to generate private profit. The members own the CLT jointly on the basis of trust – as implied in the name. Today, a primary aim of CLTs is to produce affordable living space. They are local organizations.

Florian Hertweck

Let us talk about Granby Four Streets. What was the situation in Liverpool like when you met with the residents for the first time?

Anthony Engi Meacock

I met the CLT in Liverpool for the first time in 2013. It is important to emphasize that Liverpool's population was shrinking until 2010. The population had peaked shortly before the financial crisis of 2008; it declined steadily thereafter. It rose again for the first time in 2010, but today it remains below half its peak.

British Prime Minister Margaret Thatcher in the Patterson family's apartment in Romford, near London, after Thatcher had presented them with a certificate from the Greater London Council as the 12,000th purchasers of an apartment under her right-to-buy policy.

«No Substitute for Social Housing» / Interview

This demographic depletion had the consequence of a huge vacancy rate. Both the city administration and the municipal government agreed on a program to purchase the empty, boarded-up townhouses, raze them, and replace them with new, lower-density buildings. Many of these new buildings were very low in quality, and they did not function well in many respects. The situation deteriorated further when the city administration ran out of money and was not even able to develop new buildings. All over the city you saw empty, boarded-up buildings. Granby Four Streets took its name from the last four streets of Victorian houses that survived in a district that used to be full of townhouses. For various reasons, there was a handful of residents who initially were not able or willing to move; for example, some did not want to sell because the price they were offered was so low that they could not get anything for it elsewhere. After years of campaigning, they founded the CLT because they found themselves bound to their neighborhood without any viable alternatives.

Florian Hertweck

Are all residents of Granby Four Streets members of the CLT?

Anthony Engi Meacock

A lot of them are. The structure of the CLT is quite fluid. It creates a basis of trust that makes it impossible for the land to be sold at a later date. What is interesting about the CLT is that it differentiates between individual property and community property. An individual member cannot benefit from a potential appreciation in value. Each member gets out only what they originally paid in. It is not an investment. Only people who believe in the community can participate.

Florian Hertweck

As a result, any speculation is precluded, even passive speculation by owner-occupiers?

Anthony Engi Meacock

That's precisely the point. The CLT emphasizes the community spirit much more than private property, and does so in the context of a society in which private property rights are quite well protected by law.

Florian Hertweck

Both components are anchored in the German constitution, the protection of private property as well as its social responsibility. Property entails obligations, as stated in the German Basic Law. Yet in fact, Germany's political history has taken private property into account much more strongly than communal interests, especially since the 1980s. Addressing the question of land thus means once again strengthening the social dimension of property. This is why we are so interested in your story about Liverpool, because the residents took charge of their own fates and familiarized themselves with complex economic processes, ultimately to own communal property. In a certain sense they became experts in order to favor a communal legal instrument over individual property.

Anthony Engi Meacock

In Liverpool we work with a group of amazing people, who come from a milieu that was always politically active and fairly left-oriented. Granby has always been multicultural and progressive; its vicinity to the harbor played a considerable role in its identity. At the same time, it was also a historical necessity – considering the negative development of the district – to try out alternative models. The previous attempts had not worked, and the city administration had a stock of housing whose protection and maintenance cost a great deal of money.

The CLT was also a reaction to the hopelessness of the city administration, which had apparently given up on the district. Streetlights were broken, there was no more trash pickup, public spaces were no longer cared for or maintained. The city administration was consciously letting the area deteriorate in order to rid itself of its responsibility.

Until the remaining residents began taking care of quite elementary things themselves: painting buildings, planting trees, and so on – things that are not really significant for urban development, but which created a consciousness here for community property. These actions then evolved into a CLT as a formal structure, because a community spirit had emerged about which the people were proud.

Florian Hertweck

At some stage, though, they felt they needed architects.

Anthony Engi Meacock

Yes, that's when we came into the picture. Our approach was to initially spend a significant amount of time listening to the CLT. In the process, a number of ideas and wishes were formulated which we then developed into spatial proposals. We worked with them to create a document on the basis of which they could negotiate with the city administration. What we proposed was, in a certain way, a gradual process of repair. Rather than coming in here to tear everything down and start over from nothing, we endeavored to identify a range of possible actions on site. And then, over the course of time, to review these possibilities, to change things gradually, and develop them further.

Florian Hertweck

A constant process that does not end with just handing over the keys.

Anthony Engi Meacock

I should mention that we are not the only group of actors working in this process. There are many people doing truly interesting projects. I am completely convinced that the CLT has changed the tone of conversations so that such projects have become possible. Yet, I also think that we should be realistic in estimating the scope of this project.

Florian Hertweck

You mean the extent to which it can be applied on a larger scale?

Anthony Engi Meacock

I am not sure whether the CLT model can be scaled. It obviously depends a great deal on individual persons and their individual skills. I also think that there is no substitute for proper government funding of social housing. I do not believe that thousands of these CLTs will suddenly appear and solve the housing problem without significant inward investment. Most CLTs perform amazing work, but on their own the model is not the fundamental solution I would imagine.

Florian Hertweck

And what, in your view, is the solution in Great Britain?

Anthony Engi Meacock

Large-scale, state-financed social housing. Of course, CLTs can be part of this mix, but there are certain restrictions regarding the scope in which the CLT model can operate. Nevertheless, I believe that we need projects like Granby Four Streets to show that alternatives are actually possible. That is why CLTs, no matter how small, are so valuable.

Granby Four Streets, Liverpool since 2012

While Ex-Rotaprint was able to assert itself in a real estate market that was taking off, the story of Granby Four Streets emerged from a context of property contraction. Originally, Granby Street was the high street of the densely populated, inner-city area of Toxteth in Liverpool, which was once settled by dockworkers, domestic servants and craftsmen in Victorian townhouses. It is home to the oldest continuous African community in England. The structural changes of the 1970s brought high unemployment, poverty, and a lack of prospects to the area, along with a general atmosphere of hopelessness. On July 4, 1981 riots broke out, leaving destroyed businesses and burned-out cars in their wake. In the 1980s, the densely populated area of Toxteth lost a third of its population. Only a few of the 80 businesses originally located on Granby Street remained. After the Housing Act introduced by the Thatcher government in 1988, housing associations focused ever more on new buildings, not least at Granby Triangle. Even more people moved away, leaving the area to ruin and decay. In this apocalyptic situation, the city bought the empty buildings, intending not to conduct the necessary renovations but to raze the buildings, street by street. The city's attempt to expropriate the buildings by force foundered in the face of resistance from the residents, who took their case to court and won. According to one resident, «all of Granby Street was boarded up, the streets were filthy.

Living in that place was physically degrading.»[1]

After winning the 2002 election, Labour launched the Housing Market Renewal Initiative, a program that subsidized the demolition, restoration, and new construction of housing. The goal was to upgrade central areas in intrinsically attractive locations like Granby Triangle. Although the residents negotiated with the city administration and proposed alternatives to demolition, the city continued tearing down the entire area, street by street, down to the final four streets. When politics withdrew from urban development programs after the Conservative-Liberal coalition took power after the 2010 election, the residents of Granby Four Streets seized their opportunity. They went on the offensive to protect their homes, by painting the remaining houses, planting trees and shrubs, removing debris, and organizing markets. The street was occupied and «shared with others as a democratic space.»[2] In 2012, with the support of a social investor, they founded a Community Land Trust.[3] The city administration, which had purchased nearly all of the real estate in the area with the intention of selling it to a developer, acquiesced to the residents' demands: The value of the buildings was set to zero and their ownership transferred to the CLT for one pound. The residents worked with the architectural collective Assemble to develop intermediate uses for the dilapidated buildings. The residents' initiative also opened up a market for cooperatives and housing associations, which are now participating in the restoration of 180 houses. Most of the buildings owned by the CLT are rented, with several even offered for sale as «affordable housing» – at 80 percent of the market price. To prevent the houses from falling into the hands of speculators, the purchase contracts stipulate that the resale price may not increase at a rate any higher than the average local income. The CLT uses the income from home sales to finance further renovation projects; like the ExRotaprint project, the money is to remain in local circulation to the greatest extent possible.

The story of Granby Four Streets is reminiscent of the «restorational squatting» that took place in West Berlin in the 1970s and 1980s, when opposition to wholesale redevelopment arose in the alternative scene and prompted residents to repair their deteriorating buildings themselves, ultimately leading to the institutionalization of the process in the «IBA-Altbau.» In the case of the Granby Four Streets project, the communally organized society of residents was able to win control over the real property as well as the buildings. In both cases – the ExRotaprint site and Granby Four Streets – the activists have become experts (in organizing associations and nonprofit societies, in the renovation of buildings, in holding various events). Yet both stories make clear that, in the face of political resistance, support is required, from foundations or investors who do not merely target the highest possible profits.

Florian Hertweck

Conversion of the ruins of
a house in Granby Four
Streets into an indoor garden.
Architects: Assemble,
London

1
Martina Groß, «Auferstanden.
Die Granby Four Streets
in Liverpool,» Deutschland-
funk 2016, manuscript,
p. 16, https://www.
deutschlandfunkkultur.de/
granby-four-streets-
in-liverpool-vier-strassen-
werden-zum.3720.de.html?
dram:article_id=370771.
2
Ibid., p. 18.
3
In England there are
170 Community Land Trusts
(CLTs). The idea originally
came from the US: Founding
a CLT entailed purchasing
farmland, which was then
rezoned as building land and
thus increased so much in
value that banks granted
credit for house construction.
CLTs are becoming ever more
active in urban areas as well.

Stefan Rettich
Building a Nation.
The Importance of Public Housing for Singaporean Unity

«Change, change, change!» – With this emphatic slogan in his inaugural address, Lee Kuan Yew, the founder and first prime minister of the small island state of Singapore, decreed a rapid course of modernization that continues even today. This politically initiated project of permanent transformation initially had the goal of bringing peace to a divided, multiethnic society. To achieve this goal, Lee and his People's Action Party (PAP), which continues to rule autonomously today, used social housing construction as a central key for the formation of a national identity. Singapore's social prosperity is thus also manifested in a continual improvement of the standard of living.

Today, 80 percent of the 4.4 million Singaporeans[1] live in homes built by the Housing & Development Board (HDB), the statutory board responsible for public housing. Ninety percent of them even own their own homes, which are allocated via state leasing contracts for a term of 99 years. This shows how closely the links between the city-state and its citizens are forged. Yet it also demonstrates how an authoritarian government, which runs the state according to the principles of «corporate socialism,» can deploy humanist instruments like social housing construction for state control and to preserve its power. This practice has occasionally led to violent unrest, especially in the initial phase.

Arrival City
This history of Singapore is a history of immigration: people from the south of China, from Malaysia and India moved into the relatively young harbor city that was founded in 1819 and has increasingly prospered ever since. Under British colonial rule, which was established in 1867 and lasted until 1963, the city was separated into ethnic districts. The migrant population lived in informal urban *kampongs,* villages arranged in a ring around the city center. Upon independence, an independent nation based on the model of Western national states was to emerge, which was unified in its culture, territory, and political administration – considering the complex immigration history, quite a difficult undertaking. The new political elites saw a solution in the resolute destruction of the migrant-based city structures. They based their

1
Singapore has a total
of 5.6 million inhabitants,
1.2 m of whom are guest
workers and foreigners.

Stefan Rettich / Building a Nation

Pinnacle@Duxton:
Next-generation housing
with Sky Gardens, 2009

Stefan Rettich / Building a Nation

program on a model that had already been introduced in the late 1940s by the British colonial government and its urban development authority, the Singapore Improvement Trust (SIT): the British «new town.» In the subsequent period, no stone was left unturned. Today, Singapore is composed of 23 loosely connected Modernist new towns and three estates, which are linked with each other by a dense network of highways. The last *kampong* was approved for demolition in 2008, but for three decades now, the original new towns have also been subject to a trans-formation process, governed by the inherent principle of a radical *tabula rasa* with the goal of progressive concentration.

From the Earth into the Sky

The British colonial government had already undertaken a number of interventions in order to improve the infra-structure and hygienic conditions in the city. Geographer Brenda Yeoh demonstrated how social conflicts in colonial Singapore between the urban elites and the sub-ordinated classes repeatedly erupted around issues of housing: the «Asian housing problem.»[2] Poor sanitation, diseases, and a use of verandas and semipublic spaces regarded as «problematic» by the elites offered repeated occasions for the city administration and the SIT to initiate urban planning and settlement projects in order to take control of such spaces in entire districts. Paving the way for these political interventions was the public image of the *kampong* as a hotbed of disease, filth, and backward-ness – as the opposite of civilization and cleanliness.[3] The 1947 Housing Report refers to this background when it proposes: «The only solution to this problem is demolition and rehousing.»[4] On this foundation, the SIT began to erect large-scale housing complexes based on the model of British «new towns.» After independence and the victory of the PAP in 1959, the successor to the SIT was founded, the Housing & Development Board (HDB), which has been responsible ever since for the planning, regulation, and supervision of public housing construction.

The fire that destroyed the kampong Bukit Ho Swee in May 1961, which brought the resettlement of many inhabitants to the new housing built by the HDB, is now

2
Brenda S.A. Yeoh, *Contested Space in Colonial Singapore. Power Relations in the Urban Built Environment,* Singapore 2003.
3
Lo Hah Seng, *Black Areas. The Urban Kampongs and Power Relations in Post-War Singapore Historiography,* Working Paper, No. 137/2006, Murdoch University, Perth.
4
Singapore Housing Report 1947, Singapore 1947, p. 6.

Stefan Rettich / Building a Nation

considered by researchers to have launched the era of public social housing construction in Singapore.

The state's decision to resettle the population in the highly concentrated high-rise complexes of the new towns went hand in hand with a destruction of the local communities and reliable neighborhood relationships that had emerged back under British colonial rule. Thus, the leap from the urban *kampong* into the new high-rises of Queenstown, from the «earth to the sky,» was ambivalent: the amenities of sanitary facilities, modern installations, and improved infrastructure were offset by the experience of isolation and anonymity. The Forfar House in Queenstown, one of the modern icons of this new town, gained sad notoriety for the many suicides committed there.[5]

Housing a Nation

The HDB adapted and refined the public housing construction program, which was notably characterized by the integration of institutional mechanisms and specific urban planning strategies. The continual adjustment of the overall strategy and its successes are documented in a series of reports still issued today. «Housing a Nation» was the title of one of the first reports, which was still entirely focused on propagating the necessity of mass housing construction. It is striking that the program relied from the very outset on promoting residential property in order to mix the ethnically segregated society and forge a connection among the residents of the newly populated buildings. The strategy of the Home Ownership Scheme launched in 1964 was initially highly unpopular, however, and was not able to gain acceptance until the introduction of the Central Provident Fund (CPF). The CPF, the origins of which can be traced back to the pension fund of the colonial period, combines all of the country's social security systems. All employees were initially required to pay 20 percent of their income into the social fund. In 1968 the PAP expanded the taxes to enable employees to aspire to and purchase residential property. This transformed the CPF into a state-mandated building loan contract, and helped lower the costs for the public housing construction program to under 3 percent of the state budget. Today employees pay taxes amounting to 40 percent of gross

5
Calvin Low, *10-Stories.
Queenstown through the
Years,* Singapore 2007.

wages; however, these contributions are reduced steadily down to 10 percent at retirement age. In addition to accounts for pensions and disease prevention, the «ordinary account» is also a kind of savings account. The state works with this money and pays interest on the deposits (currently at a rate of 3.5 percent), with which citizens can finance costs for education, or, naturally, to purchase a public or private apartment. The CPF thus secures a continuous cash flow for public housing construction, which is not public housing construction in the strict sense, but merely uses the social security system as interim financing and to encourage private residential property. «My main concern was to give every citizen a share of the land and their own future. I wanted a kind of society of homeowners,» founding father Lee Kuan Yew relates in his memoirs.[6]

The second pillar is the HDB, which is responsible for the construction, marketing, and maintenance of residential real estate, and currently manages one million housing units, 90 percent of which are the individual property of citizens.[7] It must be kept in mind that the land remains public property, with the real estate allocated for 99 years on the basis of a lease agreement. After this term it is returned to the state, which has the express intention of granting each generation the same chances and right to self-determined housing. During the period of the lease the HDB apartments can even be resold – after a retention period, for instance, in order to purchase a larger apartment or an apartment on the private market. However, the deal is closed by the HDB, meaning that the state acts as interim owner, regulates the prices and decides on the reallocation.

The fact that the HDB was able to erect so many housing units on state land is anything but trivial, for in 1949, while Singapore was still British-ruled, only 31 percent of the land was public; through continuous purchases, this percentage rose to 90 by 2002. The introduction of a Land Acquisition Act in 1966, which made comprehensive expropriation of land possible at the current market value, greatly facilitated this development. Many public author- ities were able to benefit from this law, including the HDB and its counterpart for industrial development, Jurong

6
Lee Kuan Yew, *From Third World to First, Singapore and the Asian Economic Boom*, New York, 2011, p. 95, cited here in: Andrew Purves, «Die Modelle Hong Kong und Singapore – Staatliche Landverpachtung statt Verkauf,» in: Brigitta Gerber, Ulrich Kriese (eds.), *Boden behalten – Stadt gestalten*, Zurich 2019, p. 99.
7
In 2003 the construction company of the HDB was outsourced; since 2005 it has been called Surbana Jurong. [online] https://surbanajurong.com/our-history.

Stefan Rettich / Building a Nation

Town Cooperation (JTC).[8] The law was based on Lee Kuan Yew's conviction that the private sector was not entitled to unearned profits generated by public investments: «I saw no reason why private landowners should profit from a rise in land values that had been achieved through economic development and the infrastructure financed with public funds.»[9] In order to manage Singapore's integrated urban development beyond the individual new towns, in 1974 the Urban Redevelopment Agency (URA) was ultimately founded, with the goal of systematic overall development of the city-state.

Ethnic Integration Policy

In 1989 the housing construction program was expanded by the Ethnic Integration Policy (EIP), with which the government reacted to the ethnic conflicts that still simmered beneath the surface. Singapore's 5.6 million inhabitants (1.2 million of them guest workers and foreigners) belong to various ethnic groups: Chinese (76.8 percent), Malays (13.8 percent), Indians (7.9 percent), and other Southeast Asian groups belonging to various religions; the majority is Buddhist, but there are also Muslims, Taoists, Hindus, and Christians. The EIP introduced a quota that regulates the ethnic composition of every single housing block according to the share of the population as a whole. Even today, this quota determines to whom HDB housing is made available, and has led to thorough mixing of neighborhoods, all the way down to each individual building. In the foyer of HDB headquarters – a gigantic, impressive administrative complex – the newly developed housing complexes are marketed. Above the models monitors are suspended, displaying in real time how many apartments are available in the various complexes for each of the ethnic groups. Multiethnic families are also proudly featured in the HDB's brochures and promotional films; here, the family is considered to be the basis of a harmonious society purged of conflict.

Upgrading and the SERS Program

The poor structures of the early new towns were the trigger for an Upgrading Program in 1993, intended to renew the stock of buildings. A short time later it was replaced by the

8
Purves 2019 (see note 6), p. 96.
9
Quoted here in ibid.

Stefan Rettich / Building a Nation

Selective En bloc Redevelopment Scheme (SERS), which aimed to completely restructure neighborhoods: entire city districts were resettled, torn down, and rebuilt. Since the apartments were privately owned, a participatory process was introduced, with levels extending from the direct neighborhood all the way into parliament.

This process provided the opportunity for all residents to comment on and evaluate the measures planned by the URA, HDB, and the parliament, and thus to contribute to the new legislation pertaining to the new towns. The higher standard of the new housing, which increased its value, gave the residents a major incentive to participate. Whether this compensates for the loss of their familiar neighborhood remains an open question. Statistics, at least, published in the annual reports that the HDB has issued since its founding, indicate that satisfaction with housing continues to remain high. These comprehensive studies – in addition to the housing programs, and financing through the CPF – thus constitute the third pillar of this social-technological project that conceives of society as completely controllable and plannable.

From Mass Housing to Home of Choice

The signs of the times point to individualization, in Singapore as well. Just as in Western societies, the promise of welfare oriented to standardization and mass consumption has been eroding for quite some time. The changed rhetoric in the exhibition on the 2008 Master Plan is one indication – here the talk is no longer of «mass housing» but of a «home of choice.» Back in the 1990s a new program was launched to offer apartments in privately developed «condominiums,» with a higher housing standard, more individual floor plans, their own swimming pools, leisure and sport facilities, and amenities that worked well. Today, the housing projects of the HDB are oriented to these standards. Planning, too, is generally outsourced to private architecture firms. This shift can be seen in the urban architecture, in the further concentration of the districts: today, new housing blocks are 40 to 60, sometimes even 80, stories tall. While the new towns were small (satellite) cities, these new developments are «vertical towns.» With their high-rise units connected to each other by four

Stefan Rettich / Building a Nation

to eight bridges, they bring to mind the urban visions of the Metabolists. Every twentieth story or so is left completely free, full of plants like the «sky garden» on the roof, and is intended to replace the communal spaces previously located on the ground floor. The background of this trend is, above all, the shortage of space in the island state, which cannot be compensated for even despite gigantic land reclamation projects – which tie up a great deal of resources. For the same reason, land is granted to private entities only in the form of a ground lease. The advantages that this offers, aside from the rental payments, became apparent in the global financial crisis, which hit especially hard in Singapore, as a banking location with large-scale urban planning development projects like Marina Bay. Since the state owned all of the real estate, including spaces that had not yet been developed, land could be taken off the market to artificially cut supply in order to stabilize the situation.

Singapore as a Model?

The comprehensive social engineering that the city-state uses to implement its housing and land policy, and also to preserve its power in a democracy with a glaring authoritarian and illiberal streak, is alarming from the Western perspective, and cannot serve as a management model. Yet there are several fundamental aspects worth considering. For instance, it appears to make sense to separate land from its use and to allocate its value added to the state and its public interests. Similarly, it is worth discussing whether the right to housing, connected with the right to acquire residential property, should be integrated into social security systems. Yet this would entail unpopular tax hikes. The current situation in Germany, however, offers a unique opportunity to redirect an already existing tax. The «solidarity surcharge,» originally introduced to finance the costs of German reunification, brought in tax revenue of 17.95 billion euros in 2017. In the face of the current housing crisis, many citizens would certainly agree to continuing levying this surcharge if the funds were used to build housing, which they would have the right to purchase at a discount.

The text is based on an article by Regina Bittner, Wilfried Hackenbroich, and Stefan Rettich, which appeared in *ARCH+*, No. 203/2011, and summarizes the international studies on the new towns of the postwar modern era in the framework of the CIAM urbanism graduate program run by the Bauhaus Dessau Foundation. The research on the Singapore case study was performed by Roberta Barone, Onur Ekmekci, Karen Henrique, Horst Nickels, Karin Schwambach, and Meltem Sentür.

«A Form of Ultra-State Capitalism that Draws Its Income from Land Commercialization»

Interview with Françoise Ged (Observatoire de Chine, Paris) and land-law expert Miguel Elosua by Florian Hertweck on land policy in China

Florian Hertweck

Does China differentiate between land in the city and land in the country-side?

Miguel Elosua

Yes; generally, urban land belongs to the state, while rural land belongs to the collective.

Florian Hertweck

The collective means the communities?

Miguel Elosua

No, this is a concept that was established along with the collectiv-ization of the means of production after the Communist Party (CP) took power. The collective is a body that represents farmers. Accordingly, one could say that the agricultural lands on the periphery of the cities belong to the farmers. But the farmers are represented by the collective, which is recommended by a committee in every village. The law prescribes that these committees be democratically elected by the villagers, but in truth they are controlled by the CP. In reality, therefore, the members of the party decide how to deal with the land.

Florian Hertweck

Let us first talk about the cities. You already stated that urban land is nationalized.

Françoise Ged

The definition of the vocabulary helps to understand the complexity of Chinese cities according to their administrative definition and hierarchy. Since the reforms of the 1980s, land and real estate speculation has been a driver for economic development. «Urbanizing» a rural place is sometimes merely a way to give its population urban status: this place is transformed into an «urban area»; that means its residents can obtain the envied urban *hukou* (residence card). So the administrative boundaries are often subject to change.

Florian Hertweck

What happens then with the new urban land?

Miguel Elosua

It is expropriated. Some of this land is agricultural, some of it is building land. The state prefers to expropriate agricultural land, because the amount of compensation due is much lower. Up until 1982 this process was not called expropriation but rather «prevention of the right to land use.» The land was nationalized, so to speak, but agricultural land was acknowledged to be the property of the collective. There was no desire to start a fight with the farmers over an issue that was at the very heart of their support of the Communist Party before coming to power. It should be stressed that in 1978 China was eminently rural, with 82 percent of its population living in rural areas. In 2004 the constitution was changed. Private property was recognized for the first time. Since then the Chinese have spoken of expropriation and compensation. But the compensations are usually quite low, especially in the periphery where rural land is converted to urban land, and vary widely from one region to the next. The local governments set the level of compensation payments. This creates many problems. I have just returned from Shanghai, where a developer from the city administration was tasked with setting and disbursing compensation payments and tearing down existing buildings in order to develop his project. There are some residents who do not want to relocate, usually because they are not fully satisfied with the compensation offered. But there has been a positive evolution through time, especially in cases of relocating urban residents of old neighborhoods.

Florian Hertweck

Because the compensation is so low and is paid to the collective, while at the same time the land is nationalized? Does this mean the farmer gets nothing?

Miguel Elosua

Some benefit from the situation because they have personal relationships that allow them to negotiate. And one must not forget that as soon as rural residents officially become urban residents, they receive access to the health care system, to good hospitals and schools, and in some cases even to public housing. However, farmers want to maximize value, and

value these urban benefits only when they are available in big cities such as Shanghai, where an urban residence permit is very hard to get and the health system has a good reputation and is highly regarded.

Françoise Ged

We could imagine the whole process as a business. The status of the land is usually changed because a half-public, half-private developer wants to build there. The local authorities grant the developer development rights to properties that were previously nationalized, via a call for tender or in the framework of an auction. The building rights are temporally restricted, depending on the use: to 70 years for housing, to 50 years for industrial use, to 30 for trade and commerce. In China, the distinction between land and what is built on land, as well as the rights associated with land, have a long tradition; even the Jesuits left writings on this subject.

Miguel Elosua

When the CP decided in 1978 to open China up to the principle of a free market, there was no intention of privatizing land, which was to remain the property of the state. Instead, the state granted rights to build privately owned buildings on land for a certain period. Up until the real rights law of 2007 there were many voices raised against the privatization of use rights, because it ran counter to social justice.

Françoise Ged

The decisive question is not to whom

An almost entirely demolished
quarter of Zhengzhou's old
town. According to the 2010
census, of the city's 12 million
inhabitants, four million live
in newly built neighborhoods.

land belongs, but who receives access to its use. The use rights are granted to developers who build infrastructure (roads, networks) and then commercialize land. They build large apartments, which are rapidly increasing in value against a backdrop of rapid economic growth. In this period of strong growth, home buyers, through the very acquisition of an apartment, climb in the social hierarchy. Access to property has been a form of «social elevator.» On the other hand, the rent of land allows large-scale infrastructure projects to be realized. Thus one could argue that it is a win-win process. Where the urban administration is good, everything does work out well for everyone. But if it is not well managed, which is frequently the case, then there are few facilities and infrastructure for residents.

Florian Hertweck

Because the rent of land is not distributed over years?

Miguel Elosua

Exactly. Whoever acquires the use rights immediately transfers the entire sum of use fees as a lump sum. Thirty percent of it goes to the state, 70 percent to the city. This throws the gates wide open for corruption. And subsequently, hardly any taxes are collected. This is a major problem, because the local authorities depend on this income. On average, half of the city budget is generated with rent of land.

Florian Hertweck

This is a major difference from the European ground lease, which distrib-

utes interest over 99 years, through which the initial costs are much lower. This has the further consequence that rents can be calculated at lower rates, or young families are more likely to gain access to residential property. Such effects are unlikely, of course, where a lump-sum payment is due.

Françoise Ged

Local authorities use land rents to generate wealth through the marketing of housing, but also to build the transport infrastructure and network that the country was virtually devoid of in the early 1980s. This «developmental state,» whose political structure has changed little in recent decades, has encouraged growth through consumption and the personal enrichment of city dwellers, in the form of ultra-capitalism rather than «socialism.» Moreover, because mayors and representatives of local authorities are in office for relatively short periods of time, they are obliged to produce results during their term of office.

Florian Hertweck

So how are schools, kindergartens and social institutions built and repaired?

Françoise Ged

Chinese society may have grown a great deal in recent decades, but it has also aged considerably. In cities, the tendency is to close schools because there are ever fewer children. And in rural areas they are being merged into nearby medium-sized cities. Education, from primary school to university, as well as health care, is no longer a truly socialist system; instead, there are health and education «businesses.»

Miguel Elosua

Back then the state decided to nationalize land in order to leave the development of cities up to the private sector. Thus the state still had the opportunity to reappropriate these properties after 70 years at the latest. It is not yet decided how the fees for further use will be calculated. The first use contracts ran out in the past year. They had been granted not for 70 years, but for 20. A fierce controversy in the entire country ensued, because nobody really knew how much would be charged to renew the use contracts. Then the government decided that the fee should amount to one third the current market value. That would have meant that the user would have to pay something like 100 times the original fee. The users would probably not have had the funds to pay such amounts. Finally, the ministry responsible decided to allow the use rights to continue automatically for the time being, and not to charge any additional fees. This eliminated the problem in the short term, but without creating any real solution.

Florian Hertweck

Besides the amount of fees, are there other criteria stipulated in the use contracts?

Miguel Elosua

When the contracts were granted, the kind and degree of use was already prescribed by the land-use plan.

Florian Hertweck

And if the public needs change at a certain location after 30, 50, or 70 years, can the uses then be adjusted?

Françoise Ged

In China it is difficult to look so far ahead. It would be pointless to design a set of rules for such a long period of time, since it is highly probably that it would soon be obsolete. Therefore planning proceeds one step at a time.

Florian Hertweck

But you could say that, after 50 years, for instance, no industry will be needed in a certain location, but rather public housing.

Françoise Ged

Public housing construction is not bound to land use rights. There is a law that obligates cities to generate a certain amount of public housing. This housing is easy to recognize through its high density and its distance from public transport systems.

Miguel Elosua

It has since become the highest priority for every Chinese citizen to own their own residential property.
Large investors and small, everyone is focusing on the real estate market.

Françoise Ged

In China, the highest profits are made in the real estate market, considerably more than in other markets.

Florian Hertweck

In the general population, what is the

relationship between tenants and owners of residential property?

Miguel Elosua

There are very few tenants. Many people invest in real estate, but do not rent it. These apartments are simply empty. The rental income is not attractive for these investors. And the state does not levy any tax on empty apartment, in other words on strictly speculative objects.

Florian Hertweck

What explains the great imbalance between the extremely low bank costs and – depending on the location – the tremendously high sales prices for housing? Are they due only to the low labor costs and high demand?

Françoise Ged

As mentioned, the costs include infrastructure construction costs, taxes, and costs related to the management of the residential complex, as most have integrated property managers. They are not really «gated communities,» as they are often called, because these companies do not own the land, and the complexes do not operate as entities autonomous from the rest of the city. The housing estates are protected and monitored by private companies in charge of maintenance, in a country where monitoring is a common practice. Finally, these housing complexes may include playgrounds, sport fields, gardens, and community facilities for festivities, all of which contribute to their status level.

Florian Hertweck

But the project developer does receive a considerable margin?

Françoise Ged

That is the root of this crazy acceleration in the construction sector. In an economy growing so quickly an apartment can double in value within five years. Purchasing real estate is an investment that is sometimes used to accommodate family members nearby, like children or the grandparents. The situation today is entirely different than 10 years ago. Finding an apartment in a large city has become very difficult. For the ordinary population, teachers, for instance, it is practically impossible.

Florian Hertweck

So private persons are participating in speculation?

Françoise Ged

Lock, stock and barrel. This is why there are no revolts, because on the whole, a majority of city dwellers have benefited so far, in one way or another. The fact that practically no taxes are levied on the sale of real estate encourages this trend, which the authorities have tried to change in Shanghai, but without success.

Florian Hertweck

But are the developers' profits taxed?

Miguel Elosua

There is a «business tax,» which real estate developers also have to pay. But what is dramatic about the current situation is that the farmers, who are actually the owners of the land that is now being developed, get virtually nothing: just six percent of the average price paid by developers to the government for expropriated land.

Florian Hertweck

The separation between land and use rights was introduced to promote the country's urbanization. In crass opposition to an egalitarian urban structure, the location becomes decisive.

Françoise Ged

In China the location is of fundamental importance, especially with regard to schools and the public transport network. These are the criteria of highest priority for real estate agents as well. With just one child, the investment in children – and the pressure exerted on them – is very high.

Florian Hertweck

What tendencies do you see in the future as regards land and urban development?

Françoise Ged

A paradigm shift already took place in 2018, when a new ministry was created that is responsible for natural resources, agricultural land, and for rural and urban planning. Primarily for reasons of food policy and ecology, for it must not be forgotten that nearly one quarter of the global population lives in China, which has only around 7 percent of the world's agriculturally used land. This is why the management of urban *and* rural development is of paramount importance.

Urban Utopias

Urban Utopias

Urban Utopias

Many protomodern and modern utopians founded their projections of a better society on a complete reordering of land ownership in a space that was without context from the outset. Liberated from land being subdivided into plots, and accordingly also from inequitable land ownership, they took up theories put forward by land reformers such as Henry George, Herbert Spencer, or Silvio Gesell. The notion of land as a commons was transposed into its spatial dimension in different ways: Arturo Soria y Mata and Frank Lloyd Wright divided up the land, giving everyone more or less the same amount, Tony Garnier and Le Corbusier conceived of land as a continuous, flowing space in public ownership. Whereas the classical utopians preferred to develop their designs on a *tabula rasa,* the anti-utopians of the sixties and seventies included the existing urban landscape in their work, at least as a foil. Megastructuralists such as Yona Friedman or Constant projected a new urban structure with new common levels above the existing urban landscape – separated from the ground and its traditional ownership structures. Oswald Mathias Ungers even included the existing transportation system in his reorganization of the territory; dissolution of location was his answer to the land question. Utopian and anti-utopian schemes have become rare since the eighties, just as the discussion of the land question has waned. Andrea Branzi's *Agronica* is fascinating not least for this reason: it counters the prevailing pragmatism anew with a fundamental idea. Critical utopias or anti-utopias like these should not be misinterpreted as projects. They are critical reflections on the state of society, cities, and landscapes that can broaden the horizon of our present-day work. *Agronica* is also notable because following the focus on cities, Branzi re-emphasizes the significance of the landscape and agriculture for spatial production. The same is true of the question of land: originally discussed in relation to the countryside, it was thought about in connection with urban development in the nineteenth and twentieth centuries because it was linked to the question of housing. Today we are confronted with the task of conceiving of what is built and what is unbuilt as one when it comes to the land question (and

Urban Utopias

generally in urban planning) – no longer considering the city only from the perspective of building, but from the perspective of the landscape, and factoring in agriculture. Yet the twenty-first-century land question requires a critical counternarrative to the political economy of neoliberalism. Reflective images with a «utopian impulse» – in Fredric Jameson's words – can make important contributions here. They have the potential to move the debate forward by presenting more current concepts and models of land as a commons.

Urban Utopias

Ildefons Cerdà
L'Eixample
1860

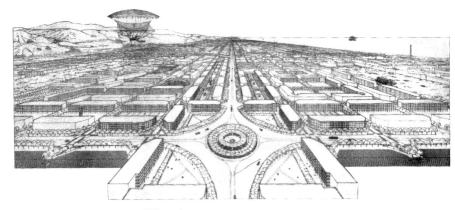

Barcelona's planned Eixample district is often used as the model *par excellence* for the reconstruction of the «European city» because of its structure of blocks built up on all sides and with chamfered corners; in the end, the model's strategy of reconstructing perimeter blocks also entailed the privatization of the city. Yet Ildefons Cerdà (1815–1876), who was active in Spain's liberal party as a representative of the leftist wing, understood the isomorphic grid in an entirely different way – namely, as an expression of an egalitarian social order. The squares, whose sides are 113 meters long, were subdivided such that either two opposite sides of each block were to be built up, or two in an L shape, or in some cases three in a U shape. The central area was to be landscaped as a public space – following Cerdà's motto: «bringing the landscape into the city and the city into the landscape.» In the end, the overall plan was for separate buildings, not for each block to be developed on all sides. Land speculation was to be made impossible on the open spaces; they were to represent a spatial continuum, offering an alternative to the sidewalks for people making their way across the city. The land to be built up was divided into plots with direct access to the street, in contrast to the many plots tucked away in courtyards set back farther in the old town. Cerdà aimed to secure the plan against excessive land and real estate speculation by making the plots practically the same size and the same quality. In *Teoría general de la urbanización* he bemoaned the fact that everyone paid taxes to finance the infrastructure for urban development, but that some profited more from it than others. Accordingly, he intended his plan not only to offer uniform sanitary standards but also «the same and appropriate surplus value to all owners.»[1] This was Cerdà's compelling response to the conditions of early capitalism, when land was included in the legal concept of individual property and «fully integrated in the economic system of exploitation in this form.»[2] His project of a flowing urban landscape was ultimately attacked and rejected by an alliance of local politicians, private real estate owners, real estate companies, the local press, and even the chamber of architects. The blocks were built up on all sides, density was increased substantially and the differentiation of the plots encouraged real estate speculation.

FH

Arturo Soria y Mata
Ciudad lineal
1884

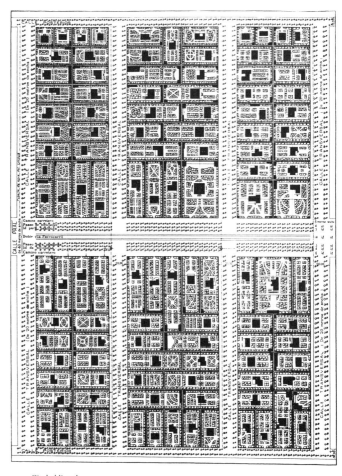

Designed by Arturo Soria y Mata (1844–1920), the *Ciudad lineal,* or Linear City, sought to counter the precarious living conditions in the major cities of the time with socially balanced housing in the landscape. It was called the last utopia of the nineteenth century. Influenced directly by reading Henry George, Soria y Mata pursued the ideal of a «just distribution of the Earth.» The Linear City was to extend along a central axis that connected existing cities and accommodated all the infrastructures of the day (railroads, roads, sewerage and telephone lines). Tracts measuring 1 kilometer by 300 meters on either side of the axis were to be built up; Soria y Mata separated them with cul-de-sacs and divided them into parcels of more or less the same size for families to use. The smallest plots, for poorer strata of the population, were to measure 400 square meters; the better-off could have plots one and a half; twice; or, in exceptional cases, even three times that size. In contrast to vertical segregation in the old city, Soria y Mata wanted to achieve a horizontal mixture in the Linear City so that «the poor and the rich live close to one another without losing their independence.»[3] The footprint of each house was to cover at most one fifth of the plot. The rest of the area was to be used by the family for keeping animals, growing fruit trees and vegetables, and as an ornamental garden. At the same time, the houses were to be separated from each other; the reason Soria y Mata gave was fire protection and the high cost of fire insurance. The land required for the Linear City was to be purchased at market value prior to beginning the project, i.e., as agricultural land. A company established specifically for the project was then to provide access and sell the land to the residents. Less privileged people interested in living there who could not afford to buy a plot were to be given the opportunity to pay off the sum over 20 years. The costs of building the infrastructure and connecting it to the individual plots were to be financed by the difference between the costs of buying and reselling the land. Soria y Mata's ideal was to make use of the economy of straight lines and pipes and thus have the Linear City follow a perfectly straight line. However, this was to depend on the availability and the topography of the land. Even as he conceptualized the Linear City, Soria y Mata sensed it would be difficult to purchase the land required for his project in reality. This was proven true when the concept was realized for the first time, near Madrid. Many landowners resisted selling at the limited price, for which reason Soria y Mata demanded that the state should declare the Linear City to be in the public interest so that a law would force the landowners to sell the land at its current price. He argued that after all, the state or the municipality themselves would profit from the Linear City because they could take over the infrastructure produced by the developer, as well as land for public institutions, practically for free once the Linear City had been completed.

On the territorial level, Soria y Mata imagined the Linear City to be a link between all the existing communities. That would have produced a structure of triangles – with nodes consisting of the existing communities and lines of the Linear City, whose homogeneous building structure would dampen the sharp rise in land prices on the continuum from the countryside to the city. He also dreamed of realizing the Linear City in other countries: he wanted to transfer the idea to the colonies of Latin America and to sparsely populated areas lacking infrastructure in Russia and China. Although in fact only a 5-kilometer section of the Linear City was realized in a Madrid suburb, Soria y Mata influenced many later models of the linear city such as those by Le Corbusier, Michel Écochard, and by Ralf Schüler and Ursulina Schüler-Witte. Ivan Leonidov, who also sought to overcome the dichotomy of the city and the countryside with his 1930 design for a linear city in Magnitogorsk (which was never realized), was theoretically free to make decisions about the land, which had been transferred to state ownership following Lenin's 1917 Decree on Land.

FH

Ebenezer Howard
Garden City
1898/1902

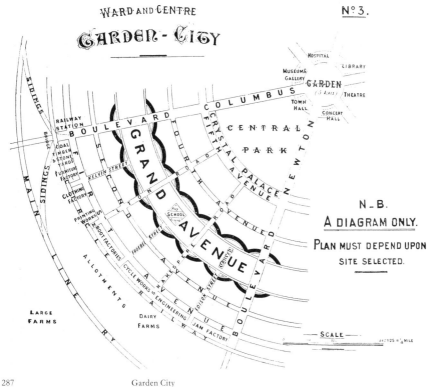

In 1898, Ebenezer Howard (1850–1928), the pioneer of the garden city movement, described valuable approaches for how we manage land today in *To-morrow: A Peaceful Path to Real Reform*.[4] Howard presented his ideas about municipal land management using the example of the garden city. It was supposed to function as a countermodel to living in the rapidly growing industrial cities in England, with their high land prices and poor housing and living conditions. Howard sketched out a model of polycentral, autonomous garden cities of roughly 32,000, the spread of which was limited by an agricultural belt. The area of the garden city to be given over to residential development averaged 400 hectares and featured low density, an abundance of open space with public buildings, and managed traffic conditions. Howard's garden city idea centered around socio-economic considerations, including aspects of municipal ownership of land as well as notions of private ownership of buildings and means of production. One premise of the model was that the garden city would be implemented and financed on land previously used for agriculture. It was to be administered and controlled by a municipal land company founded by the residents; the «trustees» were to be «four gentlemen of responsible position and of undoubted probity and honour.» The municipal land company was to buy the land, as Howard distanced himself from the necessity of expropriation, and to manage the land and the rents of land to be paid by the future residents. Accordingly, the land remained in the common ownership of the land company. Plots were to be allocated exclusively on the basis of ground leases, with the fees being calculated on the basis of the annual yield of the plot in question. All revenues of the garden city thus came from fees from ground leases. The profit remaining after interest and repayment of mortgages was to be used by the company to build public facilities such as schools, parks, and roads. A model of public co-determination was to ensure that existing organizations and land-owners, factory owners, as well as the new leaseholders were involved in planning and designing the city. Howard's idea of the garden city indirectly followed the concepts of various early nineteenth-century writers and social critics who focused on the land question – for example, Edward Gibbon Wakefield's and Alfred Marshall's deliberations on optimum settlement processes, Thomas Spence's model of the socialization of land, and Herbert Spencer's principles of land national-ization as the only possible type of ownership, which were based on Spence. His work was also influenced by James Silk Buckingham's 1848 model of an ideal industrial community, Henry George's writings on socializing land rent and taxes on real estate as a single tax, and, finally, Pyotr Kropotkin's model of the free community. Howard combined these ideas in his garden city, which he himself called a «unique combination of proposals» of various approaches to land reform. In contrast to his predecessors, Howard was the first to formulate the relationship between the city and the countryside in such a detailed manner that his plans could be made concrete and be visualized on the basis of plans and calculations. Howard's garden city subsequently became one of the prevailing models for planning «a city in a garden» and attracted great attention, particularly in Europe. The community model was implemented most clearly in the first garden cities to be built in England, Letchworth (1903) and Welwyn Garden City (1919), and later in numerous other European garden cities. The first two garden cities are exemplars of Howard's social reformist vision of a settlement organized as a cooperative in which the land is owned jointly and rented out to individuals, but in which the freedom of industrial and business entrepreneurs remains intact nonetheless. After the Second World War, as garden cities were emulated worldwide, the basic idea lost some completeness and coherence in practice. One result of the marked increase in density and the increasing privatization of land – in particular in conurbations – was that Howard's core ideas were often disregarded – for example, the ways of financing and organizing the garden city and limits on its size. Instead, Howard's garden city idea became a synonym for a suburban settlement with garden-oriented housing, in which individualism took the place of the community idea and communal land ownership.

Ivonne Weichold

Tony Garnier
Une cité industrielle
1901–1904
(published in 1917)

Tony Garnier (1869–1948) planned his industrial city and designed it down to architectural details on a fictitious site that was framed by a reservoir for energy supply and a river for sewerage and transporting goods. Freeways connect three areas in his utopia: a business district, a research district and a residential district. The business district is developed around a central rail station and links up with an – also fictitious – historic district; a nearby industrial quarter with various factories; in the west the largest district with housing and various public institutions; and finally a district with hospitals, institutions for invalids, and a center for light therapy. Garnier designed each of the buildings individually. His utopia of a workers' city with no need for police, jails, or barracks was designed for a population of 35,000, roughly the same size as Howard's contemporary model of the garden city. In his brief explanation of the project, he wrote that social progress, especially concerning land, was a precondition for it: «Society then would have free reign over the distribution of land.» He proposed various typologies for the residential neighborhoods: collective residential buildings, but mostly single-family dwellings that were to be built on plots 13 × 15 meters in size. The footprint of the house was allowed to cover at most half of the plot, and the remainder – both in front of the house and behind it – was to be accessible by the public. Garnier did not envisage private gardens; people were to be able to walk across the entire city in all directions independently of the streets – an idea that was already visible in Ildefons Cerdà's plan for Barcelona and later in the work of reformers such as Hermann Jansen. The city was to be a «great park, without any wall or enclosure limiting the terrain,»[5] Garnier wrote. The industrial city differs markedly from the garden city in that it has neither gardens nor agriculture, but land is considered a common good in both models. The influence of the industrial city on the classical modern style must not be underestimated. Garnier's powerful images impressed Le Corbusier in particular, inspiring the latter to separate functions and envisage the free availability of land in his modern urban design – which did, however, consider the role of agriculture more specifically.

FH

Le Corbusier
Ville contemporaine
1922

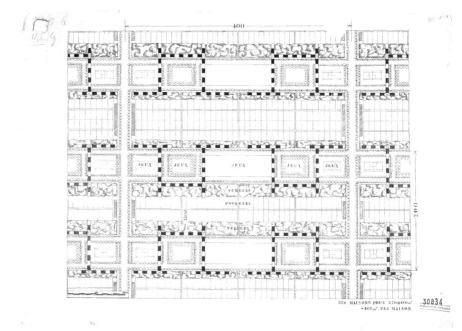

In contrast to the very small ideal cities devised by Howard and Garnier on the margins of an existing major city or located far from it, Le Corbusier (1887–1965) tackled the replanning of the major city itself. Of course, he had a new Paris in mind – a city he both hated and loved. Its population was about 3 million at the time. «Therefore my settled opinion,…» he wrote in *The City of To-morrow and Its Planning,* which was published in 1925, «is that the centres of our great cities must be pulled down and rebuilt.»[6] His utopia had a clear geometric structure with three sections: the downtown with 60-story office towers roughly 250 meters high for 500,000 to 800,000 people in the city center, grouped around a traffic hub, including an airport, which – as Wolfgang Pehnt emphasized sardonically – was «drawn like an academic's design for a huge neo-Baroque fountain basin,»[7] as well as urban residential buildings for 500,000 people arranged around it in linear blocks with setbacks and in city blocks developed on all sides. Surrounding the compact city, Le Corbusier placed garden cities for 2.5 million residents and, in the east, an industrial quarter with docks and a freight depot. His basic idea was to achieve high building density while simultaneously unsealing the ground of the city. Compared with the Paris of his day, density was to increase fourfold but buildings were to cover only 5 percent of the previously built-up land. The best way to reduce coverage while simultaneously increasing floor area was to use a typology of high-rises, then linear blocks with setbacks, and, finally blocks in a honeycomb pattern, each of which was developed on all sides. This was intended to reduce distances within the city and at the same time intensify public transport. As in Garnier's design, the city would be transformed into a vast park, or in Le Corbusier's metaphorical words: «the City of To-morrow could be set *entirely* in the midst of green open spaces.»[8] The blocks in the honeycomb pattern and the linear blocks with setbacks were designed like stacked-up single-family homes, and were interspersed with sports facilities and contiguous vegetable gardens that could be watered and fertilized automatically. «The inhabitant comes back from his factory or office, and with the renewed strength given him by his games, sets to work on his garden.»[9] To the master of the Modern Movement, the resident of the city of 3 million was self-sufficient in this sense. Le Corbusier mentions Haussmann's renovation of Paris, which he considered positive at least in economic terms, as his model for putting his prodigious plan into practice – «My scheme is brutal, because town existence and life itself are brutal.»[10] In contrast to Haussmann, Le Corbusier sought to increase not only quality but also quantity – which, he believed,would make the surplus value of urban land soar. Like Haussmann, he envisaged expropriation of land. The project was to be financed using the gains in surplus value between the value of the existing buildings and that of the new developments, which would be much higher. It is not quite clear how land was to be managed later. In some places, Le Corbusier spoke of municipal land ownership and ground leases, in others of selling the land to investors from abroad, which he believed would guarantee that foreign troops would never be able to attack Paris. He wanted to leave an intermediate zone between the city and the garden cities undeveloped; in case the city needed to grow, it could expand into that zone. «If the centres of our cities have become a sort of intensely active form of capital for the mad speculation of private enterprise [...], this projected zone would represent a formidable financial reserve among the resources of municipalities.»[11] He was convinced that the value of land would soon increase tenfold. The criticism of Le Corbusier's urban design is still valid today: his *tabula rasa* philosophy; the schematic nature of his geometric layout, which, unlike Howard, he considered not simply a diagram but a concrete urban design; the monumentality and homogeneity of his urban design, with the same building typologies repeated over and over; the urban design of the elevated central platform; the separation of the functions of working and housing, and of the building from the street; and, not least, his esoteric and patronizing rhetoric. But it is also worthwhile to shift our view from the macro level to the micro perspective of his urban design: how he masterfully stacked serially fabricated single-family homes within a single building and defined their relationship to the open spaces; integrated community functions and urban agriculture into urban planning, with the ideal of self-sufficiency; and, finally, reduced the footprint and generally the amount of sealed land while simultaneously increasing density.

FH

This is how Le Corbusier
imagined the land of
the future big city. In his book
*The City of To-morrow and
Its Planning*, published in
1925, he showed this image
of Parc Monceau twice.

Ville contemporaine

Frank Lloyd Wright
Broadacre City
1932–1958

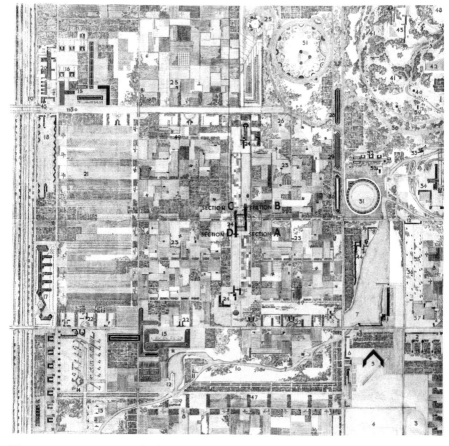

«When every man, woman, and child may be born to put his feet on his own acres and every unborn child finds his acre waiting for him when he is born – then democracy will have been realized»[12]… and they should be «entitled to ‹own› an acre of ground so long as they live on it or use it.»[13] «Agriculture and manufacturing… have been made a blessing by three principal freedoms: free ground, free education, and a free medium of exchange for all labor or commodities. This means entire freedom from speculation. There can be no speculation in any three of these essentials to the commonwealth essentially by way of which the commonwealth lives. Broadacre City is still a true capitalist system wherein private ownership is based upon personal use and public service: genuine Capitalism. Capitalism made organic since it is broadly based upon the ground and the individual upon the ground.»[14] Frank Lloyd Wright (1867–1959) used these words to explain his utopia Broadacre City to his fellow architect Ludwig Mies van der Rohe – his translation into space of ideas of two theoreticians who influenced him greatly: Henry George with respect to treating land as a commons, without expropriating and municipalizing it; Silvio Gesell in terms of interweaving land and the economy as anti-speculative fields in which goods can be exchanged fairly. Wright envisaged «[n]o private ownership of public needs,» and «[n]o public ownership of private needs.»[15] He presented his idea at Rockefeller Center in New York in 1935, during the Great Depression. He developed his thinking consequentially, from dividing up the surface of the Earth more or less equally into a decentralized, horizontal urban design without hierarchies, in which the various communities were to be based on local agriculture and production. He projected an image of the city diametrically opposed to that of his archenemy Le Corbusier (even though both did consider agriculture to be an important component of the city, and Wright's designs also included individual high-rises). Wright was certainly not opposed to technical innovations: he envisaged flying taxis and nuclear-powered automobiles that were to guarantee individuals limitless mobility. As to be expected, he assigned architects a special role in his conception of the landscape: as community architects, they were to divide up, distribute, and administer the land.

FH

Oswald Mathias Ungers
Network City[16]
1968

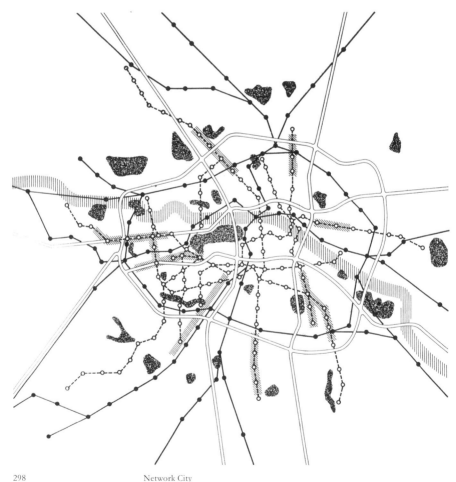

When it comes to buying and selling land, the decisive factor for its value is location. In Cologne, for example, the average price of land for one- or two-family homes was 1,640 euros per square meter in good locations and just 400 euros per square meter in average locations in 2019.[17] Prices have not only risen exponentially in very good locations in recent years but have also remained high in city centers. Major cities are increasingly becoming pyramidal structures with a golden center in the middle. Oswald Mathias Ungers (1926–2007) had critically observed this tendency as early as the sixties, when he linked his teaching at the Technische Universität with research on the city of Berlin, even though it was a shrinking and decidedly polycentric city at the time. For example, West Berlin's upper middle class and upper class lived mostly in the exclusive neighborhoods to the west. The «problem of location,» Ungers was convinced, could be «reduced by a high-performance transport network.» So, seven years after the Berlin Wall was built, he and his students and academic staff developed a more or less isomorphic transport network for all of Berlin (West and East), in which high-density nodes were to be connected to each other through infrastructures. The center was divided into subcenters that were to be distributed across the territory of the city without creating a hierarchical order. That would make the various urban services and activities equally accessible to all the city's residents, regardless of where they lived: «It gives [every resident] the freedom to choose his location wherever he desires, and also to change it at any time for any purpose.» Ungers used his own route to a department store as an example: «In Berlin, I reach the food hall of the KaDeWe [Kaufhaus des Westens, a major department store] directly from my apartment. I take my car, drive to the department store's fourth parking level, and arrive at the food hall offering a vast range of items via a covered bridge. Apartment–car–street–parking garage–bridge–department store form a uniform system.»[18] It is typical that Ungers first had infrastructure for cars in mind for his network city during expansion of Berlin's Stadtautobahn. In 1965/66, the design assignment he gave his students for their degree projects was to directly connect urban functions such as a new university, a police headquarters, or an amusement park with the transport network for cars. His focus three years later was on the city's public transportation system. He asked his students to design buildings above light rail and subway stations, demanding that they place new stops inside buildings in order to achieve the highest density possible on the transportation network and to transform it to a uniform system – just like the trip from his garage to the food hall. Even if Ungers did not directly address the land question, he did grapple with questions of land and housing in his research and teaching. Although the purpose of relativizing location was to equalize land prices within the city, he cleverly avoided the problem of expropriating land by proposing buildings on top of (public) transportation hubs and the megastructure put forward in *Berlin 1995*. Ungers was clearer regarding the question of housing: housing was to be conceived of as infrastructure and therefore to be provided by the public sector (privatizing infrastructures would not have crossed his mind). It is no accident that he also devoted himself to analyzing the not-for-profit Karl Marx Hof in Vienna, which could be built only because the municipality made the land available. In *City in the City,* which Ungers developed in collaboration with Rem Koolhaas in 1977, proposing unbuilding Berlin and transforming it into a green archipelago, he again disregarded the question of how the owners of the buildings to be returned to nature were to be induced to unbuild them, if not by expropriation. The whole idea of a green archipelago is imaginable only if the public sector has power over land.

FH

Berlin 1995,
Oswald Mathias Ungers /
Technische Universität Berlin,
1969

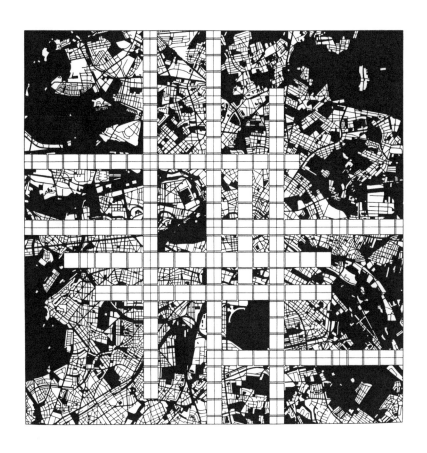

Andrea Branzi
Agronica
1994

Agronica marks the decline of the urban utopia as an all-encompassing, global, and ultimately exhaustive image.[19] At the same time, it asserts that the contemporary urban condition is gradually emerging as a partial, fragmented and inchoate figure. Indeed, Andrea Branzi (born 1938), the main author of *Agronica,* defines it as an incomplete utopia that does not seek to replace what exists today, but rather to complement the large palette of existing urban forms such as the metropolis, the city, the village, mobility systems, or the market.[20] More precisely, in *Agronica,* Branzi and his team propose a diffusely urbanized pattern of agriculture that combines productive farmlands with a mobile system of architectural elements. These move around on *pilotis* and offer reversible distributed urban services across the territory.[21] In other words: *Agronica* is a landscape as urban as it is agricultural, in which existing settlements are repurposed and reused, and new architectural facilities blur the lines between public and private as well as between inside and outside.[22]

This is a condition in which everything is flexible, whereby the interactions between form and function fade away, permitting dynamic and seasonal adaptation, temporary repurposing, and continuous reversibility. In such a context, Branzi introduces mobile buildings and infrastructures, and thus separates the land from the architecture and the background from the foreground. This defines the contemporary territory more as a boundless system of relational forces and flows rather than as a collection of objects firmly entrenched in portions of land.[23] In this perspective, *Agronica* comprises a notion of land as a neutral support for a collection of elements whose open and mobile aggregation not only dissipates the question of ownership into that of a commons but also discloses the demise of typologies as core elements of architecture and urbanism.[24] According to Branzi, the form and organization of territory indeed fade away in *Agronica.*[25] As a consequence, its structure is no longer defined by a morphological order, while land ownership no longer structures the form of the territory.

Chiara Cavalieri

Florian Hertweck
Freilandstadt
2019

The Anthropocene will be followed by the Symbiocene. Humankind will no longer dominate the planet but will live symbiotically with its flora and fauna, its resources and elements. Not only will land no longer be a commodity, it will also no longer be abused by humankind for constructing infrastructures and buildings and for mining geological resources. The surface of the Earth will be declared World Heritage, it will be unsealed and renaturalized. Streets and foundation slabs will no longer exist. Each cubic meter of earth will be plowed through by 300 worms. Water will no longer evaporate, but only seep into the ground. The best projects historically developed for the elevated typology will grow upward, forming the *Freilandstadt* – not as a contiguous megastructure, but as distinct objects. They will host manifold uses, like cities within the city. The most important building material will be wood; the selection of other materials will be limited to a very small repertoire, as was traditionally the case. The *Freilandstadt* will epitomize the promise of high density with a simultaneously reduced footprint. Because the ground will be renaturalized, it will no longer be necessary to green façades, roofs, balconies, or terraces. People will have to travel only short distances to the most varied land uses, and their journeys will no longer be fragmented by infrastructures, fences, and walls. Drones will deliver non-biological products, and people will grow their own organic produce. They will feel that working in community gardens provides balance to their virtual jobs and makes them happy. At the scale of the body, people will walk or ride horses or mountain bikes; at the regional level, they will use aerial taxis; and at the supraregional level, they will enjoy short travel times on maglev trains and hyperloops that connect all *Freilandstädte* with each other. Locational problems will be a thing of the past because of the high degree of functional diversity. Virtual communication will be wireless, but the great desire for real communication will be satisfied by the density of uses in the buildings and the open public spaces. Animals will no longer be killed for consumption, but only as necessary to maintain the ecological equilibrium. Their wanderings will no longer be restricted at all. In the *Freilandstadt,* people will be decelerated by enhanced contact with other living beings, and they will abandon their mania to optimize everything. Seemingly purposeless activities in the fresh air and the open countryside will become meaningful once more.

FH

Ildefons Cerdà
L'Eixample
1860
1
Laurent Coudroy de Lille, «Ildefons Cerdà,» in: Thierry Paquot (ed.), *Les faiseurs de villes 1850–1950*, Gollion 2010, p. 116.
2
Juan Rodriguez-Lores, «Die Grundfrage der Grundrente. Stadtplanung von Ildefonso Cerdà für Barcelona und James Hobrecht für Berlin,» in: *Stadtbauwelt*, No. 65/1980, p. 31.

Arturo Soria y Mata
Ciudad lineal
1884
3
Arturo Soria y Mata, *La cité linéaire. Nouvelle architecture de villes*, Paris 1979 [first edition 1884], p. 18.

Ebenezer Howard
Garden City
1898/1902
4
It was only the second edition of 1902 that was titled *Garden Cities of To-morrow*. Cf. *Ebenezer Howard, Gartenstädte von Morgen: Das Buch und seine Geschichte* [1902], ed. by Julius Posener, Basel/Berlin/Boston 2015.

Tony Garnier
Une cité industrielle
1901–1904
(published in 1917)
5
Tony Garnier, *Une cité industrielle*, translation: Marguerite McGoldrick, New York 1989 [first edition 1917], p. 13.

Le Corbusier
Ville contemporaine
1922
6
Le Corbusier, *The City of To-morrow and Its Planning*, translated from the 8th French edition of *Urbanisme* by Frederick Etchells, London 1971 [first edition 1925], p. 98.
7
Wolfgang Pehnt, «Der Prophet der ‹strahlenden Stadt›. Vorwort zum Reprint 2015,» in: Le Corbusier, *Städtebau* [1925], translated and edited by Hans Hildebrandt, Munich 2015, no page number.
8
Le Corbusier 1925 (see note 6), p. 80.

9
Ibid., p. 206.
10
Ibid., p. 298.
11
Ibid., p. 98.

Frank Lloyd Wright
Broadacre City
1932–1958
12
Frank Lloyd Wright, *The Living City*, New York 1958, p. 119.
13
Ibid., p. 51.
14
Bruce Brooks Pfeiffer, *Frank Lloyd Wright Collected Writings, Volume 4: 1939–1949*, New York 1994, p. 53.
15
Frank Lloyd Wright, *The Disappearing City*, New York 1932, on the plan, no page number.

Oswald Mathias Ungers
Network City
1968
16
Ungers did not use this term – he laconically called his plan «*Gesamtplan*» (Overall Plan, for Berlin) – but the editor of this volume believes it expresses the core idea best (Ungers did use the term *Netzwerk* [network] regularly, for example in the megastructure *Berlin 1995*). Franz Oswald, who had worked with Ungers, later developed the model of the *Netzstadt* (net city) in collaboration with chemist Peter Baccini.
17
Grundstücksmarktbericht 2019 für die Stadt Köln, ed. by the Gutachterausschuss für Grundstückswerte in der Stadt Köln, 2019, p. 25.
18
Oswald Mathias Ungers/TU Berlin (eds.), *Veröffentlichungen zur Architektur*, issue no. 21/1968 «Schnellbahn und Gebäude,» pp. 1–2.

Andrea Branzi
Agronica
1994
19
Agronica was conceived and designed in 1994 at the Domus Academy for Philips Electronics.
20
Rather as a positive utopia, such as the Ville Radieuse, or as a critical utopia, such as No Stop City. See Andrea

Branzi et al., «Symbiotic Metropolis: Agronica» in: Ezio Manzini, Marco Susani (eds.), *The Solid Side. The Search for Consistency in a Changing World. Projects and Proposals*, New Delhi 1995, pp. 101–120.
21
Andrea Branzi, «Preliminary Notes for a Master Plan» and «Master Plan Strijp Philips, Eindhoven 1999,» in: *Lotus*, no. 107/2000, pp. 110–123.
22
See Charles Waldheim, «Industrial Economy and Agrarian Urbanism,» in: Paola Viganò, Chiara Cavalieri, Martina Barcelloni Corte (eds.), *The Horizontal Metropolis between Urbanism and Urbanization*, Berlin 2018, pp. 47–53.
23
Ibid.
24
See Andrea Branzi, «On Agronica,» in the video presented at the exhibition «The Horizontal Metropolis: A Radical Project,» Venice Biennale of Architecture 2016.
25
See Branzi et al. 1995 (see note 20), pp. 101–120.

Florian Hertweck
Freilandstadt
2019
Text and design: Florian Hertweck. Dragos Ghioca was involved in designing and realizing the illustration.

Urban Utopias / Notes

Urbanism and Architecture

Urbanism and Architecture

Architectural Models

Two architectural approaches to solving the problem of land as a commons can be distinguished. The first unfolds over time, the second in space. In terms of time, it is about legally separating the land from the building: the land remains in public ownership or – in the case of foundations, for example – in private, not-for-profit ownership. It is then made available to a user or an investor for a limited period of time through usage rights or ground leases. This approach enables lessors who are bound to the public interest to use contractual provisions to guarantee reduced rents or a variety of land uses, for example, and in return, they can rely on low-risk revenues in the long term. In addition, they can use the plot again after the contract has run out and can negotiate new urban development goals in advance of that time. If all land were to remain municipal property and were made available to third parties through ground leases, and if all these contracts had to be renewed or renegotiated at the same time, this would enable dynamic urban planning, which would be capable of reacting more directly to processes of growth or shrinkage and to various social challenges. Inflexible master plans and land speculation would cease to be effective. Ground leases are much more effective than land use plans for guiding land use, densification, the social and functional mix, and housing supply. In this book, we present some places and projects on this spectrum: from the medina in Casablanca and the European commons to current projects such as Granby Four Streets in Liverpool and Lysbüchel Süd in Basel.

Of course, the great majority of architects operates on the second spectrum – space – pursuing either a minimalist or a radical approach. The minimalist approach comprises projects in which the footprints of the buildings are reduced and the land not covered by the building is made accessible to the public, not only to the users of the building. The radical approach includes projects in which the buildings are elevated above the land (in the spatial sense). The land is then considered to be a continuous plane, both physically and symbolically, which – even in the case of private ownership – is made available to the public and is not built up. This refers

Architectural typologies: the land question

Reduction of the footprint
/
Public space inside
a perimeter block
/
Plateau urbanism
/
Integration of public space
/
Mounting the building
on *pilotis* (columns)
to make the land available

Architectural Models

above all to the typology of Modernism *par excellence:* Le Corbusier's *pilotis;* he sought to «liberate» the land (*libération du sol*). However, the closer we get to the present day as we review such projects, the less laden by ideology the elevated projects become.

The projects presented do not promote universal solutions, but are to be understood as statements. The fact that practically all land available for building is private does not necessarily mean that public access is increasingly restricted. There are conceptual ways to make land and space accessible to the public. Elevated buildings – which may take any of various architectural forms – certainly can contribute to offering more space to the public in high-density locations, even though they are practically banished from architectural production in Europe today. This can succeed only if architects' clients share this aspiration from the outset or agree to it in – often difficult – negotiations. Architects can contribute to solving the land question – not only by engaging in the political discourse but specifically also in their core competence, the process of planning buildings.

We will begin thinking here about a synthesis, namely by intertwining the two spectra: expressing time-limited access to land architecturally, constructively and spatially. How will people deal with the real estate once the ground lease has run out, and if the concept for use has changed? Planners have two options in this procedure: when they conceptualize the building itself, to additionally conceptualize how it will be unbuilt or how it will be re-purposed. In the context of the land question, «recycling» buildings gains new meaning.

Architecture and Land Separated in Terms of Time

Architectural Models / Architecture and Land Separated in Terms of Time

Commons

The village green in
Berlin-Marzahn is still
discernible today
(photograph from 1990).

Commons

Commons – historically also known as common land – are those portions of a resource that are common property. Commons are a «third space» between potentially freely available, in a sense public resource space on the one hand and private space for individual use on the other. The resource spaces can also be immaterial; thus, the «third space» can be of a physical or virtual nature. As the jointly managed and administered part of the resource, a commons is differentiated from a fourth space, a «club» to which access is limited, especially by the fact that access to the commons is potentially free to all.[1] Although «club» spaces are also used jointly, they are not managed jointly. In other words, a commons is that area in which the yields are shared by everyone involved.

The significance and prevalence of commons have changed many times in the course of history. This type of space emerged in the medieval feudal system; it denoted the undivided land that the peasantry cultivated jointly, which was usually tolerated by its legal owner, the feudal lord. It was called *gemeent* in Dutch, *obștie* in Romanian, *usi civici* in Italian, *Allmende* in German, and commons in English. In late medieval Europe, these jointly managed woodlands, rangelands or alpine pastures were enclosed and privatized, usually by force. Karl Marx described this process as primitive accumulation or originary accumulation, which constituted the foundation of the capitalist economic system. Silvia Federici added the aspect of the

dissolution of the social bonds within the commons to this interpretation.[2]

A comparison of historical types of commons shows the relationship between the social practices and the spaces resulting from them. Each type is distinguished not only by its spatial relationship to the settled area but also by the frequency of use and the degree to which commoners, the people involved in the commons, identified with their common area. Four types of commons in German-speaking countries – *Alm, Hutweide, Vöde,* and *Anger* – developed chronologically in this order and can be interpreted as steps along a development path in which the spatial relationship to the settled area became stronger, the uses of the commons became more diversified, and the interactions between the resource space, the users, and the rules for using it became increasingly complex. This development corresponds to a process of increasing urbanization of the commons, which are constituted in ever new forms even today, despite enclosures. Their current-day variant can be considered to be the many forms of urban commons. The location of the *Alm* in the mountains far away from the village made it necessary to organize its use on a seasonal basis. Since the *Hutweide* was located on otherwise unused agricultural land near the village, people went there weekly or daily to tend to their animals. The *Vöde,* as a regional type of a «wandering» commons, was located on different fallow fields from one year to the next, which required more complex organization, including agreements between peasants who did and those who did not own land. The jointly used green area in the *Angerdorf,* a widespread type of village in central and eastern Europe through the nineteenth century, was located in the middle of the village, forming the most urban form of the commons.[3]

Numerous examples of the *Anger* that still exist today show that it is a mature type of urban open space that is usually embedded in the middle of the village's system of streets and is therefore accessible to everyone. Today, these public, green village centers are managed and maintained by the municipalities; in other words, common practices are no longer required to preserve them as open spaces. However, because of its spatial location within the settlement, the *Anger* raises new questions today about managing our resources: central location, spatial embedded-ness, unsealed land surface, and open access make it a potential commons space for negotiating the most diverse interests among local residents, the municipality, and urban society.

Hardly any of the open spaces that were originally managed as commons are still in common ownership today. Enclosures transferred them to private (*Alm, Hutweide*) or public (*Vöde, Anger*) ownership. Time and again, however, processes of commoning result in the formation of new commons, which in turn are constantly being enclosed and privatized again – regardless of whether the prevailing legal system provides for a legally defined form of common property or not.[4]

Especially since the early 1990s, processes of continually exacerbated resource scarcity in the economic, ecological, and social realms have contributed to giving commons new meaning again, both in research and in everyday practice. In the tension between the disengagement of the state from regulating the privatization and financialization of urban spaces on the one hand, and civil-society demands for participation in planning decisions on the other, the question about concrete models that can be described spatially and experienced concretely and that can be used for organizing communal life is taking on new urgency.

Dagmar Pelger

The Medina of Casablanca

The Medina of Casablanca

Sultan Mohamed Ben Abdellah had the medina in Casablanca reerected, beginning in 1770, to protect the city's Atlantic coast from foreign invasions. The sultan had it conform to the existing model of the Maghrebian city, first erecting a fortified wall, the *sqala,* and then various public institutions: the grand mosque, the *medersa* (a kind of comprehensive school), the pasha's house, steam baths, and traditional ovens. In the early twentieth century, the medina consisted of three areas: the residential quarters of the Muslims and the European traders, where Sultan Mohamed Ben Abdellah's initial buildings are located beside residential buildings, consulates, hotels, and administrative buildings; the *tnakers,* precarious huts made of reeds for the poorest segment of the population; and finally the *mellah,* the Jewish quarter.

In morphological terms, Casablanca's medina presents itself as a compact mass of 50 hectares with a central core for trading. The urban form is characterized by an enclosure wall with gates opening onto the maze of streets; the civil and religious institutions as well as shops are located on the central arteries, which link up with the narrower lanes and one-way streets that in turn provide access to the residential buildings. All the residential buildings and shops were built on public land by the people using them, who received usage rights for the land from the sultan. When density increased sharply in the late nineteenth century, Sultan Hassan I mobilized public land for an expansion to the west.

Two kinds of ownership can be differentiated in the medina of Casablanca: the plots owned by the state and the plots owned by *habous* – not-for-profit foundations that administer land bequeathed to them by wealthy individuals. Private ownership of land is very rare: these plots were made available to the residents for erecting their buildings. They benefit from a traditional right called *zina,* which is similar to European ground leases: they have certain ownership rights to the building and to improvements they make to the land. According to *zina,* the people using land can sell and mortgage their buildings. Although this right was previously unrestricted, it is limited to 40 years today.[5]

The introduction of a land register in Morocco during the French Protectorate resulted in a duality and in «modern» private ownership of land inspired by the Australian Torrens Act, coexisting with traditional Moroccan law that continues to apply – especially to old urban structures such as the medina and to collective agricultural land. Since then, traditional usage rights such as the land owned by the *habous* foundations or the collective *djemâa* landholdings (similar to commons) can be entered into the land registry, just as traditional usage rights can be applied to new plots of land. Today many private landowners grant usage rights to third parties.

Karim Rouissi

The Hirzbrunnenquartier in Basel
1924–1930

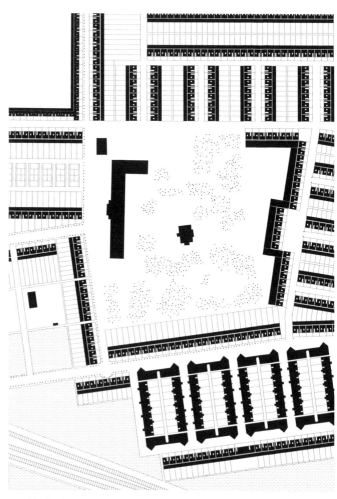

Between 1924 and 1930, architects Hans Bernoulli (1876–1959), August Künzel (1888–1965), and Hans von der Mühll (1887–1953) designed the Hirzbrunnenquartier (Hirzbrunnen Quarter) directly neighboring the Badischer Bahnhof (Basel German Station) on what was then the urban fringe of Basel. They achieved their ambitious goals of constructing a contiguous housing development at particularly affordable prices, both for rentals and condominiums, in the period following World War I when the economic situation was very difficult and there was a major housing shortage. In this sense, the project can be read as a model for Bernoulli's hypotheses in his 1946 book *Towns and the Land,* in which he argues for combating land speculation, making plots available for a time-limited right to build and setting rents at levels that merely cover costs – i.e., that do not look to generate profits. However, this attitude toward the land question was put to a hard test when this development was built. The architects headed the establishment of a cooperative to develop the area, which was to purchase the former estate and build the development in various stages over a six-year period using loan guarantees, mortgages, and shares in the cooperative. They had to adapt their plans multiple times because the development's location on the outskirts made it seem a risky investment in the context of the fragile capital market in the twenties. In the end, the centerpiece of the design – the communal open space at the center of the settlement (originally offered for sale to the City of Basel as collateral for a loan) – was sold to a Catholic hospital association that built a hospital enclosed by a fence rather than a publicly accessible park. Despite this setback, three cooperative developments; private row houses; a kindergarten; a school; a shop; tennis courts; and individual private homes, including that of the Bernoulli family, were realized in the following six years. Despite the scarce funds and the no-frills standard of construction, the architects pursued high architectural quality for the buildings and did not once exceed their budget or the tight time frame. There was nothing extravagant about the architecture, and it fulfilled the basic needs for clean air, open space and optimal lighting, expressed in a materiality that was as durable and as low-maintenance as possible. By designing a neighborhood for a variety of living standards with various floor heights, typologies and amenities, and featuring fine gradations from the communal to the private, the architects created a form of cooperative housing that is unrivaled to this day.

Metaxia Markaki, Ferdinand v. Pappenheim

Archigram
Control and Choice
1967

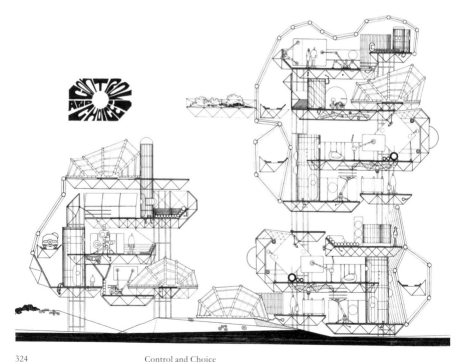

On one decisive point, *Control and Choice* contradicts Ralph Wilcoxon's well-known definition of a mega-structure. It is indeed «constructed of modular units» and «capable of great extension» (building as expansion), and it is designed as a spatial framework into which «smaller units [can be] built.»[6] But unlike a mega-structure, here the supporting structure is not «expected to have a useful life much longer than that of the smaller units.» Unlike Yona Friedman, Constant or Eckhard Schulze-Fielitz's large-scale structures, which remain stable while the capsules or filling units are more ephemeral and interchangeable, *Control and Choice* is the visualization of a nomadic building, which – when it is no longer needed in a particular place, or has become disruptive – can be completely dismantled and rebuilt elsewhere. With its radical interpretation of mega-structural principles of flexibility, modularity and mobility, Archigram marked the beginning of the end of the mega-structure; around the same time, Michael Webb's *Cushicle* took these too far on a small scale, while Ron Herron's *Walking City* took them too far on a large scale. With these three projects, the «need for drift of a nomadic and individualistic generation, which should be released from society's gravity and sedentari-ness,» was transferred to architecture in its entirety.[7] But while the phrase hardly applies to Webb's mobile living room or Herron's ambulatory cities, it can very much be applied to *Control and Choice*. In contrast to Peter Cook's idea of a «time-space-atmosphere sequence,»[8] in which the structure would be in a constant state of change and motion, *Control and Choice* could be a model for an architecture which endures for a long time in constructional and material terms but is nonetheless capable of being dismantled and rebuilt, given new and changed uses. This dismountable and remountable architecture would be suitable for sites where users are only granted use or ground lease rights for a limited period. Unlike Archigram, which «accepts the capitalist system of production and consumption,»[9] this reusability would undermine the chain of production, use and disposal, and meet the needs of changed functional requirements and ecological necessities. Around 70 percent of the trash created worldwide is still generated by the construction industry. Structures must be conceived sustainably in a twofold sense: first, that they last a long time, and second, that they can also be removed.

FH

Gisa Rothe
Housing Development at Rupenhorn[10]
1967

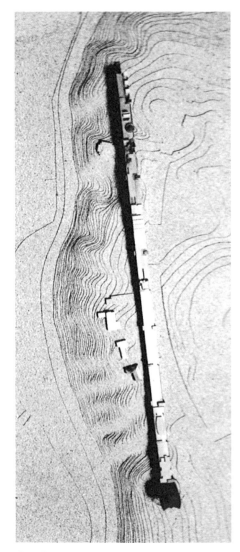

In 1967, Oswald Mathias Ungers devoted the work of his chair at Technische Universität Berlin to Rupenhorn in Berlin. In issue 10 of his *Veröffentlichungen zur Architektur* series, titled «Living by the Park,» Ungers gives a detailed description of the historical transformation of the area under study: «Rupenhorn is one of the residential areas in the west of Berlin with the most beautiful landscape. … Its development began in the twenties. The houses stood on ridge-like ledges on large plots – making the most of the topography. … The pattern changed after 1945. The previously large buildings fell into disrepair, were put to other uses, divided up, or disappeared. The land freed up in this way was filled with small private homes. … In recent years, another development has slowly prevailed: large companies have purchased the plots. Numerous plots are owned by the same entity, and plans can treat them as one. At the same time, the high land costs necessitate higher density. The consequence: single-family homes are replaced by apartment blocks, be they rentals or condominiums. … The three phases played out over a period of just 40 years. New phases began every 10 to 15 years. During each phase, the structures of ownership changed completely. … In other words, three turnovers in terms of the residents' social strata, the forms of land use, and the structure of the buildings. That also means three shifts in thinking about planning and method in a single generation – from the indi- vidualized design to the standardized design to the construction system; technology – from individual production by artisans to economical floor plans to industrial production; and responsibility – from the individual client to the purchaser of a fully planned home to the anony- mous renter. It is already possible to discern a fourth phase of develop- ment with considerable certainty today. The higher density and thus greater concentration of housing will attract stores, kindergartens, perhaps restaurants, etc. … It will be necessary to leave space for some of these institutions in the buildings to be planned: an open ground floor or roof. … The ability to assimilate is an important demand placed on the new development.»[11]

In this passage, Ungers not only described the transformation of land ownership structures from smaller to larger structures but also the necessity arising from it to design architecture in such a way that it would be able to adapt to these transformation processes. In contrast to Mies's universal space, certain functions such as housing were pre- determined and architecturally designed, leaving sufficient space for communal, commercial, and public land uses. This was about clearly structured buildings with ground floor zones dimensioned so that they could incorporate these new functions. Ungers' students' projects differed from those of the Metabolists and Archigram in that they did not aesthetically idealize the technology or the modularity of capsules and pipes. Gisa Rothe's degree project was a slender, but extremely long elevated block whose open ground floor zone was to be filled over time with the functions needed.

FH

Frei Otto
Ökohäuser (Eco Houses), Berlin
1981–1990

The IBA Berlin (Internationale Bau-ausstellung Berlin, International Building Exhibition Berlin) 1984–1987 went down in history as the first major urban repair experiment that was actually built. In the section devoted to existing buildings, this achievement was manifested by preserving and cautiously repairing the old apart-ment buildings whose users received professional consulting services – a shining hour of institutionally promoted participation. In the section devoted to new buildings, it became apparent through the care with which the new projects were integrated into the urban context – that is, into the cubage of the premodern block structures and the historic morphol-ogy of the plazas and streets that were thereby repaired. From the perspective of the land question, however, the IBA program and its way of managing land proved more fruitful than its typo-morphological aspect. For one thing, IBA was one of the most important municipal social housing initiatives; for another, most projects involved ground leases. The city of Berlin granted usage rights to housing companies – an instrument effective in the long term, as proven by the fact that some housing companies involved at the time have since been privatized.

Nobody realized IBA's various aspects – participation, not-for-profit housing, socially just land use – more convincingly in a project than Frei Otto. He had already developed the basic idea in 1959 when he designed three high-rises in New York; users could design their apartments freely within the skeleton of the building. In Berlin, Otto was originally supposed to build on Askanischer Platz, but then that plot was assigned to Ungers. In return, Otto was given a smaller plot in the southern part of Tiergarten district.

His plan for the Askanischer Platz site was for a significantly higher complex (taking up a neighboring high-rise; after all, it was a principle of IBA to use the typological context for orientation); he designed a lower and smaller project for the new site: three solitary residential buildings in an area whose typology is characterized by villas. Otto's idea was for «garden shelves» consisting of floor slabs and columns made of reinforced concrete. «The future residents could acquire ‹floor plots› [of this skeleton] on a 75-year lease and install their own individual home, either building it themselves or with the assistance of an architect of their choice.»[12] Since the slabs were statically over-dimensioned, residents were completely free to choose where to place interior walls and could plant as much greenery as they wanted on the terraces. As Otto multiplied the site in the vertical dimension, the paths, stairwells, and arcades became common property. Thus, this development displays a novel kind of structure moving from the public (plot) to the community (infra-structure) to the private (housing).[13] Construction began only in 1988, not least because of the complex planning process, which took eight years.

Ökohäuser (Eco Houses), Berlin

The location of IBA's social housing is a historical stroke of luck: into the seventies, policymakers in the West still thought that German unification might come about, but later considered it less and less likely. For that reason, land previously kept vacant in the center of the former capital, but close to the Berlin Wall and therefore at the periphery of West Berlin, was made available for IBA to develop. The Wall actually fell while some IBA projects were still being finalized. Whereas the central and northern parts of Friedrichstrasse, which were previously in East Berlin, saw increased density in the nineties as Senate Director of Building Hans Stimmann oversaw the development of quasi monofunctional and monostylistic market-rate buildings on the perimeters of the city blocks with not a single affordable apartment, a large number of heterogeneous social housing units still exist in the southern part of the same street – in the heart of the German capital. Unfortunately, this situation is practically unique.

FH

Social Housing, Steinsel
Christian Bauer
2001–2007

Examples showing how socially just land use and architectural experiments can create affordable housing can be found in Luxembourg as well. Almost 20 years ago, the municipality of Steinsel, which is not far from the capital of Luxembourg and has a population of 6,000, was able to purchase a large plot of land at a preferential price. The plan prepared by the Luxembourg architectural firm Christian Bauer & Associés Architectes took the region's dominating typology – row houses – to its limits. It divided the land into 28 narrow plots, 18.6 meters long and 4 meters wide, for row houses. The municipality built the necessary infrastructure and functioned as the builder. Since it sought to retain rights over the land and to grant ground leases to the owners of the houses, the government of Luxembourg subsidized half the costs for purchasing the land and providing infrastructure. The purchasers of the houses had to contribute one quarter of the costs to build the infrastructure: the street, the sewer lines, etc. Christian Bauer designed the homes, grouping six or eight houses together. The compact structure and the serial production of the houses made it possible to reduce building costs by roughly 20,000 euros per house, compared with the already low estimate. At a purchase price of approximately 220,000 euros per 133-square-meter row house, including the infrastructure costs mentioned above, or 1,655 euros per square meter, this development is significantly cheaper than the Luxembourg average, which amounted to 6,900 euros per square meter for new buildings in 2017 (a building of this size would generally cost more than 900,000 euros). The purchasers are bound to the conditions of Luxembourg's social housing program. They must live in these homes for at least 10 years. After that period, the owners can sell their houses, including the ground leases, to interested parties who must also fulfill the conditions for social housing, for the same price plus the average national inflation rate. Despite the low construction costs, Bauer succeeded in creating aesthetic diversity reminiscent of Bruno Taut's housing developments within a coherent urban figure by varying the serial elements and the colors.

FH

Architecture and Land Separated in Terms of Space

El Lissitzky
Wolkenbügel
1924

Wolkenbügel

In 1924, El Lissitzky (1890–1941)
introduced a new typology in
the form of the *Wolkenbügel,* the horizontal skyscraper, or «sky-hook.»
He positioned three interconnected
office tracts on three offset piers.
The vertical access located in the piers
was intended to connect directly with
existing underground railway stations.
With this design, El Lissitzky aimed
to create usable space above existing
buildings or infrastructure without
having the site completely enclosed –
as an alternative model to skyscrapers
in Chicago and New York, which
are designed to fill in the ground area
of the site as fully as possible. The
Wolkenbügel was designed to contribute to «a horizontal commonality»
in contrast to «vertical willfulness.»
«The static architecture of the
Egyptian pyramids has been super-
seded,» El Lissitzky proclaimed, «our
architecture revolves, swims, flies.»[14]
In collaboration with the Swiss
engineer Emil Roth, he developed
a construction that enabled immense
cantilevers to be employed, allowed
for movable walls, and even included
the later dismantling of the building.

FH

Le Corbusier
L'Îlot insalubre no. 6
1937

22038

With Îlot insalubre no. 6, part of his Paris Plan of 1937, Le Corbusier (1887–1965) turned to his deliberations on the Contemporary City for Three Million Inhabitants, his Plan Voisin, and the Athens Charter. Two 16-story-high residential buildings spanning four city blocks were to be developed independently of the existing street grid. The special feature about Îlot insalubre no. 6 was that by elevating the buildings on *piloti* columns – even including the flanking parking spaces – Le Corbusier left space free not only on the entire ground-floor zone but on the first floor as well, which, like the accessible roof terrace, was to be used for various communal functions. The intention was to landscape the ground level with paths and vegetation exclusively for the use of pedestrians and cyclists and connect it with complementary facilities such as a public swimming pool, kindergartens, daycare centers for children, primary schools, work-shops, clubs, cinemas, and libraries. It was envisaged that the multistory slabs would contain a variety of housing forms, ranging from studio flats, through full-length three-room apartments, to spacious maisonettes.

FH

Paul Rudolph
Trailer Tower
1954

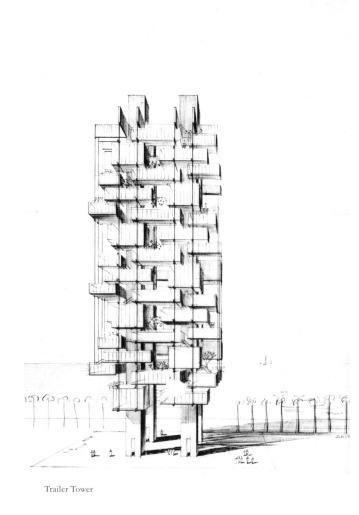

The Trailer Tower was the first high-rise project by Paul Rudolph (1918–1997). It was informed by his fascination for affordable, prefabricated trailer homes, which were extremely popular in the US in the 1950s. Rudolph developed the project for Sarasota, Florida, home to the world's largest trailer city, the Sarasota Tourist Park, which the caravan owners administered themselves, even managing their own police and fire department. Rudolph projected the idea of prefabricated, mobile units into the vertical. Prefabricated volumes were to be hung and removed as required from cantilevered, reinforced concrete beams connecting four pillars. The dwellings were designed in varying sizes, ranging from single-story apartments to maisonettes. The distinct separation of the different apartment volumes created versatile interspaces that could be used as terraces and loggias. Rudolph's Sarasota Tower provided the model for projects by the Japanese Metabolists and European Megastructuralists of the 1960s and 1970s.

FH

Nathan Osterman
Habitat of the Future
1956

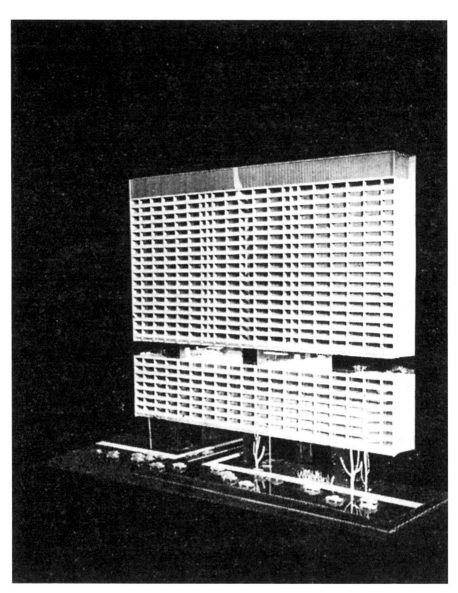

When Soviet architecture opened up to modern influences after the death of Stalin in 1953, Nathan Osterman (1916–1969) experimented with a variety of design concepts for housing of the future. For reasons of economy, the proposals aimed, on the one hand, to engage with the archetypal Soviet concept of a standardized architecture and, on the other, to follow the aspiration of the new generation of architects to respond to the heterogeneity of Soviet society. He planned an abundance of apartments of different sizes, which were to take into account the different family constellations and life phases of the residents. One of these designs shows a wide, multistory building subdivided into two tracts, in which a massive elevation was to create two free spaces, one on the ground level and one above the seventh floor. In the tradition of Le Corbusier, Osterman intended to service the apartments with collective amenities, which could also be distributed vertically in the building. The aim of this new architecture was, in his words, to unite work and living, emancipate women from household tasks, increase the offer of leisure activities, and respect the environment.

FH

Aldo Rossi
Locomotiva 2
1962

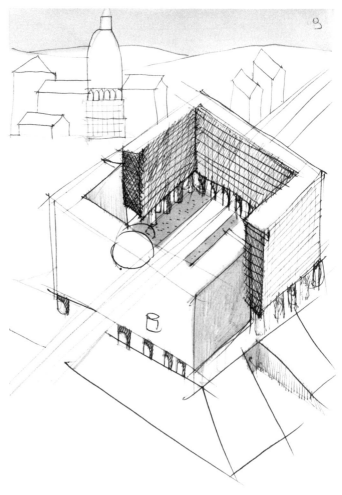

.SPACCATO ASSONOMETRICO

73, ^ mar ordineud dependes . RR

Four years before Aldo Rossi
(1931–1997) published his book
The Architecture of the City (*L'architettura
della città,* 1966), his Locomotiva 2,
a competition entry for a new central
business district in Turin, proposed
a hybrid typology of closed-perimeter
development, elevation and plateau
urbanism. As a counterpoint to
the suburban development of Turin,
but derived from the Roman grid,
Rossi (together with Luca Mesa and
Gianugo Polesello), with a nod
to Étienne-Louis Boullée, proposed
a gigantic object in the form
of a block spanning 300 meters with
an interior courtyard, which would
be elevated to a height of 30 meters
above a complex plinth using 12
round supports. The complex was to
house public institutions and allow
the passage of motorized and public
transport routes on different levels.
The surface of the plinth – the courtyard of the mega-building – was
to function as a series of urban plazas
flanked by shops and businesses on
the one hand, and by a congress hall,
theaters, and cinemas on the other.
Rossi intended to create recreational
uses on top of the building, which
itself was to provide office space for
private and public service providers.

FH

Egon Eiermann
Hängehochhaus
1965

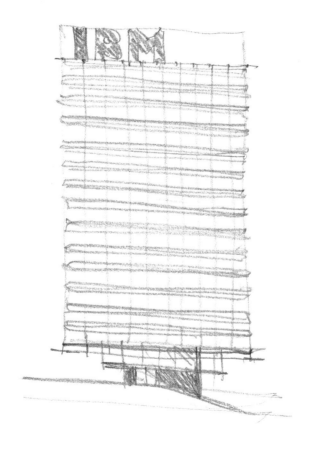

As one of the most influential European postwar architects, who brought elegance, lightness, and understatement back into German architecture after the Second World War, Egon Eiermann (1904–1970) experimented with a variety of high-rise towers in the mid-sixties. In addition to the goblet-shaped tower he designed for typewriter manufacturer and computer pioneer Olivetti in Frankfurt am Main, he concentrated on designing suspended high-rise towers, among others for IBM. By means of cables in the façade, all the floors were to be suspended from a cantilever roof-level construction on the top floor, which rested on a central core. This structural principle was designed not only to allow the floors to be used flexibly but also to dispense with all load-bearing elements in the lower section, apart from the access core. The ground floor would remain free for other purposes. Because the company-owned factory site in Böblingen was large enough to build a low-rise building, IBM abandoned its plans for erecting the suspended high-rise tower. For reasons of economy, Olivetti also eventually decided to implement the goblet-shaped tower design just twice, once as an administrative building and once as a guest house.

FH

Kevin Roche
Federal Reserve Bank
1969

Federal Reserve Bank

Kevin Roche (1922–2019) was already a renowned corporate architect in the US when he was entrusted with the extension of the Federal Reserve Bank in Manhattan. Roche was commissioned to design a high-rise building with 80,825 square meters of effective floor space on the 2,100-square-meter site adjacent to the bank. «[T]he site was small, the program large,» Roche recounts, «and, although they were not bound by New York zoning laws, the bank wished to be good citizens.» What Roche is referring to here is the clients' intention to maintain part of the site as a public plaza. After conducting morphological studies that could not satisfy the requirements of having a large amount of floor space as well as keeping the ground floor free, Roche ultimately conceived the idea of raising the entire tower to the level of the eaves of the existing adjacent building. The plaza would then take up almost the entire surface of the site and extend to a height of 47 meters. Excavation for the tower had already begun when a nearby building became available, which the bank ultimately moved into, rendering Roche's plans obsolete.

FH

SITE / James Wines
Highrise of Homes
1981

Similar to the Urban Villas developed by Oswald Mathias Ungers four years previously, Highrise of Homes by James Wines (born 1932) is an attempt to reconcile the widespread desire for individuality with the necessity for densification in view of American society's land consumption. Based on a critique of both the banality of late Functionalist apartment blocks and landscape-destroying detached houses shortly after the 1979 oil crisis, Wines imagined a 10- to 25-story structure that stacked a variety of detached houses and their gardens one above the other. The houses were not to be planned by the same architect but created by the residents themselves using a catalog of components. Wines, who was a founding member of the SITE (Sculpture In The Environment) architectural group, proposed a variety of uses for the land: small auditoriums, restaurants, a health club and communal outdoor facilities. In this interplay of public land, communal structure and individual housing, along with the modified role of the architect in dialog with the users, Highrise of Homes serves as inspiration for Frei Otto's ecological housing project in Berlin and many contemporary co-housing projects.

FH

HHF
Parking & More
2014

Parking & More

Parking & More, by HHF Architects (Tilo Herlach, born 1972; Simon Hartmann, born 1974; and Simon Frommenwiler, born 1972), takes up the idea of an elevated parking lot as developed by Louis Kahn for Philadelphia, enriching it with a variety of functions and activities. While a motel and a fitness center are planned for the upper floor of the converted structure, small shops, restaurants, and bars are to be built on the ground floor. Where no fixed structures are planned, the ground floor becomes a threshold-free community space with sports facilities and pop-up stores. Parking & More manifests the architects' engagement with the issue of purely purpose-built and infra-structural buildings, with structures that allow them to be constantly adapted to new usage requirements. The project site, located in the Dreispitz quarter in Basel, is devel-oping in slow stages, both temporally and spatially, from a purely industrial and commercial area to a mixed-use city district. The entire district belongs to the Basel-based Christoph Merian Foundation, which is why the projects can only be constructed subject to ground lease law or, as in the case of the parking lot, prefinanced by the foundation itself.

FH

University of Luxembourg
Slab
2018

Slab

The «Slab» of the University of Luxembourg, an experimental project cofinanced by the European Union, takes up the principles of the history of ideas projects that have been selected here: a large, effective floor area with a minimal footprint, individual types of accommodation with communal activities, large-scale structures for flexible usage; and, finally, a variety of types of modular and prefabricated construction methods, of recycling and of repurposing which address the time dimension of ground lease contracts and social change in Luxembourg.

The 11-story Slab is a response to the changing demographic structure of Luxembourg, where almost half of all newcomers are single parents or people living alone. A core of steel-reinforced concrete contains vertical and horizontal access as well as various small communal amenities such as laundries and bicycle parking. Prefabricated wooden residential units extending over two floors are positioned between the reinforced concrete ceilings. These are made up of modules that are modern and minimal in their use of space. Consisting of small kitchen units, bathrooms, bedrooms, and living rooms, they can be vertically or horizontally combined in different ways without enlarging the living area. In return, on the top floor there are generous communal areas with outdoor spaces: in one tract there is a common living room with communal kitchen; for additional tracts, there is the option of a media center with co-working space, an Internet-free analog room with library and/or a wellness area with sauna, gym, and pool. The ground floor is initially to remain open between the entrance areas of the cores, but can later be laid out in a variety of ways – with shops in urban settings, with open spaces in situations with high building density, and with offices in suburban areas.

FH

Commons
1
Vincent Ostrom, Elinor
Ostrom, «Public Goods and
Public Choices,» in:
E.S. Savas (ed.), *Alternatives
for Delivering Public
Services; Toward Improved
Performance.* Boulder,
Colorado 1977.
2
Silvia Federici, *Caliban and
the Witch: Women, the Body
and Primitive Accumulation,*
New York 2004.
3
Dagmar Pelger, Anita Kaspar,
Jörg Stollmann (eds.), *Spatial
Commons. Städtische Frei-
räume als Ressource,* Berlin
2016.
4
Peter Linebaugh, *The Magna
Carta Manifesto: Liberties and
Commons for All,* Berkeley,
California 2008.

The Medina of Casablanca
5
Cf. Paul Decroux, *Droit foncier
marocain,* Rabat 1977.

Archigram
Control and Choice
1966
6
Ralph Wilcoxon, *A Short
Bibliography on Mega-
structures,* Charlottesville,
Virginia 1968, p. 2.
7
François Barré, *Archigram,*
exhibition catalog for the
exhibition of the same name,
Centre Pompidou, Paris
1994, p. 7.
8
Peter Cook, in: ibid., p. 124.
9
Dominique Rouillard, «La
planète interdite,» in: ibid.,
p. 22.

Gisa Rothe
**Housing Development at
Rupenhorn**
1967
10
This was Rothe's final project
for her architecture degree
under Oswald Mathias Ungers
at Technische Universität
Berlin.
11
Oswald Mathias Ungers, Gisa
Rothe, «Rupenhorn» [1967],
in: *ARCH+,* No. 181/182/
2006, pp. 102–103.

Frei Otto
Ökohäuser (Eco Houses)
Berlin
1981–1990

12
Irene Meissner, «Eco-Houses
in Berlin-Tiergarten,» in:
Winfried Nerdinger (ed.), *Frei
Otto. Complete Works. Light-
weight Construction, Natural
Design,* Basel/Boston/Berlin
2005, p. 312.
13
See Fee Kyriakopolous,
«Die Ökohäuser von Frei Otto
in Berlin Tiergarten,» in:
Arno Brandlhuber, Florian
Hertweck, Thomas Mayfried
(eds.), *The Dialogic City.
Berlin wird Berlin,* Cologne
2015, pp. 601–609.

El Lissitzky
Wolkenbügel
1924
14
Quoted in *El Lissitzky, Maler,
Architekt, Typograf,
Fotograf – Erinnerungen,
Briefe, Schriften,* shared with
the author by Sophie
Lissitzky-Küppers, Dresden
1967, p. 330.

Luxembourg

Luxembourg

Introduction

The population of the Grand Duchy of Luxembourg is currently approximately 600,000; almost half are not citizens of the country. Almost exactly the same size as the German state of Saarland, Luxembourg covers 2,585 square kilometers, and its population density is 228 persons per square kilometer, significantly lower than Saarland's 385 persons per square kilometer. Since the sixties, the Grand Duchy has evolved from an agricultural and industrial country into a financial and administrative hub. Today a number of EU institutions are located here, alongside 142 banks and almost 4,000 registered investment funds, which have made Luxembourg the most important trading center for financial instruments in Europe. In recent years many digital companies have also settled in Luxembourg: Amazon, eBay, PayPal, Skype, and the satellite operator SES. As a result, Luxembourg has a strong labor market. In the past 20 years, the number of jobs has practically doubled to more than 432,000. It is estimated that the population would almost double by 2060 if growth were to continue at its current pace. However, the lack of housing is an acute problem even today. In Luxembourg City, the focal point of the labor market, the average rent for apartments is 23 euros per square meter, and the average purchase price for a house is more than 1 million euros. Across the country, the price for a square meter of newly constructed housing averages 6,900 euros. Even though many salaries are high, housing costs account for an average of 38 percent of household income. An estimated 7,000 new units per year would be needed to house newcomers, but only 2,600 units are actually built. Not least because of the lack of housing, 42 percent of employees commute from nearby Belgium, France, and Germany, where housing prices are much lower. At the same time, a marked asymmetry of supply is a distinguishing feature of the housing market: whereas the share of social housing is less than 3 percent and not a single housing cooperative exists, most new housing is constructed by developers who offer most of it for sale. Accordingly, the home-ownership rate is high: 73 percent as of 2015. The fact that too little housing is built is due mostly to the difficulty of mobilizing land for this

Luxembourg

purpose. An estimated 100,000 people could be housed in 50,000 to 80,000 apartments if the land zoned for housing were actually developed. The inequitable distribution of land plays a role here: whereas only 10 percent of land ready for construction is owned by the public sector, 1 percent of the population owns roughly one quarter of the entire country. The lack of a significant tax on land and the strong appreciation in the value of land ready for development make it lucrative for land owners to leave their land undeveloped.

Florian Hertweck

Luxembourg

References: LISER,
Luxembourg Institute of
Socio-Economic Research;
STATEC, government
statistics service
of Luxembourg; and
Observatoire de l'Habitat,
Ministry of Housing,
Grand Duchy of Luxembourg

Luxembourg

«Our Priority is to Contain Land Speculation»

Sam Tanson (Minister of Housing) and Mike Mathias (Member of the Council of State) in a conversation with Christine Muller and Florian Hertweck about the question of land and housing in Luxembourg

Florian Hertweck

Madame Minister, how significant is the question of land in Luxembourg?

Sam Tanson

Of course, this problem has various facets in Luxembourg, as it does elsewhere, but the Ministry of Housing can build on the important fact that across the country – and in relation to our country's relatively small land area – a lot of land is zoned for housing in the municipal plans. However, only about 10 percent of that land is owned by the public sector. Our challenge is to create more affordable housing on that land – infill housing could be built immediately on one third of it – and to gain public ownership of more such land.

Florian Hertweck

So your focus is on land ready for building. According to an estimate by the Luxembourg Institute for Socio-Economic Research (LISER), at least 100,000 people could be housed if all the land ready for building across Luxembourg were developed. That would solve the housing problem.

Sam Tanson

We think it is important to concentrate on this land to avoid promoting even more sprawl. We must create a balance between the production of affordable housing on the one hand, which also helps manage mobility, and preserving nature and preventing sprawl on the other. That is why we are initially focusing on the agglomerations. We will build housing where people work, in order to cut their commuting distances. Simply creating housing for 100,000 people in a short time would not solve the housing problem in Luxembourg. Most of all, we need affordable housing for low- and middle-income households.

Florian Hertweck

If you seek to prioritize development within built-up areas, which we all welcome, then you are faced with the problem of having authority over only 10 percent of the land ready for building. How will you mobilize the other 90 percent for the purposes of social urban development, specifically to create affordable housing?

Sam Tanson

There are various levels of action. First, we must position ourselves so that the state housing companies promote the construction of not-for-profit housing on the 10 percent publicly held land. Many of these plots are owned by the municipalities, which are important actors. We must make funds available to the municipalities so that they can both develop housing and also manage it later. About the other 90 percent: much of it is not in the hands of real estate developers, but is owned by private individuals, especially in the rural

«Our Priority is to Contain Land Speculation» / Interview

areas. Land is their most important investment because it yields returns they cannot achieve elsewhere.

Christine Muller

But if this land is not developed, then these returns are only theoretical.

Mike Mathias

They may actually be more than theoretical returns: after all, no landowner would give them up, and all of them have already factored them in. These returns also create a lot of political pressure, especially in Luxembourg. That is why it is difficult to adopt measures for distributing this rent of land in a such way that the general public also profits from it. For example, increasing pressure on landowners to actually build on the developable land in the short term, including at least some affordable housing.

Florian Hertweck

The people who own this land do not see any need today to develop it.

Sam Tanson

And no need to sell, either. They don't need money, and they don't want money because it doesn't yield surplus value if they put it in the bank. The only thing they might consider is a swap. Another factor is that taxes on real estate are very low in Luxembourg. If landowners simply do nothing with their land, it costs them practically nothing.

Christine Muller

There is also a psychological component: as long as families don't have cash assets, they avoid arguments. I advise many small landowners whom I accompany to meetings with asset managers or banks, and then I see that the decisive reason why they don't want to sell the land, aside from devaluation of money, is they fear family disputes. For example, their son will want to buy a Porsche, and then the trouble starts. That's why I think the question of land is emotionally loaded in Luxembourg. What's more, our society here isn't really an urban society interested in the city as such. My generation preferred to move to the country and build a house with a garden. So there isn't much identification across generations with the city or with urban development.

Sam Tanson

But in the past 20 years, the population of the city of Luxembourg has exploded, from just under 80,000 in 2000 to more than 116,000 today. New people keep moving in, even if they only stay for an average of five years.

Florian Hertweck

And these new residents don't own land. I moved to Luxembourg with my family three years ago. First we rented a small townhouse in Luxembourg City. Because of the sky-high rent, we realized pretty quickly that that wouldn't make sense long-term. Then we wanted to buy, but even with my income as a university professor, it was absolutely impossible to purchase

«Our Priority is to Contain Land Speculation» / Interview

a home in Luxembourg City. The problem wasn't just the dizzying prices, there was practically nothing available on the market. We then found a home in the southern part of the country, about a 20-minute drive from the capital, or 40 minutes by train. My point here is: living in the city is out of the question for newcomers up to the upper middle class. That is why 42 percent of the people who work in Luxembourg live across the border – half of them in France, a quarter each in Belgium and Germany – and commute in and back out every day.

Mike Mathias
You have to take into consideration that the country is small and that its commuter belt isn't larger than in other urban centers. But in the case of Luxembourg, commuters cross borders to other countries. This situation is exacerbated by the fact that compared to the size of their populations, the urban centers in Luxembourg have relatively small amounts of developable land and therefore also relatively less growth potential than rural towns. That is another reason why living in the city and the secondary urban centers has become unaffordable for many people. The fact that we have so much developable land in rural communities is because we didn't actually do any spatial planning covering the entire country for decades. We now have to deal with this legacy. For one thing, it is very difficult to mobilize the developable land because we don't

have the legal instruments to do so; for another, building plots are particularly scarce and expensive in the centers, where we ought to focus our priorities for development.

Christine Muller
In rural regions, politics and policies have always been seen as a means to an end and have been implemented very pragmatically. People focus on self-interest and mutual assistance. Historically speaking, land use policy and agricultural policy have always been closely connected. Farmers have long based their creditworthiness, which is essential for their survival, on owning developable land. After all, farms have to be modernized and expanded if they are to remain competitive. We mustn't lose sight of the historical importance of agriculture and the mentality it entails here in Luxembourg.

Florian Hertweck
What about the industrial wastelands that are often close to urban areas, for example in Esch-sur-Alzette?

Sam Tanson
The land that can potentially be converted from industrial to other uses is indeed an important factor for urban development. It accounts for much of the 10 percent publicly owned land mentioned a few moments ago, some of which is currently under development. Developing this land is high on our list of priorities. On the other hand, we don't want to fully exploit all the developable land in rural areas.

If it doesn't make much sense from an overall planning perspective to develop housing in a particular place, then we don't force it. That is why it is so important to think about urban development and spatial planning for the entire country as one. We can also consider zoning more land for development, but also only where it makes sense.

Florian Hertweck

What measures do you want to take to mobilize the developable land that is not publicly owned?

Sam Tanson

First of all, we would like to build up the public reservoir of land in general. So we worked with the state Comité d'Acquisition to empower us to assess land specifically as to its qualities for housing and then to buy it if appropriate. This land would then be reserved for building affordable or not-for-profit housing. We would then make it available to the public housing companies. However, it's pointless to try to buy land in the urban centers, especially in good locations, simply because the prices are much too high. And we don't want to push prices up. In addition, we want it to be less worthwhile for landowners to simply leave their land undeveloped. If that were to cost money, then they would manage their land in a different way. This government is planning a major tax reform for this legislative period that also affects taxes on real estate. Our priority is to contain land speculation. We're working on this tax reform now.

Florian Hertweck

The land question always implicitly involves the question: Do we as a society want to increase taxes on labor, or rather on windfall profits arising from land speculation? This question was already posed by Henry George, and he proposed a single tax. He argued for abolishing all other taxes because the rent of land is more than sufficient for the state to function. It sounds absurd, but Swiss parliamentarian Jacqueline Badran recently calculated that the value of all land and real estate in Switzerland, taken together, is 4 trillion Swiss francs plus interest. If it were taxed at a rate of just 2 percent, Switzerland could abolish all other taxes and would still have more money available than it does today.

Christine Muller

I think the problem is too complex for us to work with just a single remedy. We need many different measures at different levels, and we shouldn't underestimate the issue of increasing density in traditional neighborhoods with single-family homes. If you permit an apartment on each floor in such areas, and also require fewer parking spaces, as the City of Luxembourg has done, then that results in additional housing in areas that are already well served. To be precise: that's housing in line with the demographic reality. Because of the large number of small households, we

«Our Priority is to Contain Land Speculation» / Interview

need compact apartments in attractive surroundings. In areas with municipal protection of historic buildings, it is easier to convince the owners of listed buildings to create housing within the existing building stock if they do not need to provide expensive underground parking, or any additional parking at all. These simple measures often bring about better results than one big blanket solution.

Florian Hertweck

But would that be enough? I know expropriation is an ugly word and that it triggers a lot of resentment, especially in a country as liberal as Luxembourg, where property is sacred. But when the plateau on top of Kirchberg in Luxembourg City was developed as an administrative and financial center in the sixties, many landowners who did not want to sell were expropriated.

Christine Muller

Nonetheless, Luxembourg has no tradition of that kind of approach. For a long time, people were unable to imagine how things would develop. Up until 20 years ago, nobody was talking about growth here. Today, we are actually a metropolitan region, albeit a small one. We simply aren't a rural area any more with one or two medium-sized cities and a lot of villages. There wasn't a housing problem in the past and, accordingly, nobody asked questions about who owned the land and whether it would make sense to transfer more land to the public sector.

Mike Mathias

I don't think we can change the tax on real estate to such an extent that that would make landowners develop undeveloped land. A higher tax on real estate certainly makes sense in order to show how valuable and scarce land actually is. It can also serve as collateral for municipal finances long-term – following the example of Ireland during the financial crisis. There are many good arguments in favor of reforming the tax on real estate. But I doubt that it would result in mobilizing a massive amount of additional land for development. That isn't the primary purpose of that tax, after all. We must also keep in mind that a large fraction of Luxembourg's revenues come from external rather than domestic economic activity – people from neighboring countries filling their gas tanks here and international bank deals cut on Kirchberg, but not stemming directly from Luxembourg's economy. The tax on labor is relatively low, as are social welfare contributions.

Florian Hertweck

It wouldn't even be possible to introduce a land appreciation tax?

Mike Mathias

When it comes to that particular tax, the question always arises how it should be levied and for what purpose. If we impose a substantial land appreciation tax, then the state does take in revenues, but we still haven't used them to create affordable housing. On the contrary, we would even fuel high-priced building. That is why we definitely have to think about an alternative, namely that owners of large tracts of land have to reserve 20, 30, or 40 percent of the land for affordable or social housing. This can take the form of reserving it for low-income renters for 20 years, or having Luxembourg's two public housing companies build the housing to have not-for-profit housing in the long term. It really is unacceptable that landowners rake in the entire rent of land at the expense of the rest of society. Demanding 10 percent affordable housing in new construction projects seems to me to be the right approach.

Florian Hertweck

In my opinion, 10 percent is far too little.

Mike Mathias

Yes, it isn't enough, especially in a European comparison, but it's the right approach. We should build on this strategy and round it out with a land appreciation tax, if appropriate.

Sam Tanson

The Sectoral Housing Plan now provides for 30 percent affordable housing for larger projects. Besides, the 10 percent we had in the past was often not implemented properly. For one thing, the law isn't formulated clearly, and for another, there are no sanctions if developers don't comply with the rule. We would like to support the municipalities in making full use of the tools at hand, and we will also revise the rule.

Christine Muller

The municipalities have a lot of scope for action when they prepare their land use plans, but they don't exploit it fully. For example, you can start with moderate density in areas for new development, and then, during the public participation process and talks with the land-owners, link an increase in density to the condition that the share of subsidized housing be increased from 10 to 20 percent. If the developers get more out of the deal, then you can come to an agreement beneficial to everyone involved. The municipalities should also do more to buy land reserved for subsidized housing. That would mean that creating subsidized housing is in the hands of the public, not in the hands of the developers, which obviously impacts prices. Of course, that doesn't mean that the private sector should not be involved in creating affordable housing. There certainly is room for intelligent partnerships.

Sam Tanson

In fact, the municipalities have a lot more scope for action than they are often aware of. We are in the process of completely revising the Housing Pact. If you look at the original Housing Pact that entered into force about 20 years ago, you understand where we're coming from. It says that if a municipality's population increases, it receives more money from the state – regardless of who builds the new housing and who moves in there. A better name than «Housing Pact» would have been «Demography Pact.» We want a paradigm shift here; it has to be about creating affordable housing. We will use the Climate Pact for orientation in terms of methodology: the municipality receives financial and logistical support from us for measures that specifically benefit affordable housing and the quality of housing. We want there to be housing consultants supporting the municipalities in these questions, like the climate consultants today.

Florian Hertweck

My colleagues and I at the university sometimes consult municipalities on how they can best create affordable housing. Various models exist. If they buy the land and build the housing, then they get up to 75 percent of the costs back from the state; that applies to the costs of construction, access, and planning as well as the costs of buying the land. Those subsidies are astoundingly high. But they have to do all the work, and also manage the housing.

Mike Mathias

This law is from 1979, and it also shows where we're coming from. At the time, social housing policy meant: There may be a few people who have difficulties finding housing, and the state will provide subsidies either for rental apartments or for condominiums. People thought that this would solve the problem and that it would make people strong enough for the market-rate housing market. One consequence of this policy is that we only have about 2 percent social rental units today. The rest have become part of the free market.

Florian Hertweck

How can we move from the imbalance in housing supply, with a marginal amount of social housing and the absolute dominance of market-rate housing, to a healthier one? After all, various possibilities exist between the two poles of social housing and housing built by developers – for example, cooperatives, co-housing ventures (*Baugruppen*), and company-owned rental units.

Sam Tanson

Cooperatives will be part of the picture. We are currently examining how we can support local initiatives. I personally have a very positive view of cooperatives, because the quality of life is very high within the community they provide. The question of quality is often neglected in this entire discussion. But cooperatives are not a panacea, and we shouldn't focus exclusively on them. There are 3,000 people on the waiting list for the housing company, and the number of available apartments is far lower.

Christine Muller

We shouldn't forget at this point that a lot of people – and experience shows that includes many younger people – still have a very antiquated notion of housing.

Sam Tanson

But people also have different conceptions of living here in Luxembourg. When I was a member of the city council of Luxembourg City, we made two plots available for joint building ventures (*Baugemeinschaften*). The response was overwhelming. We had significantly more applicants than we could serve. But we simply also need affordable rental housing relatively quickly, and we need to manage it relatively flexibly too. As I mentioned: a lot of people are here for just a short time. We will support joint building ventures and cooperatives, but considering where we're starting, we will not become a second Viennese Model.

Florian Hertweck

What can one ask of private developers in Luxembourg?

Sam Tanson

We are in talks with them, and I am very confident that we can draw up a set of rules that applies to everyone and that is transparent, and that the private developers will make their contributions.

Christine Muller

We are currently working on some housing in Cologne. Our client is devoted almost exclusively to social housing. He is happy with the yields from social housing, which are much lower, because he has a long-term perspective.

Mike Mathias

Well, there are different business models in market-rate housing. Some people invest and intend to sell the housing right away. Their aim is a relatively high yield...

Florian Hertweck

... quick and dirty. That's the dominating business model here.

Mike Mathias

And in Germany, there is also the business model of investors who invest long-term in rental housing. The rent may be capped, but investors can rely on secure income. And when the period where social housing is reserved for low-income people is over, they can rent them out for higher rents, or sell them.

Florian Hertweck

In Munich, the city introduced the model of Socially Just Land Use (SoBoN) in the early nineties. It means that the developer has to build 30 percent – by now 40 percent – not-for-profit housing in market-rate housing construction projects. Christine Thalgott, previously Munich's director of urban planning, invented this model. She explained to us that it was accepted not least because it was transparent and because it applied equally to all investors.

Mike Mathias

I can well imagine that families who

privately own land would be interested in models involving long-term investments, especially if they didn't have to deal with managing the buildings and the rents. In this way, we might be able to get people on board who leave their land undeveloped today.

Florian Hertweck

Of course, the idea of a long-term solid investment is the basis for ground leases – even if the land belongs to private owners.
In Switzerland, not-for-profit foundations take this role. Either they use the long-term investment to finance social and cultural projects, or they mandate beneficial land uses required for social urban development in the ground lease agreements. All landowners in Luxembourg who do not want to build or sell could enter into ground lease agreements for their land. Then they would keep the land and earn money off it, and it would be developed nonetheless.

Mike Mathias

In Luxembourg, ground leases are used mainly by public builders applying a very low fee. Private individuals and companies could handle that differently. The law mandates that ground leases in residential areas must run for at least 50 years.
And whether private individuals and companies are willing to agree to such a long time period remains to be seen. In that regard, the model of a land trust might be another approach. In a model similar to ground leases, individuals could hand their land over to a foundation, receive a monthly yield, and be sure that the land and any buildings built on it are managed according to the rules for not-for-profit organizations. However, that does institutionalize the rent of land.

Florian Hertweck

How about «people's shares» for land? All of the land would belong to the community, and its members would receive shares – as far as I'm concerned, those people who own more today could receive more shares than others.

Mike Mathias

Like in Greenland.

Sam Tanson

They want Greenland to be sold now too.

Florian Hertweck, Andrea Rumpf
The Architecture of the Common Ground. Luxembourg's Contribution to the 16th Venice Biennale of Architecture

Many European cities that are under high developmental pressure, like Luxembourg, have practically no more land of their own available for construction. Although this problem is primarily a challenge for politics, many architects are also addressing it from a design perspective. The Luxembourg Pavilion engages with the most radical of these approaches – elevated buildings that allow land space to remain open, both physically and symbolically. Various projects from the history of ideas enter into dialog with contemporary experiments that share the aspiration of making land accessible to public uses. In so doing, they are resisting an alleged logic that has led to the almost universal privatization of land in cities, creating isolated enclaves and reducing the public sphere. The Architecture of the Common Ground is not a plea for a thoroughly elevated city, but an appeal to understand that finite and indispensable land is an inalienable common good, like air and water. Only then will we be in a position to further develop our cities in socially and environmentally sustainable ways.

On the first level, the exhibition uses a spatial installation to tangibly illustrate the issue of the privatization of land. Right at the start, visitors are led into a central corridor which opens up only to the exhibition space at the other end. The corridor takes up 8 percent of the floor area of the entire exhibition space. This projects the situation in Luxembourg onto the exhibition space, illustrating that public authorities have only 8 percent of building land remaining at their disposal. Positioned around this installation, in the form of models on a scale of 1:33, is a selection of 13 as yet unrealized elevated projects from the history of ideas, ranging from a model of Kevin Roche's Federal Reserve Bank soaring 5 meters into the exhibition space to Egon Eiermann's suspended *Hängehochhaus*. The focus here is less on the objects themselves than on the space between land and object, which is made available to the public even in the context of a privately owned property. The various projects not only clearly illustrate how much variety the elevated building typology can yield – from slab buildings and towers to clusters and urban block developments – but also how manifold the design and use of this porous ground-floor space can be.

«The Architecture
of the Common Ground,»
Luxembourg Pavilion, Venice
Biennale of Architecture
2018

Florian Hertweck, Andrea Rumpf / The Architecture of the Common Ground

Florian Hertweck, Andrea Rumpf / The Architecture of the Common Ground

Organizer:
LUCA Luxembourg Center for
Architecture
/
Curators:
Master in Architecture –
University of Luxembourg,
Florian Hertweck /
LUCA Luxembourg Center for
Architecture, Andrea Rumpf
/
Co-curator:
Philippe Nathan
/
Visual Identity:
Thomas Mayfried & Swantje
Grundler
/
Commissioner:
Luxembourg Ministry of
Culture
/
Team:
LUCA Luxembourg Center for
Architecture:
Stéphanie Baustert, Bastien
Fréard, Lili Krack, Pascale
Kauffman, Thomas Miller /
Maribel Casas /
Master in Architecture,
European Urbanisation,
Globalisation –
University of Luxembourg:
Marielle Ferreira Silva,
Markus Hesse, Nikos Katsikis,
Christoph Odenbreit, Carole
Schmit, Christian Schulz,
Sara Volterrani, Ivonne
Weichold /
Institute of Civil Engineering
and Environment: Research
Project «Eco-Construction of
Sustainable Development»:
Danièle Waldmann /
Luxembourg Institute of
Socio-Economic Research:
Julien Licheron, Antoine
Décoville, Valérie Feltgen,
Olivier Klein
/
Coordination in Venice:
Alvise Pagnacco
/
Experts:
Alain Guiheux, Dirk Löhr,
Christine Muller,
Anh-Linh Ngo, Véronique
Patteeuw, Beatriz Ramo,
Nico Steinmetz,
Frank Vansteenkiste
/
Production:
Prefalux, Definizioni

Glossary

Bebauungsplan

According to German planning law, a *Bebauungsplan* is a legally binding plan for an urban area with respect to the type of land use, building density, plot size, spaces for transportation, agriculture, forestry, public purposes, sports and recreation, etc.

Commons

Commons can be explained using the example of the commons in historical English villages. It was land, often in the middle of the village, used by all the villagers according to certain rules. For example, one family could graze two cows there, another family three sheep, another person could take firewood, but only during a certain month of the year. The villagers renegotiated the rules as needed. So a commons consists of a common-pool resource (in this case, the piece of land), the people managing it (the villagers), the rules by which they manage it and the social process involved. Many other forms of commons exist today – for example, digital commons. Commons may have access rules; they are not to be confused with open access resources.

Community land trust

A community land trust is a not-for-profit company that develops and manages affordable housing, communal gardens, and similar community facilities. Community land trusts generally make land available to their members on the basis of ground leases.

Cooperative

A cooperative is a company owned by its members that pursues the goal of supporting the members' economic activities or their social or cultural concerns by means of communal business operations. A housing cooperative is a cooperative form of housing company dedicated to the principles of self-help, personal responsibility, self-determination, and self-management.

Financialization

Financialization is generally considered to be the increasing dominance of the financial markets over real economies. In the urban discourse, the term refers mainly to the growing impact on land and real estate markets by investment funds and large corporations operating at an international scale and following the principle of shareholder value.

Ground lease

A ground lease allows a leaseholder (a person or a legal entity) to own a building on a site owned by a lessor. The leaseholder does not purchase the land, but normally pays an annual fee to the lessor. At the end of the ground lease contract, unless otherwise agreed, the building is returned to the owner of the land in exchange for compensation. The ground lease can be sold, inherited, or encumbered by a loan.

Hauszinssteuer

The *Hauszinssteuer,* a tax on housing built before July 1918, was levied in Germany from 1924 to 1943.

It was based on a proposal by Berlin housing commissioner Martin Wagner to have real estate owners pay a share of the costs of publicly financed housing.

Land value increment tax
The purpose of a land value increment tax is for the state to absorb increases in land value. West Germany's Social Democratic Party argued for a 30 percent land value increment tax in the early 1970s. Such a tax was levied between 1904 and 1944, but does not exist in Germany today.

Municipal land bank
A municipal land bank is a municipal agency that purchases and manages land. Where possible, it makes land available by granting ground leases rather than by selling it off, and links such agreements to certain goals relating to social factors, employment, culture, urban planning, etc.

Municipalization
Municipalization means transferring land to public – municipal – ownership.

Not-for-profit housing
Not-for-profit housing, in contrast to for-profit housing, is built and managed by a not-for-profit organization, akin to a charitable organization, which therefore receives tax breaks. Any profits must be reinvested in the housing stock; thus, rents are limited to the costs necessary to manage the housing stock. Not-for-profit status for housing existed under German law from the mid-nineteenth century to 1990; since then, this status can be granted only to cooperatives that rent out housing to their members.

Rent of land
Rent of land is the difference in rent between a piece of marginal land, which can just be managed in an economically viable way, and the piece of land in question; the difference arises because of the plot's location, quality, or intensity of use.

Right of preemption
In some cases, if justified by the common good, municipalities in Germany have the right of preemption. They can then purchase a plot of land or a building from its owner in place of a third party seeking to purchase that land or building.

SEM (*städtebauliche Entwicklungsmassnahme*)
An SEM (*städtebauliche Entwicklungsmassnahme,* urban development measure) is an instrument for urban development that facilitates the purchase of land by municipalities for major urban development projects. The SEM is considered to be the «most effective weapon» in urban planning law as, among other things, it permits the municipality to expropriate land in the absence of a *Bebauungsplan* and to capture the increased land value resulting from the urban development project.

Social housing
Social housing is publicly subsidized housing for social groups who cannot

meet their housing needs on the free market.

Verfügungseigentum and *Nutzungs-eigentum*

According to this model – which was proposed by Social Democratic politician Hans-Jochen Vogel in the early 1970s, but was not put into practice, each individual plot of land has two aspects regulating it: one aspect is the plot's ownership by the municipality and the other its use by a private individual or entity under a ground lease or similar arrangement for a limited period of time after which new land-use decisions can be made. This property regime is not suitable for property used by the owner.

Florian Hertweck, Dirk Löhr, Sandra H. Lustig

Daniela Brahm is a Berlin-based visual artist and project space producer. She studied at the Hochschule der Künste Berlin from 1988 to 1995 and has since exhibited in Germany and abroad at, among others, Künstlerhaus Bethanien Berlin (2005); Museo Tamayo Mexico City (2006); «Ideal City – Invisible Cities,» Zamosc (Poland) and Potsdam (2006); Museum of Modern Art in Warsaw (2009 and 2017); Casino Luxembourg, Luxembourg (2014); Urbane Künste Ruhr (2015). In 2004 she collaborated with the artist Les Schliesser to initiate the ExRotaprint project on the premises of the former Rotaprint factory in Berlin-Wedding, and in 2007 she co-founded and was shareholder in ExRotaprint gGmbH, where she has been a member of the planning team ever since. Brahm is actively involved in the StadtNeudenken initiative and a member of the Round Table for reorganizing Berlin's property policy. In 2018/19 she was a visiting professor for «Public Space Strategies» at the Weißensee Kunsthochschule Berlin.

Arno Brandlhuber is an architect and urban planner and has led the collaborative Brandlhuber+ (Berlin) architectural practice since 2006. His work is focused on architectural and research projects as well as publications and political interventions. In addition to his research work on «space production in the Berlin Republic,» he is also actively involved in legislative aspects of architectural and urban production. The following films have emerged from his collaboration with the artist and film director Christopher Roth: *Legislating Architecture* (2016), *The Property Drama* (2017), and *Architecting after Politics* (2018), as well as the traveling exhibition *Legislating Architecture – Architecting after Politics* (since 2018). He has been Professor of Design and Architecture at the ETH Zurich since 2017. Together with Olaf Grawert and Christopher Roth, he founded the online TV broadcaster s+ station.plus and is conducting research in the area of new media and technologies as arguments in favor of future architectures.

Chiara Cavalieri is an architect and holds a PhD in Urbanism from IUAV Venice. In recent years she has been a lecturer in the fields of architecture and urbanism at various universities, including the University of Louvain, ENSAP Lille, EPFL Lausanne, ITMO Saint Petersburg, GSD Harvard and the Università Iuav di Venezia. She has led various projects, research projects, and international workshops (with IUAV Venice, at Studio Secchi-Viganò, Lab-U, at EPFL Lausanne, at Studio Viganò, and at the University of Louvain). In 2016 she co-curated the exhibition *The Horizontal Metropolis: A Radical Project* for the 15th Venice Biennale of Architecture. She is currently Professor of Urbanism at the University of Louvain and a member of the Executive Committee of the Habitat Research Center at the École polytechnique fédérale de Lausanne (EPFL).

Sylvia Claus is an art historian and professor at Brandenburg University of Technology Cottbus-Senftenberg. From 2004 to 2018 she was director of the postgraduate Master of Advanced Studies Program (MAS ETH gta) at the Institute for the History and Theory of Architecture (GTA) at the ETH Zurich. She serves as curator for various exhibitions, research projects, and publications related to art, architecture, and town planning in the eighteenth to twenty-first centuries. Her monograph *Städtebau als politische Kultur. Der Architekt und Theoretiker Hans Bernoulli (1876–1959)* [Town planning as political culture. The architect and theoretician Hans Bernoulli], which she published with Lukas Zurfluh in 2018, deals with the work of one of the most important advocates of the municipalization of land.

Reinier de Graaf is an architect and author. He is a partner in the Office for Metropolitan Architecture (OMA), where he is in charge of projects in Europe, Russia, and the Middle East. De Graaf is cofounder of OMA's AMO think tank and

Sir Arthur Marshall Visiting Professor of Urban Design at the Department of Architecture at the University of Cambridge. He is author of the book *Four Walls and a Roof: The Complex Nature of a Simple Profession,* which was recognized by the *Financial Times* and *The Guardian* as one of the best books on architecture in 2017.

Franziska Eichstädt-Bohlig is an urban planner and retired politician, and is in private practice in Berlin. Her areas of focus are urban development, housing policy, and land policy. From 1989 to 2011 she was actively involved in political work for Alliance 90/ The Greens. From 1989 to 1990 she was urban planning director in Berlin-Kreuzberg, from 1994 to 2005 Member of the German Federal Parliament, from 2006 through 2011 Member of the Berlin State Parliament, and, for a time, chair of the parliamentary group. From 1983 to 1989 she worked as manager of «Stattbau,» the organization responsible for the resident-oriented renovation of previously occupied houses in Berlin-Kreuzberg. In 2005/06 she worked on the Special Commission «The New Face of the City – Strategies for the Future of Cities in the 21st Century» of the Heinrich Böll Foundation, and in 2016/17 on the expert commission «Shared Spaces – Strategies for Greater Social and Spatial Integration.» The Heinrich Böll Foundation documented her political work in *Die Gründungsgeneration der Grünen – Acht Interviews* [The founding generation of the Greens – Eight interviews].

Miguel Elosua is a lawyer with a doctorate from the École des hautes études en sciences sociales (EHESS) and the East China University for Political Science and Law in Shanghai. He is currently a researcher at the Paris Center for Modern and Contemporary China Research (Centre d'études de la Chine moderne et contemporaine). From 2012 to 2015, he was senior researcher in the research project financed by the European Union, «UrbaChina:

Sustainable Urbanization in China from Historical and Comparative Perspectives, Mega-Trends towards 2050.» Among other things he worked on basic principles of urbanization and on political institutions in Shanghai and Chongqing.

Simon Frommenwiler is an architect and lecturer at various universities and tertiary institutions in Germany and in other countries (among others, in 2013–2018 associate professor at the ENSA Strasbourg, in 2014 lecturer in Architecture at the Massachusetts Institute of Technology, and since 2018 visiting professor at the Harvard Graduate School of Design). With the partners Tilo Herlach and Simon Hartmann, he founded the architectural firm HHF Architekten in Basel. They carry out projects in Switzerland, China, Germany, France, Mexico, and the US, with commissions ranging from new buildings and internal fit-outs, planning activities for public spaces, all the way to buildings in public spaces. HHF Architects deliberately seek out collaboration with other architects and artists, including cooperation with the Chinese conceptual artist Ai Weiwei since 2005. Their work has been awarded several national and international prizes, including the American Architecture Award (2009, 2014) and the Swiss Architecture Award (2014).

Andreas Garkisch studied Architecture in Munich at the Technical University and Philosophy and Sociology at the Ludwig-Maximilian University. Since 1998 he has led Büro 03 Architekten in Munich together with Karin Schmid and Michael Wimmer. He is a member of the Bavarian Chamber of Architects, the German Academy for Urban Development and Land Use Planning (DASL), the Association of German Architects (BDA), the City Planner List, and is on the Steering Committee and in the Bavarian State group of the German Academy for Urban Development and Land Use Planning (DASL). In 2012 he was Visiting Professor of Design and Housing Develop-

ment at the Technical University Darmstadt, and in 2014 also a Visiting Professor of Urban Planning at the Leibniz University Hannover. He has been a member of the Baukollegium Berlin since 2017. He has been Professor of Urban Architecture in the Faculty of Architecture and Urbanism of the Bauhaus-Universität Weimar since 2019.

Françoise Ged is an architect and director of the Observatoire de Chine at the Cité de l'Architecture in Paris. In 1997 she received a doctorate from the École des hautes études en sciences sociales (EHESS) for a study of town planning in Shanghai 1842–1995. Her postdoctoral dissertation involved a study of Chinese policy on the preservation of historical monuments. She has led numerous French-Chinese cooperative projects. Currently, she is working in two French research programs of the Agence Nationale de la Recherche: «Patrimondi» on the relationship of globalization, tourism and preservation of historical monuments; and «City-Nkor» with a team of researchers from South Korea. Her work on China and the preservation of historical monuments has been widely published. She has been a member of the European Research Program INTREPID on interdisciplinarity since 2015. Françoise Ged was awarded the French Order of Merit in 2008. She has been a member of the Académie d'Architecture since 2014.

Tanja Herdt is an architect with a specialization in urban planning and is Professor of Theory and Methods of Urban Design at the TU Delft in Holland. She studied architecture with a major in Urban Planning at the TU Darmstadt, and obtained her doctorate from the ETH Zurich in 2012. In her work she focuses on sustainable housing development – especially development within city boundaries (in Germany, interior-zone development [Innenentwicklung pursuant to Section 34 BauGB]), and both living and public spaces. The focus of her work is social-space

issues in current transformation processes in the cities, and in connection with the environment, health, and building culture. In her research she examines especially the further development of methods and instruments of town planning and its cultural and historical implications. Since 2014 she has been active in practice with the Metron AG in the area of urban planning. In that organization she worked as project manager at, among others, the Stiftung Habitat on the project Lysbüchel Süd. Her book Die Stadt und die Architektur des Wandels. Radikale Projekte und Visionen des britischen Architekten Cedric Price [The city and the architecture of change. Radical projects and visions of the British architect Cedric Price] was published in 2017.

Florian Hertweck is an architect and professor at the University of Luxembourg, where he is director of the master's program Architecture, European Urbanization, Globalization. In 2016 he founded the planning office Studio Hertweck Architecture Urbanism in Luxembourg. In 2018 he curated the Luxembourg Pavilion at the 16th Venice Biennale of Architecture on land issues with Andrea Rumpf. Currently he is heading up a planner and researcher consortium on planning perspectives for greater Geneva with Milica Topalovic. His most important publications include: Positions on Emancipation. Architecture between Aesthetics and Politics (2018, with Nikos Katsikis); The Dialogic City. Berlin wird Berlin (2015, with Arno Brandlhuber and Thomas Mayfried); The City in the City. Berlin: A Green Archipelago (2013, critical new edition of Oswald Mathias Ungers's and Rem Koolhaas's Manifest of 1977, with Sébastien Marot); and Der Berliner Architekturstreit (2010).

Markus Hesse is a geographer and space planner who works as Professor of Urban Research at the University of Luxembourg, and before that at the Free University in Berlin, as well as actively

pursuing non-university research. He focuses on urban and economic geography, spatial planning, and problems at the interface between science and practice. One current research project involves studying rapidly growing, strongly internationalized («relational») cities, with a focus on their integration into global economic processes and its consequences for land use and real estate markets (Geneva, Luxembourg City, Singapore). He is a full member of the Academy for Spatial Research and Planning (ARL), is widely published in scientific journals, books and public media, and blogs with Constance Carr at http://sustaingov.blogspot.com/.

Klaus Hubmann completed formal training as a bank clerk before earning a degree in business economics HWV/FH at what is now the UBS. He then worked in the area of culture (film distribution, film production) and media (monthly cultural news in Basel). After working on rental and finance issues at cooperatives, he then focused on the issue of affordable public housing. Since 2004 Hubmann has been a member of the board of trustees and, since 2007, also Managing Director of the Stiftung Habitat in Basel, which uses its own properties and construction and land development projects to promote affordable housing and a livable city environment. With others, he founded the «Gemeingut Boden» information network and was a co-initiator of the Bodeninitiative (land initiative) in Basel, and headed its campaign office.

Manuela Kölke is a freelance architect, author, and translator in Berlin. Her work investigates contradictions in planning practices, forms of self-organization, the achievement of justice in space, and anarchy theory and practice at the interface of post-humanist and decolonial science and space production. In the context of her PhD at the European Graduate School (Switzerland/Malta) she is currently studying the concept and significance of

Biographies

non-planning – the negation of every kind of planning – in the kaleidoscope of philosophy, theology, and political theory. Her publications include: *Ontic Flows: From Digital Humanities to Post-humanities* (2016, with Matt Bernico), *Radical Standard – zur städtebaulichen Umsetzung von Spatial Justice* [Urban planning implementation of spatial justice] (2012, TU Braunschweig), and contributions on subversive space practices. Since 2017 she has translated, among others, *Revolutionären Schriften* [Revolutionary writings] for the first English translation of the *Complete Works of Rosa Luxemburg* (in press, published by Peter Hudis et al.).

Nikolaus Kuhnert is an architect and since 1975 has been editor and since 1983 co-publisher of the journal *ARCH+*. In 1978 he obtained his PhD on *Soziale Elemente der Architektur: Typus und Typusbegriffe im Kontext der Rationalen Architektur* [Social elements of architecture: Types and type concepts in the context of rational architecture]. In addition to his work as an editor, he has conceived and organized various symposia, including, with Otl Aicher, the «Berlin-modell Industriekultur» symposium (1988). He was a member of the board of trustees of «Shrinking Cities» (2002–2006) and until 2010 a member of the Advisory Board of the Goethe Institute. In 1996 his work as publisher and editor of *ARCH+* was honored with the Erich Schelling Architecture Prize in the area of architectural theory.

Giovanni La Varra is an architect with a PhD in Spatial planning. Since 2014 he has been Associate Professor of Architectural Design at the University of Udine, and also teaches at the Luiss in Rome. At the Polytechnic in Milan he coordinated research on the Metroposco Project (funded by the Province of Milan) and on the «Milan Chronicles of Living,» and set up the feasibility study on the restoration of the Sant'Elia district of Cagliari. He curated the exhibition *Post It City,* based on a study of contemporary and self-organized forms of use of public space, sponsored by the Center of Contemporary Culture of Barcelona (catalog 2008). From 2009 to 2011 he was a member of the planning office of Expo2015 Milan. He has published contributions, essays, and book reviews in *Casabella, Domus, Abitare, Territorio, Il Sole 24 ore, Urbanistica quaderni, Paesaggio urbano* and *Arch'it.*

Dirk Löhr is Professor of Tax Studies and Ecological Economics at the University of Trier, Environment Campus Birkenfeld. He completed doctoral and postdoctoral studies at the Ruhr University Bochum. At the Environment Campus Birkenfeld he is Chair of the Center for Land Research. He works as a freelance tax adviser and consultant for municipal councils. In addition, he is a member of the committee of valuation experts for Rhein-hessen-Nahe and of the higher committee of valuation experts for Rheinland-Pfalz. Among other things, he is member of the Building Land Commission of the German Federal Government and the related expert dialog on ground lease law. He is also a member of the Committee on Land Policy of the German Academy for Urban and Regional Spatial Planning and of the governing board of the International Union for Land Value Taxation. Löhr was one of the initiators of the «Land Tax: Up to date!» initiative, which is seeking to introduce a tax based on land value. In 2017 he prefaced and published a new edition of the main work of Henry George, *Fortschritt und Armut* [Progress and poverty].

Metaxia Markaki is an architect and researcher, and works in Athens and Zurich. She studied architecture at the NTU Athens and the ENSAPLV Paris, and specializes in urban and territorial studies at the ETH Zurich. She taught at the ETH Studio Basel and the Harvard GSD with Jacques Herzog and Pierre de Meuron, as well as at the ETH Architecture of Territory with Milica Topalovic. Metaxia's interest lies mainly in the tensions between territorial research and architecture and is expressed in design projects, teaching, and writing. She has been involved in various exhibitions and publications and is co-author of the book *achtung: die Landschaft* [attention: the landscape] (Lars Müller Publishers, 2015). Since 2017 she has organized and taught the course «Projects on Territory» on critical presentation of urban and territorial projects by means of silk-screen prints. Her work was exhibited in the S AM in Basel (2018) and the ZAZ in Zurich (2019). She is currently studying at the ETH Doctoral School for Landscape and Urban Research for a doctorate on the special idiosyncrasies of the Greek countryside.

Mike Mathias is a social economist and has been working as First State Secretary in the Luxembourg Ministry of Housing since February 2019. Prior to that, from 2014 to 2019 he was – nominated by the Greens – a member of the state council in, among others, the committees for the Environment, Agriculture, and Mobility and for Housing, Labor and Social Affairs. Between 2006 and 2014 he was a member of the Luxembourg Council for Sustainable Development. From 1992 to 2010 he worked as a managing director and policy officer for various organizations in the area of international development.

Thomas Mayfried is a photographer and graphic designer. Since 2016 he has taught as a contract professor on the Faculty of Design and Art at the Free University of Bozen-Bolzano, Italy. In 2015 Arno Brandlhuber invited him to the Academy of Fine Arts Nuremberg as a guest professor in the Department of Architecture and Urban Studies. Mayfried is co-editor of the book *The Dialogic City. Berlin wird Berlin,* in which he introduced the chapter on property and land. In 2018 he teamed up with Swantje Grundler to curate the exhibition *Der Komfort-Kuppel-Komplex* [The Comfort-Cupola Complex] at the Lothringer13 Halle in Munich, which presented, among other things, artistic positions on the issue of land. Mayfried designed the visual identity of the Master in Architecture program at the University of Luxembourg and was responsible for the look of the Luxembourg Pavilion at the 16th Venice Biennale of Architecture in 2018.

Elisabeth Merk has been Urban Planning Director of Munich since 2007. From 1988 to 1994 she was a freelancer in the area of architecture and maintenance of historical monuments. At the same time, she took the state examination in Florence and graduated with a doctorate in architecture. From 1995 to 2000 she was responsible for urban planning, urban conservation of historical monuments, and special projects in Munich and Regensburg. From 2000 to 2006 she was Head of the Department of Urban Development and Urban Planning in Halle/Saale. Merk has been Professor of Urban Design and Urban Planning at the Stuttgart University of Applied Sciences since 2005, and since 2015 she has been President of the German Academy for Urban Planning and Land Use Planning (DASL). In addition to her role as assessor in the Construction and Transport Committee of the German Association of Cities, she is a member of the Building and Planning Committee of the Bavarian Association of Cities, the UNESCO network on Conservation of Modern Architecture and Integrated Territorial Urban Conservation, the International Council on Monuments and Sites (ICOMOS), a board member for National Urban Development Policy and serves on the Board of Trustees of the Federal Foundation for Building Culture and of the German Werkbund.

Christine Muller is an urban planner and architect. Since 1988, together with Burkard Dewey, she has run the Dewey Muller architectural firm, with offices in Cologne and Luxembourg. Her work focuses on the symbiosis of

Biographies

the two disciplines of architecture and urban planning. Between 2005 and 2014 she was commissioned by the Ministry of Housing to work on the «Guidelines for Housing Construction» publication series for the Grand Duchy of Luxembourg. Since 2007 she has been a member of the Architectural and Urban Development Council of the City of Trier. As a member of COSIMO (Commission des Sites et Monuments Luxembourg), she is actively involved in the protection and development of the national architectural heritage. In her day-to-day work, she rejects processes that are increasingly dismembered and carefully sealed off from each other «to make things go faster.» The opposite is an integral part of her life and work philosophy: focus on the big picture and, if necessary, swim against the tide.

Werner Onken studied economics at the University of Oldenburg after completing his civilian service. Since 1982, as a member of the scientific staff of the Foundation for the Reform of the Monetary System, he has been responsible for the *Zeitschrift für Sozialökonomie,* for the special collection «Archive for monetary and land reform» in the library of the University of Oldenburg, and for the organization of the «Mündener Gespräche» conference series. Onken is editor of the collected works of Silvio Gesell and author of numerous brochures and essays on liberal alternatives to capitalism and fascism/communism, and on the capitalist form of globalization.

Ferdinand v. Pappenheim researches and works on the future of urban and rural areas. He studied Architecture at the ETH Zurich with a focus on urban planning and territorial planning. His thesis on the hidden potential of the Zurich forests was awarded the ETH Medal. He then worked for 6a architects in London and on several projects in Germany and South Africa, before resuming teaching and research at ETH in 2016. Since then, he has supervised research projects

on the metropolitan areas of Geneva and Belgrade for the Chair of Architecture and Territorial Planning and works for Pool Architekten on studies with an urban focus.

Dagmar Pelger is a guest lecturer for the Prof. Jörg Stollmann Chair of Urban Design and Urbanization at the TU Berlin, where since 2013 she has been conducting research and teaching on spatial commons, critical cartography, and cooperative processes of urbanization from landscape to neighborhood. Scientific cooperation at the HCU Hamburg, the KIT Karlsruhe and the University of Ghent, as well as practical experience as an architect in Berlin and Brussels, followed the study of architecture in Karlsruhe and Delft. Since 2017 she has been part of coop.disco (Robert Burghardt, Pedro Coelho, Anna Heilgemeir, Lisa Rochlitzer, Asli Varol), a cooperative of architects with a focus on not-for-profit urban development in Berlin. In 2016, she published «Spatial Commons» as the first part of her cumulative dissertation «Spatial Commons. Städtische Freiräume als Ressource» [Spatial commons. Urban open spaces as a resource] (edited together with Jörg Stollmann and Anita Kaspar).

Stefan Rettich is an architect and Professor of Urban Planning at the University of Kassel. From 2011 to 2016 he was Professor of Theory and Design at the University of Applied Sciences Bremen, and prior to that he taught four years at the Bauhaus Kolleg Dessau. He is a founding partner and co-owner of KARO* architects. With KARO*, Rettich has received numerous international awards (including the European Prize for Urban Public Space, the Brit Insurance Design Award) and has been invited to various international exhibitions, including the 11th and 12th Venice Biennale of Architecture. His most important projects and publications include *Lesezeichen* [the bookmark] for Salbke (2004–2009), *Republic of Harz* (2010, with Kai Dolata), and *Von A–Z –*

26 Essays zu Grundbegriffen der Architektur [From A to Z – 26 Essays on Basic Concepts of Architecture] (2004, with Mario Hohmann).

Karim Rouissi is an architect and since 2005 managing partner of the architectural office Empreinte d'Architectes, as well as of H+E architectures based in Casablanca since 2014. Since 2006 he has been teaching architecture and urban planning design as well as architectural theory at the École d'Architecture et de Paysage de Casablanca. In addition, he is active in various not-for-profit organizations, including the Bureau National du Mouvement ANFASS Démocratique, Casamémoire, and Architectes anonymes (ANA).

Andrea Rumpf is an art historian and culture manager. After working in Paris and Brussels, she has been head of the LUCA (Luxembourg Center for Architecture) since 2005. In this capacity, since 2006 she has curated events and exhibitions for her own organization as well as the Luxembourg contributions to the Venice Biennale of Architecture, and together with Florian Hertweck in 2018 a joint contribution on the land question «The Architecture of the Common Ground.» Andrea Rumpf represents both the LUCA and the Grand Duchy of Luxembourg as an active member of national and international organizations, committees, and projects, and at conferences on architecture, building culture, and architecture policy.

Carolien Schippers is Head of the Department of Urban Development of the Municipality of Amsterdam. In this role, she serves as a link between the state and other public and private players and entities. In coordination with other departments, her work also includes laying down program guidelines for (affordable) housing construction, sustainability goals, and public space.

Les Schliesser is a visual artist and space producer in Berlin. From 1986 to 1993 he studied at the State Academy of Fine Arts Stuttgart, then headed

the Projektraum Kunstit e.V. in Stuttgart and participated in exhibitions in Germany and abroad, among them: Tirana Biennale Albania (2001); *Ideal City – Invisible Cities* in Zamosc (Poland) and Potsdam (2006); Postmoscow Berlin (2008); Gallerie du Bellay Rouen (2008); 0047 Oslo (2014); and Casino Luxembourg, Luxembourg (2014). In 2004, together with Daniela Brahm, he initiated the project ExRotaprint on the site of the former Rotaprint factory in Berlin-Wedding. In 2007 he became cofounder and managing partner of ExRotaprint ggmbH and has since been part of the planning team of ExRotaprint. Schliesser advises similar projects involved in welfare-oriented urban development.

Christian Schöningh is a freelance architect in Berlin. Together with Silvia Carpaneto he founded carpaneto.schöningh architekten, and in 2007 with five partners Gesellschaft von Architekten and Co. In the nineties, he had already initiated and designed projects that turned out to be modules after the term became common. In doing so, he frequently changed roles after the initial phase and the preliminary draft to act as the builder, for example in cooperative housing in Spreefeld Berlin or for ExRotaprint (until 2013), and for the Schlachtensee student village. He is currently a director of two cooperatives, which number among «GI» (not-for-profit real estate players): the umbrella cooperative TRNSFRM eG, which is building two «experimental apartment buildings» by carpaneto.schöningh that are being sponsored as GIs, and ZKB eG – Cooperative for Urban Development, which with four not-for-profit partners is developing the Quartier Haus der Statistik on Alexanderplatz in Berlin. He is a member of, among others, the advisory group StEP Wohnen 2030 and Berlin-Strategie 2030.

Christian Schulz is an economic geographer and has been working since 2006 as a professor at the Institute of Geography and Spatial Planning at the University of

Luxembourg. He studied geography at the University of the Saarland; the Université Laval in Québec, Canada; and at the Université de Metz, France. After receiving his doctorate on intercommunal cross-border cooperation at the University of the Saarland in 1998, he completed postdoctoral studies at the University of Cologne (2004) with a thesis on industry-related environmental services. His current research interests are in environmental economic geography, in particular in the field of post-growth-oriented transformation processes. He currently heads the Post-Growth Economics working group of the Academy of Spatial Research and Planning (ARL).

Sam Tanson is a lawyer and is active as a politician for the Greens in Luxembourg. She joined the coalition government of the Democratic Party (DP), the Luxembourg Socialist Workers' Party (LSAP) and the Greens (déi gréng) on December 5, 2018 as Minister of Culture and Minister of Housing. Before that, she served as deputy mayor of Luxembourg City between 2013 and 2017, and was responsible for finance and mobility. Before she also became a Member of Parliament in 2018, she was a member of the Council of State from 2015 to 2018. From 2006 to 2007, Sam Tanson was spokesperson for the Young Greens (déi jonk gréng) and from 2009 to 2015 Party Chairman of «déi gréng.» From 2002 to 2004 she worked as a journalist at RTL Radio Lëtzebuerg. From 2005 until joining the government, Sam Tanson was a lawyer in Luxembourg.

Jacqueline Tellinga is an urban planner who promotes and manages experimental urban development on a small and large scale. She firmly believes that people should be empowered to create their own homes and living environments. Tellinga was responsible for the development of the Homerus-kwartier in Almere, the largest «self-building» area in the Netherlands. She has published in many specialist journals and is author of the books *De Grote Verbouwing* (The Great Reconstruction) and *Heilige Huisjes* (Sacred Houses). Tellinga is a member of the Netherlands National Expert Team on Housing and the UK Right to Build Task Force.

Christiane Thalgott is an architect and urban planner, and from 1992 to 2007 she was head of the Municipal Planning and Building Control Office in Munich. The Socially Just Land Use (SoBoN) program was introduced during her term of office. In addition to her work as head of the Munich City Planning Authority, Thalgott took on teaching duties at the University of Kiel and since 1996 at the Technical University of Munich, where she was appointed honorary professor in 2003. From 2003 to 2007 she was President of the German Academy for Urban Development and Land Use Planning (DASL). In 2013 she was elected to the architecture section of the Academy of Arts in Berlin.

Ivonne Weichold is an architect and has been a PhD student at the University of Luxembourg since 2017, where she teaches and conducts research in the master's program, Architecture, European Urbanisation, Globalisation. She focuses on the handling of agriculture and food systems and their integration into architecture and urban planning. Prior to joining the University of Luxembourg, Ivonne Weichold worked as a research associate at the Technical University of Braunschweig and was a lecturer at the Academy of Fine Arts in Nuremberg. After working as an architect at 51N4E and Stéphane Beel Architects since 2014 she has worked as a freelance architect in Brussels and Berlin.

Martin Weis studied architecture at the ETH Zurich and, after a few years gaining work experience with renowned architectural offices in Germany and other countries, worked as a freelance architect for 17 years. During this time, he established his architectural office, completed a large number of construction projects, and was able to achieve success in several competitions. In addition to experience in corporate management, he also acquired extensive project-management skills. Weis holds a master's degree in real estate from the University of Zurich. In 2009 he decided to take on another professional challenge and accepted a position as Portfolio Manager at Immobilien Basel-Stadt. In addition to the strategic planning of the real estate portfolio in financial assets, his responsibilities included the related long-term budgeting process. In 2012, he joined the Christoph Merian Foundation as Head of Development & Planning. Since 2015 he has been Head of Real Estate and a member of the Executive Board of the Christoph Merian Foundation.

Laura Weißmüller studied art history, law, and journalism in Berlin and Rome. Since 2009 she has worked as an editor for the features section of the *Süddeutsche Zeitung*. There, she is responsible for architecture, urban planning and design. She is particularly interested in the question of what kind of design is needed to bring people together. She looks for answers in newly built museums and high-rise apartments as well as single-family housing estates in rural areas or on benches in old city neighborhoods.

Biographies

Biographies

Acknowledgements

The question of land was broached in many conversations with colleagues, whom I thank for their impetus and tips – above all Arno Brandlhuber, Alain Guiheux, Dirk Löhr, Sébastien Marot, Thomas Mayfried, Can Onaner, Dominique Rouillard, Saskia Sassen, Milica Topalovic, Frank Vansteenkiste, and Paola Viganò. Thanks are due to Andrea Rumpf for making the topic the theme of the Luxembourg Pavilion at the 16th Venice Biennale of Architecture. The book is ultimately a result of this curatorial work and the research upon which it is based. I am very grateful for the trust and cooperation I experienced at the Biennale. In this context I would also like to take the opportunity to express my thanks to Alvise Pagnacco for his outstanding work on our pavilion in Venice.

Thanks to my team and my colleagues at the University of Luxembourg: Sara Volterrani for coordination and everyday support, Ivonne Weichold for drawings and text contributions, Nikos Katsikis for editing the conversation with Anthony Engi Meacock and Minos Leners, Dragos Ghioca for the painstaking transcription of many interviews, and Sara Werbinska for the many drawings and meticulous research on iconography. Further, I would like to thank the Dean of the Faculty of Humanities at the University of Luxembourg, Georg Mein, for his support, as well as my colleagues Markus Hesse and Christian Schulz for their contributions and constructive conversations.

Thomas Mayfried, Hans Georg Hiller von Gaertringen, Sandra Lustig, Susan Richter, Matthew Harris, Lars Müller and his team – above all, Maya Rüegg – deserve special thanks for their excellent cooperation.

And the book would be nothing without the authors, who merit thanks for their work: Daniela Brahm, Chiara Cavalieri, Sylvia Claus, Franziska Eichstädt-Bohlig, Tanja Herdt, Manuela Kölke, Giovanni La Varra, Dirk Löhr, Metaxia Markaki, Werner Onken, Ferdinand v. Pappenheim, Dagmar Pelger, Karim Rouissi, Les Schliesser, Jacqueline Tellinga, and Laura Weißmüller.

Thanks also go to the interview partners and their staff: Elisabeth Merk and her collaborator Ingo Trömer, Christiane Thalgott, Carolien Schippers and her collaborators Reena Koenjbiharie and Nanda Abhelakh, Reinier de Graaf and his collaborator Alexandru Retegan, who deserves particular recognition. I am likewise indebted to Stefan Rettich, Martin Weis and his collaborator Elisabeth Pestalozzi, Klaus Hubmann and his collaborator Urs Buomberger, and especially to Tanja Herdt and Simon Frommenwiler, Anthony Engi Meacock, Sam Tanson and Mike Mathias, Christine Muller, Françoise Ged, and Miguel Elosua.

Many institutions and colleagues with whom we have been working for years generously granted us the image rights for this publication: the Ungers Archiv für Architekturwissenschaft / Sophia Ungers and Anja Sieber-Albers, James and Suzan Wines, Kevin Roche John Dinkeloo and Associates LLC / Linda Scinto, and SAAI Südwestdeutsches Archiv für Architektur und Ingenieurbau am Karlsruher Institut für Technologie (KIT).

Last but not least, I would like to express my deepest gratitude to Maribel, who calmly put up with my alternating swings between exertion and absence, and always smiled knowingly at my insistence that this really would be the last book.

Florian Hertweck

Architecture on Common Ground
The Question of Land: Positions and Models

Editor: Florian Hertweck

Authors: Daniela Brahm, Arno Brandlhuber, Chiara Cavalieri, Sylvia Claus, Franziska Eichstädt-Bohlig, Miguel Elosua, Simon Frommenwiler, Andreas Garkisch, Françoise Ged, Reinier de Graaf, Tanja Herdt, Florian Hertweck, Markus Hesse, Klaus Hubmann, Manuela Kölke, Nikolaus Kuhnert, Dirk Löhr, Metaxia Markaki, Mike Mathias, Anthony Engi Meacock, Elisabeth Merk, Christine Muller, Werner Onken, Ferdinand v. Pappenheim, Dagmar Pelger, Stefan Rettich, Karim Rouissi, Andrea Rumpf, Carolien Schippers, Les Schliesser, Christian Schöningh, Christian Schulz, Sam Tanson, Jacqueline Tellinga, Christiane Thalgott, Giovanni La Varra, Ivonne Weichold, Martin Weis, Laura Weißmüller

Design: Thomas Mayfried

Translations: Matthew G. Harris, Buchen, Germany (the interviews by Andreas Garkisch and Florian Hertweck with Elisabeth Merk and Christiane Thalgott; by Florian Hertweck and Stefan Rettich with Reinier de Graaf and Carolien Schippers; by Simon Frommenwiler, Tanja Herdt, and Florian Hertweck with Martin Weis; by Simon Frommenwiler and Florian Hertweck with Klaus Hubmann and Tanja Herdt; as well as the biographies, from German into English); Sandra H. Lustig, Hamburg, Germany (the introduction, the «Urbanism and Architecture» and «Luxembourg» sections: the case study on Luxembourg by Florian Hertweck; the chapters by Werner Onken, Franziska Eichstädt-Bohlig, Markus Hesse, and Christian Schulz; and the interview by Christine Muller and Florian Hertweck with Sam Tanson and Mike Mathias, from German into English); Susan E. Richter, Berlin, Germany (the chapters by Sylvia Claus, Giovanni La Varra, Florian Hertweck, Laura Weißmüller, Daniele Brahm, Tanja Herdt, and Jacqueline Tellinga; and the interviews by Florian Hertweck and Nikolaus Kuhnert with Arno Brandlhuber and Christian Schöningh, and by Florian Hertweck with Anthony Engi Meacock)

Editing: Susan E. Richter
Proofreading: Ian McDonald, Matthew G. Harris
Coordination: Sara Volterrani and Maya Rüegg
Additional staff: Dragos Ghioca, Minos Leners, Sara Werbinska, Ivonne Weichold

Lithography / Printing / Binding:
DZA Druckerei zu Altenburg GmbH
Paper: 120 g/m² Munken Polar, 1.13

Lars Müller Publishers is supported by the Federal Office of Culture in Switzerland, from which it received funding for the years 2016–2020.

Lars Müller Publishers / Zurich, Switzerland
www.lars-mueller-publishers.com

Distributed in North America by ARTBOOK | D.A.P.
www.artbook.com

ISBN 978-3-03778-603-1, English
ISBN 978-3-03778-602-4, German
Printed in Germany